START LATE, FINISH RICH™

Praise for *The Automatic Millionaire*

"*The Automatic Millionaire* is an automatic winner. David Bach really cares about you: on every page you can hear him cheering you on to financial fitness. No matter who you are or what your income is, you can benefit from this easy-to-apply program. Do it now. You and your loved ones deserve big bucks!"

— Ken Blanchard, coauthor of
The One Minute Manager®

"*The Automatic Millionaire* gives you, step by step, everything you need to secure your financial future. When you do it David Bach's way, failure is not an option."

— Jean Chatzky, Financial Editor, NBC's *Today*

"Finally, a book that helps you stop sweating it when it comes to your money! *The Automatic Millionaire* is a fast, easy read that gets you to take action. David Bach is the money coach to trust year in and year out to motivate you financially."

— Richard Carlson, author of *Don't Sweat the Small Stuff*
and *Don't Sweat the Small Stuff About Money*

"David Bach's *The Automatic Millionaire* proves that you don't have to make a lot of money or have a complicated financial plan to get started— you can literally start towards your financial dreams today, in a matter of hours, with just one life-changing secret: Pay yourself first and make it automatic! Equally important, this book shows you how to simplify and automate your entire financial life."

— Harry S. Dent, Jr., investment strategist
and author of *The Roaring 2000s*

Praise for *Smart Women Finish Rich* and *Smart Couples Finish Rich*

"*Smart Couples Finish Rich* teaches women and men to work together as a team when it comes to money. Bach's nine steps are powerful, yet easy to understand and fun to implement. The entire family can benefit from this great book."

—Robert T. Kiyosaki, author of
Rich Dad, Poor Dad

"David Bach is the one expert to listen to when you're intimidated by your finances. His easy-to-understand program will show you how to afford your dreams."

—Anthony Robbins, author of
Awaken the Giant Within and *Unlimited Power*

"I know how hard it is to make a personal-finance book user-friendly. Bach has done it. *Smart Couples Finish Rich* picks up where *Smart Women Finish Rich* left off. . . . This is an easy, lively read filled with tips that made me smile and at least once made me laugh."

—*USA Weekend*

"*Smart Couples Finish Rich* is a must-read for couples. Bach is a great financial coach . . . he knows how to bring couples together on a topic that often divides them."

—John Gray, author of
Men Are From Mars, Women Are From Venus

"*Finally* a book for women that talks about money in a way that makes sense. David Bach is not just an expert in managing money—he's the ultimate motivational coach for women. I can't recommend this book enough. It's a must-read!"

—Barbara DeAngelis, Ph.D., bestselling author of
Real Moments

START LATE,
FINISH RICH

A No-Fail Plan for Achieving
Financial Freedom at Any Age

DAVID BACH

BROADWAY BOOKS   New York

Start Late, Finish Rich, The Automatic Millionaire, The Latte Factor, The Double Latte Factor, The 20/60/20 Principle, DOLP, Smart Women Finish Rich, Smart Couples Finish Rich are registered trademarks of FinishRich, Inc.

PRINTED IN THE UNITED STATES OF AMERICA

BROADWAY BOOKS and its logo, a letter B bisected on the diagonal, are trademarks of Random House, Inc.

This book is designed to provide accurate and authoritative information on the subject of personal finances. While all of the stories and anecdotes described in the book are based on true experiences, most of the names are pseudonyms, and some situations have been changed slightly for educational purposes and to protect each individual's privacy. It is sold with the understanding that neither the Author nor the Publisher is engaged in rendering legal, accounting, or other professional services by publishing this book. As each individual situation is unique, questions relevant to personal finances and specific to the individual should be addressed to an appropriate professional to ensure that the situation has been evaluated carefully and appropriately. The Author and Publisher specifically disclaim any liability, loss, or risk that is incurred as a consequence, directly or indirectly, of the use and application of any of the contents of this work.

ISBN-13: 978-0-7394-5634-7

To my wife, Michelle,
who dreams with me and holds my hand through the fires,
I love you.

To my little son, Jack—
I hope you always dance, dream,
and follow your heart.

CONTENTS

INTRODUCTION

So you feel like you've started late?

What if I told you it's not too late for you to finish rich? That even if you're in your thirties, forties, fifties—even your sixties and beyond—you've still got an opportunity to put your life on the right track financially and stop worrying about the future.

What if I told you it's possible to "catch up" on saving for the future without taking HUGE risks?

What if I told you that, even on an ordinary income, in less than a few hours you could transform how you earn, how you save, and how you invest—to the point where you really could start late and finish rich?

What if I told you that there are simple strategies you can use to make more money than you do now without quitting your job, so that you can finish even richer than you would have if you had started early?

Would you spend a few hours with me? Are you ready to start late and finish rich?

—DAVID BACH

IT'S ONLY TOO LATE IF YOU GIVE UP

I'll never forget the first time I met Harriet. She had come to me with a problem. The problem was that she was in her fifties, in debt, and hadn't saved a dime. She was losing sleep, depressed, and extremely worried about her future.

Her story changed my life.

My coaching changed hers.

Now it's your turn. . . .

Harriet was in the audience at one of my FinishRich seminars in Washington, D.C. I was just finishing up when she raised her hand and blurted out, "Can I ask you a really important question?"

I could tell she had something serious on her mind. Her face had worry written all over it.

"Of course," I replied. "What's the question?"

She said, "David, I'm 52 years old and I've done everything wrong. I'm divorced and recently remarried, and am now working 45 hours a week to make ends meet. I've got literally nothing in savings, and I don't know what to do. Last year I went to a financial planner. I paid him $500 to run a financial plan—and he came back and told me that in order to be able to retire in my sixties, I needed to start saving over $2,700 a month. Considering that after taxes I only take home about $3,500, his plan was ridiculous. You know what he said to me? He said, 'Well, I'm sorry, but that's what you have to do.' I went home furious and then I got depressed."

Harriet sighed deeply. "Now I don't know what to do. I'm losing sleep worrying that I'm going to wind up a bag lady someday. I don't know how I'm ever going to catch up on my savings." She looked at me bleakly. "What do you think? Is there any hope for me?"

IS THERE ANY HOPE FOR ME?

Looking back at Harriet, I could literally feel her pain. And I wasn't the only one. There was a strong sense of empathy in the room. My gut told me that a lot of other people in the audience were just as scared, hurt, and upset about their futures as Harriet was.

With that in mind, I answered Harriet as carefully as I could. "Of course there's hope for you!" I said. "But before we focus on why you can and should feel hopeful, first help me understand your situation better. You had a meeting with a financial planner, you paid for his advice, and then you went home mad. So after you got home, what exactly did you do? Did you change anything about the way you were handling your money? Did you follow through on any of his advice?"

"DAVID, TO TELL YOU THE TRUTH, I DID NOTHING"

Harriet shook her head. The appointment had been a year earlier, and the planner's advice had upset her so much that she hadn't been able to bring herself to do anything about her financial situation. She had come to my seminar trying to get remotivated to do something, but she still felt "stuck." "It all just seems impossible," she said.

IT'S NOT A SPRINT, IT'S A MARATHON

I wasn't surprised by how hopeless she felt. "Harriet," I said, "if you'd never run a mile and I told you to run a marathon today, that would seem impossible, too, wouldn't it? But you know how all long-distance runners start? They start by running just a block or two their first day of training. Actually, most don't run. They just jog. And some don't even jog. They just sort of walk fast. The point is, they start off going maybe two blocks, then three blocks, then a half-mile, then a mile, then a couple of miles. And before they know it, several months have passed and they've gone from being out of shape to being able to run a marathon."

I looked around the room. "What smart runners *don't* do is go out and try to sprint 26 miles the first day. They build up to it. Learning to save is a lot like exercise. If you've never exercised and I send you to the gym for three straight days and work you out for two hours a day, you're going to fall apart and be sore. You need to build up gradually. It's the same with saving. You don't go from saving nothing to saving $2,700 a month. That's absurd. You've got to start slowly. You need to keep it simple."

"HARRIET, CAN YOU SAVE $10 A DAY?"

I looked back at Harriet. "Do you understand what I'm trying to say with this exercise metaphor?"

She nodded slowly. "I think so."

"Good," I said. "So let me ask you the big question—the question that's at the bottom of all start-from-behind-and-finish-rich plans: Can you save $10 a day?"

Harriet looked surprised. "I think I could," she began, "but—"

I cut her off. "Come on, Harriet. You're 52 and sitting here broke, right? You *think* you can save $10 a day? Or you WILL save $10 a day?"

Harriet grinned in spite of herself. "I can," she said with quiet confidence. "Ten dollars a day is totally doable."

"Great," I said. "That's $3,650 a year. Now, what about your husband? Can you get him to save $10 a day?"

"Well, that's a whole other story," she replied, her grin widening. By now, the class was laughing with Harriet. At the same time, however, you could also feel the energy of hope stirring. Everyone in the room was rooting her on, wanting her to succeed.

"Yes, I can get Bill to save $10 a day," Harriet continued. "It won't be easy, but I'll make him."

"Okay, that's $7,300 a year." I walked over to the chalkboard. "Let's assume you do this right. You pay yourself first, which I discussed earlier"—and which we'll discuss later in this book—"you do it automatically so it doesn't take discipline or a budget, and you put your money in a solid diversified investment that earns a decent rate of return. Let's see what that would give you 20 years from now, when you're 72 . . ."

And I wrote on the chalkboard:

> $10 a day (both of you saving) =
> $20 a day x 365 = $7,300 (a year)

I looked at Harriet. "Let's say you averaged a 10% return, which is less than the stock market has averaged since 1926. It's not guaranteed, but I can show you how to put the odds in your favor to make it happen. Putting in $7,300 a year, can you guess how much you'd have in 20 years?"

I turned back to the chalkboard. "I happen to know this figure by heart," I said as I scribbled down a number, "because it comes up more often than you'd think."

Here's what I wrote:

> $461,947 (in 20 years)

BUT WAIT, THERE'S MORE

I put down the chalk and looked at Harriet. She was staring at the chalkboard, openmouthed.

"Now let me ask you something else," I said. "Do you and your husband both work for companies that offer retirement plans like a 401(k) plan?"

Harriet nodded. "Yes," she said, "but we don't use them."

"Do your employers have a policy of matching your contributions?"

Harriet nodded again. "I think so. If I remember correctly, they both offer to match 50% of what each employee contributes."

"Okay, then scratch the number I just wrote down. In 20 years, you and your husband could have . . ." I went back to the chalkboard and wrote:

$20 a day + 50% match =
$30 a day x 365 = $10,950 (a year)

"Okay," I continued, "at a 10% annual return for 20 years, that comes to . . ."

And I wrote:

$692,924 (in 20 years)

At first, Harriet was shocked. Then she got mad. "Why didn't the guy who I paid money to give me a plan explain it this way?" she asked angrily. "I would have done something a year ago. I mean, he made my situation seem impossible." She was silent for a moment. "You know," she said finally, "they should teach this in school. My whole life would have been different if I'd known this before."

I nodded sympathetically. "You're right," I said. "They *should* teach this stuff to us in school, and I wish I knew why they didn't. But the bottom line is not to waste time focusing on what you weren't taught, didn't know, or haven't done. You are where you are, and it's time to take action. So are you ready to get going?"

Harriet's response was simple and heartfelt. "Yes," she said.

The very next day, with a little coaching from me, Harriet had a plan in place.

IT REALLY CAN WORK—AND LYNN ON
THE OPRAH WINFREY SHOW PROVED IT

Fast-forward a few years from that moment with Harriet in Washington, D.C. It's January 2004, and I'm in a television studio in Chicago with Oprah Winfrey, doing a show about my book *The Automatic Millionaire*. Oprah is holding up a brokerage statement that shows an account worth $1.6 million. The account belongs to a woman sitting in the front row, Oprah says, and she invites the audience to guess which one.

A moment later, an unassuming woman in her sixties stands up and joins us on stage. Her name is Lynn Hadley, and Oprah explains that she came to my first "Smart Women Finish Rich" seminar when she was in her early fifties, put a plan in place, and took action. Now here she is a decade or so later, having retired a multimillionaire.

Lynn is beaming with pride—as well she should. Although she got a late start, she didn't let that stop her from taking action to catch up. She wasn't poor when I met her, but she didn't have a plan in place to *really* finish rich.

I told her as much during our first appointment. "Lynn," I said, "with what you have now, you won't starve during your retirement. You'll be able to enjoy the 'early bird special.' But you won't be traveling to Europe or taking any cruises. If you want to finish rich, you are going to need a new plan of attack."

I made it clear to her that this new plan wouldn't involve anything particularly fancy or complicated. It would all be based on common sense. The thing was, she would have to apply what I taught her. Not just pay it lip service, but actually do it.

"The choice is ultimately yours," I told her. "If you want to retire rich, we can work together to make it happen. I'll guide you, but you'll need to follow through. Otherwise, it won't work."

Lynn was up to the challenge. "Tell me what I need to do, David, and I'll do it," she said.

Fewer than 10 years later, Lynn took early retirement—rich enough to do what she wanted to do when she wanted to do it. And getting there wasn't all that difficult. In fact, the hardest thing Lynn had to do was what she did that first day we met: deciding—and then really believing—that it wasn't too late for her to be able to change her destiny.

HALF OF ALL AMERICANS FEEL
THEY ARE "STARTING LATE"

As of this writing, there are more than two million copies of my Finish-Rich® books in print, translated into more than 10 languages. But for all the positive impact my previous books have had, I keep hearing from people who are afraid it is too late for them—people who didn't start saving and investing while they were young and now fear they will never be able to get rich and realize their dreams.

The level of concern I've been sensing over the past few years has been so great that in the summer of 2004 I commissioned a nationwide survey by researchers at Temple University to find out just how worried Americans were about their financial futures and why.* What the survey revealed was truly disturbing.

THE START LATE FINISH RICH SURVEY
(THE FACTS ARE IN!)

If you are really worried about starting late, you should know you are not alone. Fully half of everyone we spoke to said they felt they were "starting late" when it came to saving for retirement. Indeed, only 56% said they were saving for retirement at all. As a result, two out of three believed they would have to continue working until they were at least 70, and 15% said they didn't expect ever to be able to retire.

Sadly, most of those surveyed had good reason for being so pessimistic.
- Half of those surveyed had less than $10,000 in total savings (not counting the value of their homes).
- Three in 10 had less than $1,000 in savings.
- Two-thirds reported having at least $5,000 in credit card debt, while a similar proportion said they used credit cards to cover daily expenses.
- *Seventy percent of the respondents said they were living paycheck to paycheck!*

---

*The Finish Rich Annual Survey™, conducted by the staff at Temple University nationwide in June 2004 on behalf of FinishRich, Inc., included more than 1,000 people between the ages of 21 and 69. (See Appendix, p. 328.) Complete results available at www.finishrich.com.

Why do people owe so much and save so little? Roughly half of all the people we polled said they were concerned about their current level of savings but didn't feel they could contribute any more because the cost of taking care of their families was too high and their incomes were too low.

If any of this sounds familiar, you've come to the right place.

DESPITE WHAT YOU MIGHT THINK, IT'S NOT TOO LATE FOR YOU

Please hear me: It is not too late for you!

I know it's not.

It's really very simple. Whether you know it or not, there is a way you can spend less and save more—and if you do that, you can almost certainly start late and finish rich. And if you spend less, save more, and EARN more, you can definitely start late and finish rich—even richer than you might have if you'd started early.

Easier said than done, you say? Absolutely. But trust me—if you do it right, it's not nearly as difficult as most people think. It's certainly not impossible.

I've seen plenty of people do it.

And I know you can do it too!

THE "FINISH RICH" PHILOSOPHY

In this book, I will teach you how to transform your dreams into reality and fulfill your desire for financial freedom—in other words, everything it takes to make up for your late start.

The "Start Late, Finish Rich" philosophy is based on the following beliefs:

- It's not too late for you to become rich—if you start today.
- Even if you are buried in debt—there is still hope.
- You don't have to make a lot of money to be rich.
- You don't have to invest in stocks to get rich.
- You can get rich in real estate—by starting small.
- You can find your Latte Factor®—and turbocharge it to get rich.
- You can start a business on the side—while you keep your old job and continue earning a paycheck.

- You can spend less, save more, and make more—and it doesn't have to hurt.
- You can and should reawaken your dreams—and go for them.

YOU'LL GET THE "START LATE" SYSTEM OF WEALTH-BUILDING TOOLS

I'm giving you the "START LATE" System in this book. It will be just as simple and straightforward as my previous books, but because it is meant specifically for people who are starting late on the journey to financial security and independence, it covers subjects I've never covered before, among them:

- How to transform your debt into wealth
- How to get rich in real estate on the weekends
- How to start a home-based business—and increase your income on the side
- How to use my simple "Perfect Pie Approach™" to wealth—so that you catch up on getting rich without too much risk
- Why your dreams don't have deadlines

What's more, it includes dozens of stories of real people who started late and are living rich now. If they can do it—you can too!

BOOKS DON'T CHANGE PEOPLE'S LIVES— PEOPLE DO

This book is divided into five major parts, each covering an area of your finances that you need to address in order to start late and finish rich.

Whether you read this book cover to cover or simply concentrate on the areas that seem really critical to you right now, I promise you this: *If you act on what you learn, your life will change.*

Books don't change people's lives. People change their own lives. The fact that you are reading this book right now is not a coincidence. There are literally millions of books out there right now that you could be reading. This one ended up in your hands for a reason. The reason is that you are ready to make some changes.

So let's get started. The new you is about to encounter a world of new and exciting possibilities. Let's go have some fun together. In just a few hours I think you'll be surprised by how far your thinking has come—and how ready you are to take action!

ONE FINAL THOUGHT
BEFORE WE REALLY GET STARTED

I believe you were put here for a reason. I believe you are special. I believe there is no one like you on this planet and that you were born with unique gifts, talents, and dreams. I know from experience that you may never have been told this—but that you feel it deep down inside of you. I promise you what you feel is real—and that the most important thing this book can do for you is help free you up to be who you really are meant to be.

You may think this book is only about money, but you will learn that it's really about a lot more. My mission is to free you to be who you were put here to be—and my experience has taught me that what holds most people back from their purpose in life are financial challenges. Break the financial handcuffs of living paycheck to paycheck, worrying about debt, and losing sleep over how you are going to survive financially in the future, and you will be able to focus on what is really most important to you. You are already rich inside—this book will help you reconnect with your inner gifts.

This book may be called *Start Late, Finish Rich*, but I know that inside you are already rich in spirit. All we need to do now is help you become materially rich so you can live the life you were meant to live.

Let's go—your future begins today.

FREE! THE "START LATE, FINISH RICH" AUDIO PROGRAM

All my books now come with free gifts. My goal is to give you much more than you could ever ask for from a book. So included with your purchase of this book is a complete audio program I've created called "The Five Secret Questions to Start Late and Finish Rich." These Five Questions are designed to get you to take immediate action toward realizing your greatest dreams—and saying good-bye to your greatest fears.

You'll find this audio program on my web site at **www.finishrich.com**. It includes a new interview with me containing additional insights about this book. Enjoy!

PART ONE

IT'S TIME
TO GET IT

CHAPTER ONE

SO YOU STARTED LATE— GIVE YOURSELF A BREAK ALREADY!

Of all the things people say to me after they've read my books, attended one of my seminars, stopped me in an airport, or called in to my radio show, there is one comment I hear more than all the others put together:

"If only I had started saving when I was younger."

SOMETIMES LIFE THROWS YOU A CURVEBALL

While some of you may blame yourselves for not having started earlier, I also know that many of you are starting late not because you were short-sighted or lazy or irresponsible, but because life threw you a curveball. I hear from people all the time who are starting late because of divorce, death, illness, disability, bankruptcy, poor career choices, lack of education—and on and on. Either way, it's time to cut to the chase. What's done is done. You can't go back and fix the past.

THE PAST IS OVER

Oh, you say, if only I knew then what I know now, my whole life would be different.

Of course it would. But guess what—*you didn't know.* Or if you did, you didn't do what you knew you needed to be doing.

So it's done. Finished. Settled.

Sometimes life is unfair.

But that's okay.

You can move on.

You can get over it.

Stop asking yourself why you didn't do what you should have done. The real question is: *What are you going to do about it now?*

NO MORE SAYING, "IF ONLY"!

For a long time now, you've been beating yourself up about what you haven't done or should have done. Some of you have been beating yourselves up for your mistakes for decades. It's unreal how tough we can be on ourselves.

We all do this. I'm no exception. I can't tell you how many times I've said to myself, "Oh, if only I hadn't sold *that house* in Danville, California." *That house* was the first house I ever owned. I bought it for $220,000 and sold it nearly five years later for $225,000. (Not exactly a Donald Trump real estate flip.) Today, *that house* is worth more than $700,000.

If only . . .

Or how about this one? If only I'd bought Dell stock when I bought my first Dell computer. A $10,000 investment in Dell back in 1994 would have been worth $963,000 at the end of 2003.

If only . . .

I could go on and on. But none of it matters. What matters is that with all the amazing mistakes I've made over the years, I still managed to become a multimillionaire. That's because rather than looking back, I focus on going forward. And here's the bottom line: *If you are not yet as rich as you want to be, stop focusing on what you haven't done and start focusing on what you want to do.* And if you're not yet who you want to be, get over that, too. You can become the person you really want to be. You start by letting go of all of the old stories you keep replaying in your head like a broken record or scratched CD.

YOU CAN'T COULDA-WOULDA-SHOULDA YOURSELF TO WEALTH OR HAPPINESS

You know what I'm talking about. So stop "shoulda-ing" all over yourself. It's messy and makes you unhappy. I know. I've been there.

Instead, decide today—right now—to let it go. We all make mistakes. I've made them. You've made them. Your parents and friends have made them. We are all human. Mistakes hurt. But let's not waste one more ounce of your energy, spirit, or time thinking about them, because all that will do is hold you back.

Keep this in mind:

**The past will continue to be your future
if you drag it along with you!**

THE FASTEST WAY TO LET IT GO

Here's an exercise I recommend you do. (Not this minute. Right now I want you to keep reading. But try it when you finish reading this chapter.) If you really want to get over something you regret, the fastest way to do it is to acknowledge the regret—and then burn it up. Literally.

Here's what you do. Get yourself a blank sheet of paper and write down a list of as many of your personal "if only's" you can think of.

If only I had saved more money.

If only I hadn't quit that job.

If only I hadn't taken the job I have.

If only I'd had kids.

If only I'd not had kids.

If only I had bet on the Yankees.

If only I hadn't bet on the Red Sox.

I'm serious about this. Really go to town with it. Free-flow. Let it all hang out. Be honest with yourself. You've been beating yourself up over this stuff for years, so you might as well as get it down on paper.

When you're finished making your list . . . *set fire to it!* I'm serious. Light a match and BURN IT UP. Let all those damn "if only's" turn into ashes.

Have a "Goodbye *If Only's*" party. Invite a friend over and do it together.

Just make sure you burn your "if only's" somewhere safe. We don't want you setting fire to your house. If burning them seems too extreme, then just tear up your "if only's" into little pieces and toss them in the garbage can.

YOUR BRAIN IS HARDWIRED, BUT IT CAN BE REPROGRAMMED

The fact is that your brain is hardwired. You wake up each day, and for the most part you rethink 90% of what you thought about yesterday! Now think about *that*! It's really quite amazing. You use the same words, you go through the same motions, and you often do the same things over and over and over again. What's ironic is that we do the same things over and over and over again and then hope for a new result. This is called insanity!

Watch a fly try to fly through a window sometime. The fly is hardwired to think that the harder it tries, the better its result will be. Well, you and I both know that the fly is not going to get through that window because *it is impossible to fly through glass!*

YOU REALLY NEED TO GIVE YOURSELF A BREAK

I started off trying to convince you to give yourself a break because I know you really need it.

The one thing I've learned from coaching so many people on their lives and money is that we are just too brutal on ourselves. And what do we do when we actually make some progress? We beat ourselves up for not doing everything perfectly.

Take it from me. You've been way too hard on yourself over the years. If a friend or relative ever said the things to you that you've been saying to yourself, you'd stop talking to them. You'd end the relationship then and there. You'd cut them out of your life.

It's a fact that no one will ever be as tough on you as you are on yourself. So give yourself a break.

Really.

OK, now let's focus on what really matters: how money can help you buy your freedom.

CHAPTER TWO

IT'S ABOUT YOUR MONEY, IT'S ABOUT YOUR FREEDOM

If I could give you only one gift, it would be the gift of freedom. The gift to be the person you were put here to be.

Why? Because you are a very special person. In fact, you're unique. There is no one like you on the planet. You were put here for a reason, and I promise you it wasn't to struggle through life.

What does any of this have to do with achieving financial security and independence? In a word, everything. If you are worried about money and your future, it's more than likely you're not living as free a life as you want. And if you're not living as free a life as you want, how can you be living the life you were put here to live?

YOU EITHER GET IT OR YOU DON'T

It may not be politically correct to say so, but the brutal reality of life is that in almost every case, if you sit down and get honest with yourself, you will find that 90% of your problems can be fixed with money.

Yes, I know we're supposed to believe that money doesn't make you happy. There are entire schools of philosophy built on that premise. Well, here's what experience has taught me: *Money may not make you happy, but LACK OF MONEY can certainly make you miserable.*

When all is said and done, the way you get your freedom is to buy it. You don't lease it. You don't wish for it. You buy it, and then you own it.

THE HANDWRITING IS ON THE WALL

In 2002 and 2003, the American Association of Retired Persons sponsored an in-depth study of baby boomers (people born between 1946 and 1964). It revealed some amazing things about their attitudes and experience. Perhaps its most significant finding was this:

Personal finance and work are among the least satisfying aspects of baby boomers' lives.

Specifically:
- While higher-earning boomers tend to be more satisfied with their lives than lower-income boomers, only about 20% of all boomers (one in five) are satisfied with their finances.
- One in four says the worst thing about their lives right now is their finances.
- One in three names personal finances as the one area of their lives they would most like to improve.
- Lack of finances makes it hard for baby boomers to enjoy leisure activities.
- Higher education is no guarantee of financial well-being. Only 20% of college-educated boomers are satisfied with their finances.
- Less-educated boomers are equally unhappy; only 22% of them said they were satisfied with their finances.

Perhaps the single most eye-opening finding of the AARP study is this:

In terms of their single largest ambition, both men and women mention dreams of an improved financial situation.

Read that again. The AARP surveyed thousands of baby boomers and found that their single biggest dream is to get their financial lives together.

Why? Because millions of them have put off saving—and now that they are getting older (and living longer), they're realizing that they face a huge problem.

What's the problem they face? Well, according to the AARP:

When contemplating their personal finances, slim majorities of younger adults (58%) and boomers (54%) and just half of older Americans (50%) believe they are likely to reach their goals in the area of personal finances.

In other words, nearly half of us—old, young, and in between—DON'T believe we'll be able to achieve our financial goals. What makes this finding so shocking is that the same AARP study found that most boomers and younger adults are confident about just about every other area of life. They believe their lives are bound to improve over the next five years in terms of relations with family and friends, mental health, religious or spiritual concerns, work or career, and physical health.

This is why it is so important for you to decide right now that even though you are starting late, YOU ARE GOING TO FINISH RICH. The race of your life is already on. You can continue to sit on the sidelines, moaning about how you should have gotten started last year or 10 years ago or 30 years ago. Or you can get up and start running.

NOW FOR THE GOOD NEWS

OK, are you ready to be motivated? Well, consider this: We are totally blessed in this country. As a society, America has achieved more financially over the last century than the entire world has in all previous centuries combined. Our standard of living is higher, our life expectancy is longer, and our educational and recreational opportunities are greater today than they've ever been.

Within your lifetime, the wealth of the United States has increased by a staggering amount—jumping from about $6 trillion 50 years ago to some $30 trillion today. And while many people are broke and struggling, a whole lot of other people are LOADED.

Indeed, never before in our planet's history have so many people been so wealthy. According to Merrill Lynch & Co.'s 2004 *World Wealth Report*, the number of millionaires in the United States (which the report defines as people with at least $1 million in financial or liquid assets) jumped by 14% to 2.27 million in 2003. In other words, one out of every 125 Americans is now a millionaire.

By way of comparison, back in 1900 there were fewer than 5,000 millionaires in the United States—or only about one out of every 15,000 Americans at the time.

And it's not just the number of millionaires that has increased. Since the 1960s, median household wealth in America has nearly tripled, growing from $29,000 in 1965 to $86,100 in 2001 (the most recent year for which data is available)—meaning that while half the nation's households were worth $29,000 or less back in the 1960s, today half are worth more than $86,100.

WHICH LIFE WILL YOU CHOOSE?

When you contrast the bad news (the paycheck-to-paycheck struggle that kills freedom) with the good news (the phenomenal wealth and opportunity that is all around us), you begin to realize that life is not fair.

The fact is, you don't get in life what you wish for. You get in life what you go for.

People choose their lives.

People choose their actions.

People choose their outcomes.

Life is a cause set in motion.

And life is not over until you quit.

MEET SOME PEOPLE WHO
STARTED LATE AND FINISHED RICH

Before we get to the specifics of exactly how you can start late and still finish rich, I want you to meet some remarkable people. What makes them remarkable is not that they did something difficult. Rather, it's that they discovered how easy it is to do something that most people *think* is difficult.

I hope their stories inspire you to really believe that it's not too late for you. Because it isn't.

$10 MILLION IN REAL ESTATE
IN LESS THAN 20 YEARS!

After my first appearance on *The Oprah Winfrey Show* in 2004, I was bombarded with e-mails. In just one week, I received more than 5,000. As my staff and I went through them trying to figure out which deserved an immediate reply, the address line on one message caught my eye: "Bob Biondi, San Francisco."

Wow, I thought. I'd always wondered how things had worked out for Dr. Biondi.

Dr. Biondi was my first client when I was selling and leasing commercial office space back in the early 1990s. (This was before I became a financial advisor.) His building in Pleasanton, California, was my very first listing, and I'd always loved working with him and his wife.

I remember him telling me how he'd purchased a small duplex a few years earlier and how that had led to him owning this nice little historic building in downtown Pleasanton. I'd always been grateful for the opportunity to list that little building, and I wondered how he'd done with that investment over the years.

So I picked up the phone and called him. Hearing his voice on the other end of the phone was like old times again.

"David," he said, "you were so great on *Oprah*. Mrs. Biondi and I are so proud of you. We always knew you'd do well."

"Well, thanks, Bob," I replied, "but tell me about you guys. How have you done? Did you retire? Do you still own that great little building in Pleasanton?"

"Oh, we sold that building a while ago—and, yes, I did retire. You know, David, real estate has been really great to us. In fact, today we have more than $10 million worth of real estate."

I was surprised in spite of myself. From a little duplex to $10 million worth of real estate. It was nothing short of amazing.

"You know," Dr. Biondi continued, "you were so right about the importance of planning my retirement. When we sold my medical practice, it was worth less than a half million. A lifetime of work, and my real-estate investments ultimately ended up being worth twenty times more than my practice. And my real estate keeps growing and paying me checks monthly!"

Later on, in Chapter Nineteen, you'll learn how you can do what Dr. Biondi did—namely, build a fortune in real estate on the weekends.

A SECOND MARRIAGE, A SECOND CAREER, A SECOND LIFE

Gail and Richard came up to me at a book signing to tell me their story. They had gotten married when they were both in their late thirties. Each had two children from a previous marriage—and because of two tough divorces, they came together with a lot of love but no assets. To make matters worse, Richard lost his job just two weeks after their wedding. For her part, Gail hadn't worked in more than 10 years.

Just when things should have been starting for the better, they seemed to be growing steadily worse. Then Gail and Richard came across an inspirational book called *Think and Grow Rich* by Napoleon Hill. Motivated to start focusing on what they wanted out of life, they made an inventory of their dreams, goals, and values. Together, they decided that they wanted to start a business in which the whole family could participate.

At first, they got jobs at a local candle shop. They worked hard, and eventually, Richard became the manager, while Gail opened a new store for the owner in a nearby neighborhood. Their kids also worked at the shops and held down other jobs (like paper routes). As a result, within seven years the family had saved enough money to be able to "go for it"—which, for them, meant buying their own candle shop franchise.

They all continued to work hard, and a decade later, they owned five candle shop franchises. A few years later, Gail and Richard sold the businesses, walking away with more than $3 million. At the ages of 55 and 58, respectively, they were able to retire to Florida as multimillionaires.

As Gail and Richard told me, it didn't happen overnight, but it did happen. "We never lost sight of our American Dream to control our own destiny by being in business for ourselves," said Gail. "Most important, we feel we've raised our kids to be hard workers. Two of them are already in business for themselves."

If Gail and Richard's story excites you, you'll appreciate Chapter Eighteen, which explains how you can go about selecting and buying a franchise business.

EVEN GRANDMAS CAN FINISH RICH

Like Lynn Hadley, Dr. Biondi, and Gail and Richard, you too can start late and finish rich. It doesn't have to be or seem impossible.

Even grandmas can start late and finish rich.

Over the years, I've shared a lot of stories about my Grandma Rose Bach. An amazing woman, she helped me make my first investment at the age of seven. (I bought one share of stock in my favorite restaurant, McDonald's.)

On her thirtieth birthday, Grandma Bach made a decision that would change the destiny of my family for generations. The decision she made was that she wanted to be rich.

Why was that a big decision? Because Grandma Bach was poor! Really poor. Renting a modest apartment, living paycheck to paycheck, always struggling to make ends meet. It wasn't an easy road, but she was determined and smart. Her desire to be rich led her to listen and learn when it came to money, and over the next several decades, Grandma Bach became a millionaire—a self-made millionaire. Later, she taught my father, my sister, and me how to look out for investment opportunities. Following her practice of keeping alert to the opportunities that were all around us, we would each become millionaires in our own right (my sister and I while we were still in our thirties).

HOW A GAME OF BRIDGE LED GRANDMA TO A SIX-FIGURE WINDFALL

My grandma was always on the lookout for investments. The big joke in our family was that Grandma Bach could find the silver lining in any problem—and also figure out a way to invest in it.

Not all of grandma's investments worked out, but then one day she came across a big one. She was playing bridge with her bridge club—and bragging about my dad (her son, the stockbroker)—when her friend Molly started talking about her son's new business, a hardware store that the friend said was growing like crazy.

That night, my grandma called my father to discuss investing in this new hardware store. My father wasn't impressed. "There's nothing exciting about hardware," he said. "I don't think you should invest."

Fortunately, my grandma didn't listen to her wise son. Instead, she bought a bunch of shares in her friend's son's hardware company. I say fortunately because the company turned out to be a little outfit called Home Depot. (Molly's son was Arthur Blank, the founder.) Within a decade, the shares my grandma bought were worth more than $500,000.

The next time Grandma Bach called my dad to discuss a potential investment, it involved a little company that sold office supplies. This time my dad listened and invested along with her. A good thing, too: The company was called Office Depot.

Later in this book, I'll cover how to play bridge with the right group of grandmas and make a fortune.

Just kidding. (I wanted to see if you were paying attention.) But I do promise you that by the time you finish this book, you'll be thinking differently about making money and building wealth—and that like my Grandma Bach, you'll always be open to and on the lookout for the next great opportunity.

BECOMING RICH IS A MATTER OF DECIDING TO BE RICH—AND ACTING!

Over the course of this book, you will meet lots of real people like Lynn Hadley, Dr. Biondi, Gail and Richard, and my Grandma Bach—people who started late with ordinary incomes but nonetheless finished rich. How? By deciding to *be* rich—and then doing something about it.

I'll share with you how to go from wanting to be rich to actually being rich like these people. At the same time, this book will show you a proven system to regain control of your life—so you can start having more of one.

The interesting thing about finishing rich is that ultimately it's not about the money. What it's about is the feeling of freedom that comes from knowing you are *doing something* about your worries and fears—that you're in control of your destiny, and not at the mercy of forces beyond your control. It's about the satisfaction that comes with "buying back your life" from living paycheck to paycheck. It's about having the security and independence to focus on LIVING MORE instead of just having more.

Having traveled the country and met tens of thousands of people at my seminars over the last few years, I've seen firsthand that what's missing in most people's lives today is not *things*—not money or stuff—but a life. Too many people (maybe you're one of them) are working so hard to pay their bills and get ahead that their lives have gone missing. It's time to change this. They—and you—deserve better.

Most people wish for a better life. Smart people learn, plan, and take action to get a better life.

PRINCIPLE PLUS ACTION EQUALS RESULTS

From here on out, each chapter will end with a summary of the key principles we've just covered, followed by a checklist of specific actions you should take to implement what you've just learned. I've organized the book this way because *Start Late, Finish Rich* isn't just about learning—it's about learning *and doing!*

You want results. That's why you spent your hard-earned money on this book. Well, to be perfectly honest, I can't give you results. All I can do is coach you. You're the one who must take action.

So read the summary of the key principles below and then act on what you've learned. Particularly if you're starting late, the only way you can live and finish rich is if you begin making it happen. The time to start is today.

KEY "START LATE" PRINCIPLES IN CHAPTERS ONE AND TWO

- Give yourself a break: everyone makes mistakes—smart people learn from them.
- The fastest way to get rid of regrets is acknowledge them . . . and "burn them up."
- It's not about the money—it's about living the life you were meant to live.
- Money buys you freedom.
- It's never too late to start.

FINISH RICH ACTION STEPS

Reviewing the principles we discussed in Chapters One and Two, here is what you should be doing right now so you can Start Late and Finish Rich. Check off each step as you accomplish it.

❑ Recognize that what matters is not what you "should have done" but what you now do.

❑ Do the "If Only . . ." challenge described on pages 15 and 16. Make your list of "if only's," burn it or shred it, and let it go. If possible, do this challenge with a close friend or someone you love. Sharing the process will help someone else, bring you closer together, and motivate you both to support each other in the future.

PART TWO

SPEND LESS

CHAPTER THREE

FIND YOUR
DOUBLE
LATTE FACTOR™

The reality of life is that just about everyone in America makes enough money to be wealthy. That's right. You read it correctly. *Just about everyone makes enough money to be wealthy.* Including people who are starting late. Including you.

IT'S NOT HOW MUCH WE EARN,
IT'S HOW MUCH WE SPEND!

Over their lifetimes, most working people will more than likely earn more than a million dollars—maybe much more. So why aren't we all rich? Why aren't *you* rich? It's simple, really. The problem isn't our income; it's what we do with our money once we get it.

If there is one key concept on which everything else I have to say about finishing rich is built, it is this: **How much you earn has almost no bearing on whether or not you can and will build wealth.**

YOU'VE BEEN PROGRAMMED
TO SPEND WHAT YOU EARN . . . AND MORE

I know it sounds far-fetched—especially if you're someone who is starting late on the journey to financial security and independence. But trust me, it's true. The reason you feel behind the financial curve—the reason you haven't been able to start saving and investing for your future the way you know you should be doing—is not that your income is too small. It's that your outgo is too big.

Are you rolling your eyes? I know—most people are convinced all their problems would disappear if, say, their income suddenly doubled. Chances are, you believe that, too. But if you do, you're hurting yourself.

WELCOME TO THE
"NEVER GET AHEAD RACE"

What happens when your income jumps? Tell the truth. Haven't you already seen your income go up only to find you're still living paycheck to paycheck? If you are at all normal, when your income jumps, so does your spending. It's just a fact. We earn more, and then we spend more. Then we need to earn even more, and then we end up spending even more.

This is what I call the "Never Get Ahead Race." Take the case of Nancy, who described herself as a typical middle-class mother of two when I met and worked with her on a television show. We were discussing how she wound up owing $29,000 on her credit cards, and she told the audience: "We always think that the next raise that my husband receives is going to ease the pressure. But we watch each raise come and go without a notice-able difference."

That's the American way: The more we make, the more we spend. And if we're not careful, the more we owe.

INTRODUCING THE LATTE FACTOR

Maybe you've heard of the Latte Factor. It's a concept I created based on the simple idea that all you need to do to finish rich is look at the small things on which you spend your money every day and see whether you could redirect that spending to yourself—putting five dollars a day away for your future, for example, rather than spending it on a fancy cup of coffee.

For most of us, there is no faster or more effective way to take control of your financial destiny than to find out exactly how much potential wealth you are squandering as a result of unnecessary spending on things like mocha lattes from Starbucks every morning on your way to work. But if you're starting late, it may not be enough simply to cut out a couple of hundred dollars a month in wasteful spending. You may need to cut your spending by $1,000 a month or more, and that's not likely to be possible if you focus solely on daily expenditures.

What you've got to do is turbocharge your Latte Factor. You've got to look at more than just the daily extravagances that drain your resources and consider as well the weekly, monthly, and even annual extravagances that you could easily live without—things like premium cable channels, extra-fancy cell phones, new wardrobes every season, and overly lavish Christmas presents.

Take the case of Sharon, whom I met on *The Oprah Winfrey Show.* I did a couple of shows with Oprah, in which we had real people come on and share their Latte Factors. Sharon was a sharp 37-year-old who earned $60,000 a year and had very little to show for it except for a big pile of bills. What we discovered when we looked into her finances was that her Latte Factor came to nearly $1,100 a month. About $250 of that was for manicures and massages, and I suggested to Sharon that she consider reducing the number of manicures and massages she had by half. "You don't have to give them up entirely," I said. "Just cut down a bit."

LOOK HOW MUCH MONEY
YOU WOULD HAVE

At that point, Oprah told Sharon she was going to show her how much she would have in 30 years if she followed my advice and took $125 of her manicure-and-massage money each month and, instead of spending it at the salon, invested it in a retirement account. As Sharon looked on open-mouthed, they wheeled out a cart stacked high with *real, hard cash*—more than $282,000 in all!

"This is how much money you'd have," Oprah announced with a wide grin.

"Oh, my God," Sharon said, blinking in disbelief. She was completely blown away.

But we were only getting started. After showing Sharon how much she could amass simply by cutting back a little, we showed her how rich she could finish if she turbocharged her Latte Factor. Say if, instead of wasting $1,100 a month on unnecessary things (like premium cable channels and eating out several times a week and wine-and-cheese parties), she put it all in a retirement account.

Do you have any idea how much saving $1,100 a month for 30 years can get you? If you invest it properly, you'd wind up with nearly *$2.7 million.*

That's right: All that "small stuff"—Sharon's Latte Factor—was actually costing her $2.7 million! Not very small when you think about it, is it?

LATTE FACTOR SUCCESS STORY

Dear David,

I'd heard about spending big money on the little things, but until you laid it out like this, I never realized how much money I've been wasting. Take today for example:

I was running late to work, so I had no time for breakfast at home (something that happens at least 3 times a week). I bought a bagel with cream cheese, coffee, and water bottle for the day.

Total for breakfast: $5.65

For the same reason as above, I bought the lunch "special" at work, which included a drink.

Total for lunch: $7.50

Now, I'm sitting here eating it, and imagining if I'd brown bagged it. I would have saved over $13 SO FAR TODAY!!! That's at least $10 that I could have put into a retirement plan. *Waking up a few minutes earlier in the morning is definitely worth a million dollars down the road.*

Thanks,

Nancy Ocampo
Los Angeles, CA

MAKE A MILLION, SPEND A MILLION—
AT THE END, YOU'RE STILL BROKE

The Latte Factor is not just about people who are getting started saving. It applies equally to poor, middle-class, and RICH people. We've all got a Latte Factor. Not long ago, in New York, I was invited to speak about my last book, *The Automatic Millionaire,* to an organization of very successful young entrepreneurs. To get into this group, you had to be under the age of 40— and you had to have started a company that was earning at least $1 million a year in gross revenues. The average was actually upward of $9 million a year.

While I was honored to be asked to address such a successful group, I was also concerned that my message might not resonate with them. Considering how rich they all had to be, could they really relate to the Latte Factor?

I mentioned my worries to a close friend of mine, and he laughed. "David," he said, "many of these guys and gals aren't actually rich."

I must have looked surprised, because my friend started laughing again. "Seriously," he said, "of the hundred people who are going to be in the room, how many of them do you actually think really are millionaires? Do you think *any* of them are like that couple you described in *The Automatic Millionaire*?" He was referring to Jim and Sue McIntyre, who managed to become genuine multimillionaires without ever earning much more than $50,000 a year their entire lives.

My first thought was that my friend was simply wrong. At least half of this group had to be millionaires. But then I thought about it some more, and the more I thought about it, the more I wondered. "New York City is a really easy city to have a really big Latte Factor, isn't it?" I asked my friend.

"The world capital," he replied.

NEW YORK CITY,
HOME OF THE $21.50 LATTE

With that in mind, I started my speech to the young entrepreneurs by discussing the Latte Factor and how in New York City you could easily spend $21.50 on your daily latte. They all laughed at that, of course. But then I got serious. "No kidding now," I said to them, "how many of you here have ever paid $17.50 for a martini?"

Ninety percent of the people in the room raised their hands.

"And how many of you eat out five nights a week?" I continued.

Eighty percent of the hands went up.

"How many of you rent your apartment?"

Seventy percent raised their hands.

NOW THE BIG QUESTION!

"Okay, now here's the big question," I said, "and for this one I don't want you to raise your hands. Just write your answer on the blank card we left on your plates. Excluding the value of your business and your home, are you worth at least $1 million?"

A small murmur went through the room.

"That's right," I said. "I'm asking how many of you have assets of more than $1 million—which is to say, how many of you are *really* liquid millionaires."

The answer, when we tabulated it, surprised me. Here we were, in a room of very confident and successful company founders and CEOs, but when you measured how much they were worth (as opposed to how much their businesses might be worth), fewer than 20%, or one in five, were millionaires.

IT'S GOT NOTHING TO DO WITH
HOW MUCH YOU EARN

I'm telling you this story because I've seen this sort of thing time and time again. I've worked with people earning $50,000 a year who swore they would definitely start to save when their incomes reached $100,000—only to reach that level and not be able to save because by then they were spending more than ever. I've seen that kind of person swear to change every year—only to wind up in middle age earning more than $500,000 a year yet still unable to make ends meet. I've also worked with successful business owners who never saved any money because they assumed that someday they'd be able to sell their business for a fortune—only to see their business collapse, and along with it, their financial security.

But then there are people like Jim and Sue McIntrye, whom I featured in *The Automatic Millionaire*. They earned a totally average income, never

---

LATTE FACTOR SUCCESS STORY

Dear David,

Every morning I should be taking the train to work, but instead I wake up late (an average of 3 to 4 days a week), and I end up taking a cab. So I took the $8 (cab ride) x three days a week—this equals $24 a week of wasted money. That equals $96 a month. That equals $1,152 a year. And that equals $11,520 a decade!!

I took the train this morning!!

Patricia Pillot

Bronx, NY

---

much more than $50,000 a year, but they made a point of watching where their money went. Instead of wasting it on "small stuff," they saved it—and as a result, they became financially independent. They retired as multimillionaires, able to do what they want when they want to do it. Which is what I want for you.

Actually, I want to do more for you. I want to show you how to save more _and_ how to grow your income, because the combination will make you unstoppable.

We'll get to how you can increase your income later on, in Step Four. Right now, let's focus on how to use the Latte Factor to help you save more. What you want to keep in mind at this point is that making more money isn't the answer. At least not by itself. For this section of the book, the goal is simple:

CONTROL YOUR SPENDING AND EVERYTHING BECOMES EASIER

The point of the Latte Factor is not to get you to stop ordering _grande_ mocha lattes at Starbucks. I happen to like Starbucks, and I've been known to order the occasional fancy coffee myself. The point of the Latte Factor is to make you aware of how much money you are wasting on little extravagances—and how rich you could become if, instead of wasting all those dollars, you put them to more productive uses. It doesn't matter if you earn what you think of as a small paycheck. Regardless of how big or small your income may be, the Latte Factor can make a real difference in your life. And for people who are starting late, it is nothing short of essential.

So what exactly is the Latte Factor?

When *People* magazine wrote about the Latte Factor a couple of years ago, they summed it up this way:

"A latte spurned is a fortune earned."

As I've recounted in my earlier books, I originally got the idea a little over 10 years ago when a young woman in an investment course I was teaching challenged my suggestion that all anyone needed to finish rich was to put aside $5 to $10 a day. Her name was Kim, and her point was simple. For people who live paycheck to paycheck, she told me, saving $5 to $10 a day simply wasn't possible.

I knew Kim was sincere, but I also knew she was wrong, and to prove it, I asked her to take me through her expenses for a typical day. As it turned out, we didn't even have to go past 10 A.M. to find plenty of potential savings. Her morning routine was something like this:

Before work (Starbucks):	
Double nonfat latte	$3.50
Nonfat muffin	$1.50
10 a.m. coffee break:	
Fruit smoothie	$3.95
High-protein "juice boost"	.50
Power bar	$1.75
	$11.20

"So, Kim," I told her, "we're not even at lunch yet and you've spent more than $10. And truth be told, you haven't really had anything to eat yet!"

Even Kim was willing to admit this was pretty ridiculous. But she was really shocked when I showed her how much these small luxuries were actually costing her.

"Let's say, for the sake of argument, that today, this very day, you started to save money," I said. "I'm not saying you cut out all your spending—just that you reduce it a little. Let's say you realized you could save five dollars a day. Can we try that? Just $5 a day, okay?"

Kim nodded.

"Now you are . . . how old?"

"Twenty-three," Kim said.

I pulled out my calculator and punched in some numbers. Figuring a 10% annual return, which is what the stock market has averaged over the last 50 years, I worked out that if, instead of buying her latte and muffin every morning, Kim put $5 a day into a retirement plan, by the time she was 65, her nest egg would be worth nearly $1.2 million.

"And that's actually a lowball estimate," I told her. "As I recall, you work for a company that matches employee contributions to a 401(k) plan. That's right, isn't it?"

Kim nodded.

LATTE FACTOR SUCCESS STORY

I am a teacher and as I was reading your book, *The Automatic Millionaire*, I started doing the math for what I was spending each morning. EVERY morning, 5 days a week, I spent $1.10 on coffee plus $.99 on a pack of Hostess donuts, and another $.99 on Peanut M&M's for a little snack later on in the day. The first thing I realized was that I eat a lot of junk . . . NOT GOOD! Second thing is that I was spending $3.08 EVERY DAY . . . that's $15.40 a week, which is $61.60 a month, which is $616 during our school year (10 months). I was, and still am, absolutely sick that I've wasted that much money on coffee and snacks when I could've invested that money instead. At $616 a year, that would've been $15,400 over the next 25 years! And that's only if the prices stayed the same over time, when, of course, they will only be going up in the future. I go back to work tomorrow to start another school year and you can be sure that I won't be going for coffee and snacks anymore. The Latte Factor has opened my eyes . . . that money I used to spend on goodies is now going into an IRA for my future!

Tara Richards
Hanford, CA

"Well, if your company matched just 50% of what you put in, you'd actually be saving close to $3,000 a year. And by the time you're 65, that would add up to"—I punched some more figures into my calculator—"roughly $1,742,467!"

At this point, I could see the imaginary lightbulb go off over Kim's head. "David," she said finally, "are you trying to tell me that MY LATTES ARE COSTING ME NEARLY TWO MILLION DOLLARS!"

And so the Latte Factor was born.

BUT I DON'T DRINK LATTES, AND I'M NOT 23

Kim was lucky. She learned about the Latte Factor when she was young enough to make it work for her with virtually no impact on her lifestyle.

But what if her spending habits weren't so easy to rein in? What if, say, she wasn't the kind of person who went to Starbucks every morning? And what if she hadn't been 23 when she turned up in my investment course? What if she had been 33? Or 43? Would the Latte Factor have been of any use to her then?

Let's take the question about Kim's age first. There's no getting around it: It's a lot easier to finish rich when you start early. But just because you're starting late does NOT mean you're doomed to fail. All it means is that you are going to have to work harder at saving and investing. Kim can look forward to piling up millions merely by putting aside $5 a day, or $150 a month, because she's got 40 years or more before she reaches retirement age—plenty of time for the miracle of compound interest to work its magic. If you're in your thirties or forties or fifties and you're just getting started saving and investing, there will be less time for compound interest to grow your nest egg for you. So you'll need to sock away a lot more cash than Kim. You'll need to turbocharge your Latte Factor.

How much more will you need to put aside? The following table should give you an idea.

There's good news and bad news here—though, to my way of thinking, the good news far outweighs the bad. The bad news is that if you're, say, 40, you'll have to put away roughly four times as much money as an early starter like Kim in about half the time to wind up with a nest egg compa-

THE EARLIER YOU START, THE BIGGER YOUR NEST EGG

(Assumes 10% Annual Rate of Return)

Daily Investment	Monthly Investment	10 Years	20 Years	30 Years	40 Years	50 Years
$5	$150	$30,727	$113,905	$339,073	$948,612	$2,598,659
$10	$300	$61,453	$227,811	$678,146	$1,897,224	$5,197,317
$15	$450	$92,180	$341,716	$1,017,220	$2,845,836	$7,795,976
$20	$600	$122,907	$455,621	$1,356,293	$3,794,448	$10,394,634
$30	$900	$184,360	$683,432	$2,034,439	$5,691,672	$15,591,952
$40	$1,200	$245,814	$911,243	$2,712,586	$7,588,895	$20,789,269
$50	$1,500	$307,267	$1,139,053	$3,390,732	$9,486,119	$25,986,586

rable to hers. The good news is that even if you're starting very late, you can still amass quite a respectable amount of money.

Say you're 50 and married, and both you and your spouse are employed. If each of you were to decide today to start investing an extra $15 a day in your respective retirement accounts at work, that would amount to an additional investment of $900 a month. Multiply that by 12 and we are now talking about a yearly increase in savings of $10,800. If you continue putting money away at that rate for 20 years, the results could be truly phenomenal.

Let's assume you invest the extra money in a growth-and-income port-folio consisting of 75% stock-based mutual funds and 25% short-term bonds. (I'll explain exactly how you do this sort of thing later on in the book.) With this sort of mix, it's not unreasonable to expect to earn an annual return of around 10%. (It's not guaranteed, but that's what these investments have averaged over the last 25 years or so.) By the time you and your spouse reach 70, your extra savings should total nearly $700,000. And if your employers have a policy of matching, say, 50% of your retirement-plan contributions (which many companies today do), your total would be roughly $1,025,148. Any way you cut it, this represents a significant extra cushion for retirement.

The fact is, most people overestimate what they can do financially in a year—and underestimate what they can achieve financially in just a decade or two.

INTRODUCING
THE DOUBLE LATTE FACTOR

Big deal, you say. I don't waste 5 or 10 bucks a day at Starbucks—let alone $30 or $40—and by the looks of that chart, unless I can start saving more than $1,000 a month, I'm not going to make it. Where am I going to get that kind of money?

LATTE FACTOR SUCCESS STORY

Dear David:

I found my Latte Factor. It is lottery tickets. I spend $9 twice a week, that's $72 a month and $864 a year, and I've been doing this over 10 years—at least $8,640.

And how much have I won back? Probably under $200.

Diane Jodzio-Willson
Longmont, CO

A woman named Audrey made exactly that point at a recent seminar I gave. "I love all those cute ideas for eliminating wasteful little luxuries," she said, "but I'm 50 and cutting out muffins and lattes only goes so far. I mean, sure, it can help, but your Latte Factor just isn't going to be enough."

At which point a man across the room yelled out, "Well, lady, if the Latte Factor isn't enough, maybe you should try a Double Latte Factor!"

Everyone laughed, including Audrey, but the point was a good one.

Let's face it. If you are really starting late, you're not going to be able to catch up just by cutting out regular lattes. You're going to need to double up on your savings—and that means digging deeper into your spending. You're going to have to attack your *Double* Latte Factor™.

THE DOUBLE LATTE FACTOR™

What's the Double Latte Factor? It's all those fixed, recurring expenses we incur as a result of buying or signing up for all those modern conveniences and services now considered absolutely essential that everyone somehow

> ## LATTE FACTOR SUCCESS STORY
>
> After reading *The Automatic Millionaire*, I realized that I have my own Latte Factor. Four days a week I would eat at McDonald's on my lunch break. My meal cost me $4.76 every day. That turned out to be over $19 per week, $76 per month, and $913 per year. So I have now cut that out of my life and I am packing my lunch. I am taking my newly found $913 per year and I'm investing it into my ROTH IRA. I am 23 years old and my outlook on money has completely changed after reading this book.
>
> **Brian Lowe**
> **Miamisburg, OH**

survived perfectly well without until maybe five or ten years ago—things like satellite TV, cell phones, DVD subscriptions, health club memberships, giant pickup trucks (when you live in the suburbs!), bottled water deliveries, two cars when you only need one, that sort of thing.

Nancy and George, a wonderful couple with two kids I met doing a financial makeover on television, were a great example of the Double Latte Factor. Though they earned a decent living, Nancy and George were drowning in credit card debt.

In our discussion about how they could get out from under that burden, I introduced them to the Latte Factor. Nancy wasn't impressed. "We aren't latte people," she told me. "We don't get a coffee every day. We don't get a muffin every day."

That was true. But that didn't mean there wasn't some fat in their spending. As we worked it out, beyond the basic necessities like rent and groceries, Nancy and George were spending $500 a month on dinners out, $272 on lunches out, $80 on satellite TV, $80 for a cell phone, $45 on a high-speed Internet connection, and $150 on other phone charges. Right there, you had $1,127 going to things they didn't really need—nearly $40 a day in nonessential spending.

Many of these expenditures were for things they really liked and didn't want to have to give up. But when they saw this spending for what it was—an extravagance that was red-lining their financial lives and causing them sleepless nights—they reconsidered their attitude that they weren't "latte factor" people, and they agreed to cut back on some of the extras.

So maybe you don't spend $5 every morning on a latte and muffin.

Maybe you're a smoker. In New York, where I live, a pack of cigarettes costs $7. You do the math.

Actually, I've already done it. It came up during another television money makeover I did for a couple named Melissa and Bill who were $92,000 in debt. Looking for nonessentials we could cut from their spending, Bill volunteered that he smoked a pack a day. "Well, just from the money you're currently spending on cigarettes," I told him, "you could probably build yourself a nest egg worth more than $500,000. Not to mention the fact that if you quit, you'd stand a much better chance of actually being alive to enjoy your money when you retire."

LATTE FACTOR SUCCESS STORY

My husband and I recently came to a harsh reality. We realized that our family had been struggling with an expensive addiction ... going out to eat. Last year we spent $6,100.27 dining out. That's $508.33 per month! If we saved $6,100 a year, we would wind up with $244,000 in 40 years! If we invested this money, we would earn significantly more.

This year to date, we have already spent $3,110.97 on dining out. That is $444 per month. We have not gone out to eat since we began reading your book! We are excited now about saving instead of wasting.

Susanna and Todd Hanrath
Ann Arbor, MI

Here's how it works. If you've got a pack-a-day habit, that's $2,555 a year literally going up in smoke. If you're 35 and, instead of spending that money on cigarettes, you start putting it into investments that earn 10% a year, you'd have nearly $475,000 by the time you reached 65—more than $712,000 if you get that 50% match from your employer. In other words, kicking the habit will not only help you live longer, it could also make you rich.

A PACK A DAY KEEPS RETIREMENT AWAY

(Assumes 10% Annual Rate of Return)

A Pack a Day Costs	Over a Month That Comes to	10 Years	20 Years	30 Years	40 Years	50 Years
$7	$210	$43,017	$159,467	$474,702	$1,328,057	$3,638,122

DO YOU REMEMBER WHERE
YOU USED TO GET YOUR WATER?

Bottled water has to be the funniest Latte Factor of all, because it wasn't too long ago that just about all of us were very happy getting our water for free from a tap. In fact—we still can! Yet Americans currently spend more than $6.5 billion a year on the stuff. In fact, bottled water costs you a lot more than that. Just look at the following table:

BOTTLED WATER IS A FORTUNE DOWN THE DRAIN						
(Assumes 10% Annual Rate of Return)						
Avg. Daily Water Purchase	Over a Month That Comes to	10 Years	20 Years	30 Years	40 Years	50 Years
$1	$30	$6,145	$22,781	$67,815	$189,722	$519,732

BOTTOM LINE: IT'S NO JOKE

Whether we're talking about lattes, cigarettes, bottled water, or any other unnecessary extravagance, a few dollars a day really can add up to a fortune. It may not seem like much. Hey, it's only a few dollars, right? Well, multiply a few dollars a day by 365 days a year. Before you know it, you're talking about real money. And the truth is, we all do this. I mean, really stop for a second and be honest with yourself.

The sooner you figure out your Latte Factor—that is, identify those unnecessary expenditures—the sooner you can start eliminating them. The sooner you do that, the more extra money you'll be able to put aside. And the more extra money you can put aside, the better your chances of finishing rich.

SAVE EVEN FASTER BY FINDING YOUR
DOUBLE LATTE FACTOR

By the same token, you can transform your finances by eliminating all your nonessential fixed expenses, like the gym membership you don't really use and the extra cable boxes you insist on having even though you only watch TV in the living room—in other words, your Double Latte Factor. You may find that cutting back on just one or two things, such as cable TV service or cell phones, can literally put thousands of dollars back in your pocket over the next 12 months. And as we'll soon see, the impact of doing that on your life and your future can be awesome.

A DOUBLE LATTE FACTOR TIP

I'm really not trying to be a Scrooge here. I know you may not be ready to cut out your cell phone or your cable television. But just consider the possibility that your current Latte Factor expenses could be reduced. You may love Starbucks coffee. I certainly do, but I buy my Starbucks coffee by the pound at the grocery store and brew it myself at home. A $10 bag will last me nearly three weeks. This easily saves me $3 a day. That's $100 a month, or nearly $1,200 a year.

You can also save money on your cell phone without having to give it up. As I was researching this chapter, I called Verizon to check on my cellular plan. In five minutes, I cut the fixed cost of my phone bill by $50 a month—and increased my allowance of minutes by 500. That's a savings of at least another $500 a year. Michelle and I also called the local phone company and found a better deal for our home phones that will save us $35 a month, or another $420 a year. In 30 minutes, I saved nearly $1,000 a year with two phone calls.

What about you? Just think about it—and then try it. You may be shocked to see how much money you can save in minutes!

NO PAIN, NO GAIN

I'm a positive thinker. I have a term for negative people who seem to enjoy raining on other people's parades. I call them "dream stealers," and I try to avoid them. All the same, there is nothing to be gained trying to pretend some things are easier than they really are. So let's be honest. Starting late makes it harder to finish rich. That's a fact.

But here is another fact:

Starting late does NOT mean you're doomed to a scary, uncertain future.

To put it positively, even though you're starting late, you still can finish rich. But you've got to be serious about it. You've got to be willing to take a clear, hard look at the way you live and then make some changes—changes that will probably involve giving up some things you enjoy, like going out to dinner a few times a week or subscribing to a picture-phone service from your cellular provider.

But face it—anything worthwhile is worth a few sacrifices. And what could be more worthwhile than giving yourself a future of financial security and independence?

DOCUMENTING YOUR LATTE FACTOR

So how much money are you wasting every day? Or to put it another way, what's your Latte Factor?

You can make a rough guess, but my experience is that it's much more effective to actually document how much cash you squander on nonessentials. There is something about seeing it written down in cold, clear figures that can motivate you to make changes in the way you spend that you wouldn't normally make.

So here's what I suggest: Make a copy of the Double Latte Factor Challenge™ form on page 47 and track your expenses for one day. Take the form with you everywhere you go tomorrow and write down every penny you spend throughout the day.

And when I say everything, I mean everything: every purchase you make in cash, with a credit card, or by writing a check. If you put a lunch on your Visa card, write it down. If you pay a $3 toll to cross the George Washington Bridge, write it down. If you use your debit card to pay for your groceries at the supermarket, write it down. If you give 53 cents to a homeless person in the street, write it down. I promise you, it is truly stunning to see in black-and-white just how much you spend—and on what—over the course of a single day.

Once you've done this, add to the form all your fixed monthly expenses that could either be reduced or cut out entirely. The idea, of course, is to find out how much of the total isn't absolutely essential. This should be a little easier than documenting your regular Latte Factor, since you probably get bills for most of your fixed expenses (like rent or mortgage, car payments, Internet service, cell phones, and cable or satellite TV). Just make sure you're honest with yourself about this. Really look at your checking account and credit card bills, and find out who's attached themselves to your monthly income. I think you may be shocked to realize how many people are on your household "payroll."

If you can bring your Double Latte Factor under control in the next few weeks, you're going to find some serious extra money in your pocket that you never knew you had.

TAKE THE DOUBLE LATTE FACTOR CHALLENGE—AND WIN A
~ FREE LATTE MUG ~

You can win a free Latte Factor mug (perfect for drinking your home-brewed coffee) by sharing your Double Latte Factor experience with me. Visit my Web site at **www.finishrich.com** and click on Start Late, Finish Rich and fill out the form telling me what happened to you when you took the challenge. How much money did you find? What did you learn? Every day a winner will be selected!

Since making a similar offer in *The Automatic Millionaire,* I've received thousands of success stories from readers around the world. It's a simple idea that is really working. I urge you to visit my web site at **www.finishrich.com** and read how the Latte Factor is changing the lives of people just like you. Maybe their stories will inspire you. *Maybe your story will wind up inspiring someone else!*

IS THIS TRIP NECESSARY?

I remember my Grandma Bach telling me about how, during World War II when they had gasoline rationing, there was a billboard slogan you'd see everywhere: "Is This Trip Necessary?" The idea was to remind people not to waste fuel.

I'd suggest a similar question you should always ask yourself if you're starting late on the road to finishing rich: "Is This Purchase Necessary?"

Unless you can answer that question with an absolute, unequivocal "Yes," DON'T BUY IT! Whatever it is. If you can live without it, try to live

THE DOUBLE LATTE FACTOR CHALLENGE

Calculating your Double Latte Factor means looking not just at your daily expenses, but at your weekly, monthly, seasonal, and annual expenses to find items and services big and small that can be eliminated or reduced for big savings.

Name: _____ Day: _____ Date: _____

	Item or Service	Cost	Wasted Money?		Amount Saved	Amount Saved Monthly
	What I bought or buy	How much I spent or spend	✓ if this can be eliminated	✓ if this can be reduced!	I can save X amount by doing Y!	
Item Example	Bagel with cream cheese and small coffee	$3.50		✓	$2 per day by eating at home	$60
Service Example	Two cell phones for myself and Michelle	$200/mo. including all extra fees		✓	$50/mo. by changing service plans	$50
1						
2						
3						
4						
5						
6						
7						
8						
9						
10						
11						
12						
13						
14						
15						
My Double Latte Factor (Total Amount I Can Save Monthly)						$

without it . . . or at least try to cut back on it. This is what I mean by turbocharging your Latte Factor.

KEY "START LATE" PRINCIPLES IN CHAPTER THREE

- The secret to finishing rich is not earning more; it's spending less. How much you earn has almost no bearing on whether or not you can and will build wealth.
- "Small" expenditures can add up very quickly into some amazingly large amounts.
- If you're starting late, you need to find your *Double* Latte Factor.
- Most people underestimate what they can achieve financially in a decade or two; you'd be amazed how big a nest egg you can create saving just $10 or $20 a day.

FINISH RICH ACTION PLANS

Reviewing the principles we discussed in Chapter Three, here is what you should be doing right now so you can Start Late and Finish Rich. Check off each step as you accomplish it.

❑ Recognize that what matters is not how much you earn but how much you spend.

❑ Study the table on page 39 or use the Latte Factor Calculator at **www.finishrich.com** to see how much saving a few dollars a day can transform your future—even if you are starting late.

❑ Take the Double Latte Factor Challenge. For just one day, take a copy of the form on page 47 everywhere you go and use it to track everything you spend. Then add all your fixed monthly expenses that could either be reduced or cut out entirely.

❑ Decide immediately that you can live on a little less and start to save right now.

CHAPTER FOUR

HOW TO
TRANSFORM
YOUR DEBT
INTO WEALTH

A big part of starting late and finishing rich is learning how to deal with debt in a smart way. Unfortunately, many of you who are starting late aren't just starting from zero. You're starting from less than zero.

If this sounds like your situation, don't feel bad. You are not alone. Most people owe money on their credit cards—and a huge number don't pay much more than the minimum due when their bills arrive each month. This can create a truly hopeless feeling.

How do I know this? Because every year I hear from literally thousands of you who are struggling with just this problem. In fact, it's the number-one reason people tell me they are behind on their savings plans. In all, according to **cardweb.com**, a total of 190 million Americans have credit cards, the average cardholder carries more than seven, and the average household owes an outstanding balance of $9,000. The typical couple I've worked with on TV money makeovers owed more than $25,000 on their credit cards. Many of them had outstanding balances of more than $35,000. So if you're in debt, welcome to the club.

The fact is that America has been on a spending spree—using credit cards to party—for most of the last 20 years. Since the mid-1990s, consumer debt—which consists mainly of credit card balances and auto loans—has more than doubled, reaching a record $2 trillion in 2003. (That's *trillion*, as in a thousand billion.) And the spree shows no signs of letting up. If anything, it's getting worse, not better.

But that's the country as a whole. It doesn't have to be your reality.

THE GOOD NEWS ABOUT DEALING WITH DEBT

Dealing with debt doesn't mean putting the rest of your life on hold. If you do it properly, you can actually make dramatic progress on three key financial fronts at the same time.

• You can start paying down your credit card balances . . . immediately.
• You can start contributing to your long-overdue savings plan . . . immediately.
• You can start saving to buy your own home . . . immediately.

Over the next 100 or so pages, I'm going to lay out exactly how you do all this. We'll deal first with your credit card debt, then with savings, and then with buying a home. But don't get the wrong idea. Just because that's the order in which I'm explaining it doesn't mean that's the order in which you do it. It's *not* that you pay off your debt *and then* start saving *and then* buy a home. The point is that you can—and should—do all of it right now.

This advice is the OPPOSITE of what most experts will tell you, which is to get out of debt first and then save. If you are starting late, this is a recipe for financial failure, and I'll explain why in a few pages. In the meantime, keep reading, because you are about to learn one of the most important lessons there is about getting ahead financially.

ITS NOT THE CREDIT CARD DEBT THAT'S KILLING US—IT'S THE INTEREST

I'm starting with credit card debt because it's the single biggest thing holding most people back financially.

The reason most people find it impossible to fight their way out of credit card debt is that they're focused on the wrong enemy. Take Terry and Tammy, a debt-challenged couple I counseled who owed around $30,000 on their credit cards—a burden they couldn't seem to reduce no matter how hard they tried.

"What's killing you," I told them, "isn't the $30,000 you spent on stuff you couldn't afford. It's the interest you're paying on that debt."

Terry and Tammy's debt was spread over five different credit card accounts, which were charging them an average interest rate of 19.98% (a pretty typical rate for people in their situation). Their monthly minimum payment, which they could barely afford to make, totaled about $750. Most of that represented interest.

"You guys are getting hit with more than $500 a month in interest charges," I explained to them. "That's more than $6,000 a year. Do you realize that you've got to earn $10,000 each year just to pay the interest?"

"You mean because of the taxes?" Terry asked.

"That's right," I said. "You've got to earn $10,000 to take home $6,000. So here's the thing. We've got to do something about those interest rates you're being charged."

CUT THE INTEREST RATE AND
THE DEBT BECOMES MANAGEABLE

Tammy shook her head impatiently. "David, I'm not worried about interest rates. What we need to do is find some more money. I've already figured out how we can reduce our spending by nearly $400 a month. If you can help me find another few hundred dollars, I think we can start to make a dent in what we owe."

"Tammy, you're not listening to me," I said. "If you can reduce the interest rate you're being charged, you can start paying down your debt faster. Right now you are wasting nearly $6,000 a year on *interest* payments. You can't make progress on your debt because the money you're sending the bank each month isn't going to pay down your debt. It's going to pay the interest, so all that happens is that the bank gets richer while you and Terry stay in the hole.

"So forget about the spending issue. What we need to do right now is get your interest rate lowered. If we can take you from 19.98% to zero percent, you'll be able to pay off at least a fifth of your debt this year while making the same monthly payments. And if we can get you to up your payments, you might be able to cut your debt almost in half in less than a year!"

HOW TO SWAP HIGH INTEREST CHARGES
FOR ZERO INTEREST CHARGES

"Zero interest?" Terry asked. "I thought charging interest is how credit card companies make money. Why on earth would they agree to charge us zero interest?"

"Two reasons," I said. "First, they're desperate for customers. The credit card market is completely saturated, and the competition between companies is cutthroat. So they make a no-interest introductory offer to hook you. Second, interest charges aren't the only way credit card companies make money. They make a ton of money from late fees, and they're betting that you can't go ten months without being late on a payment. You do that and the fine print kicks in. All of a sudden, instead of zero interest, they're charging you 20%. You're late a second time, and the rate jumps to 26%."

"So why take chances?" Tammy asked.

"Because if you make every payment on time—and you *will* make every payment on time, won't you?—you can reduce your debt by 25% before the introductory period ends."

Tammy still looked skeptical. "And then what do we do?"

"We'll address that next year," I said. "By then, you'll have less debt—and it's more than likely that some other credit card company will be running a low-interest-rate promotion. Of course, because of the excellent on-time payment record you'll have compiled, you'll be able to move your debt again or negotiate with your new credit card company to keep your rates low."

THE CREDIT CARD INDUSTRY HAS
A SECRET YOU NEED TO KNOW

In order to fully understand the secret the credit card companies don't want you to know, you need to understand a little about the credit card industry and its history. So let's take a look.

HOW THE CREDIT CARD CAME TO BE

Back in the 1950s, when the modern credit card industry began, things were different. The pioneering credit card companies like Diners Club and

American Express expected customers to pay off their balances in full within 30 to 60 days, and because of that only people with excellent credit (like successful businessmen) could get a Diners or Amex card. As a result, in those days, having a credit card was a major status symbol. If you had a credit card, you were cool!

By 1960, banks had begun offering what were known as revolving credit cards, which permitted users to stretch out the payments if they wished. The first and most successful of these was Bank of America's Bank Americard. Initially, you could get a Bank Americard only in California. But in 1965, Bank of America hooked up with a number of other banks around the country, and Bank Americard became the nation's first national bank credit card. Two years later, a competing group of banks introduced the MasterCharge program, and by 1969 virtually every bank in the country was issuing either Bank Americards or MasterCharge cards. It was still cool to have a credit card, but it wasn't as special as it used to be.

In 1977, with the credit card business growing ever more global, Bank Americard changed its name to Visa. Two years later, MasterCharge renamed itself MasterCard. But the real change in the business went much deeper than just a bunch of new names. Whereas Diners, Amex, and the other old-line card companies made most of their money from membership fees and sales commissions, the newer bank cards generated most of their revenue from interest charges. Since banks were now running the business, this wasn't really surprising. Charging interest on borrowed money is how banks make money. So why should their credit card business be any different?

This change in the business had huge implications for consumers. For one thing, credit cards suddenly became incredibly easy to get. Having a credit card no longer made you cool (unless, of course, you had a gold card, later replaced by the platinum card, and now by the black card). Students could get them, kids could get them—even dead people and pets occasionally wound up getting them.

But the change had another, much more important impact on consumers. Suddenly, the credit card companies began doing everything they could to encourage customers to carry balances. Minimum payments were lowered, incentives were offered, grace periods were shortened.

What accounted for this shift? Unlike the old-style companies, which get very annoyed if you don't pay off your bill each month, the banks that issue Visa and MasterCard credit cards want you to take your time. In fact, the longer you take, the happier they are. Why? Because the longer you take, the more interest you must pay, and the more money the bank makes. They're happier still when you're late with a payment, because then they can charge you a late fee on top of the interest, which makes them even more money.

HERE'S THE CREDIT CARD INDUSTRY'S SECRET

The secret of the modern credit card industry is that many banks don't really need you to pay off your debt. Their profits go up if you only make "minimum payments." And they're smart enough to know that if they ratchet the minimum payment down low enough, you'll keep spending money and they can make a fortune on you.

Not surprisingly, they don't want you to understand this. They don't want you to know that if you borrow $10,000 on your credit cards and pay only the minimum payment with an interest rate of 19.98%, it will take you *more than 37 years* to get out of debt—and before you do, you will have forked over nearly $19,000 in interest charges.

HERE'S ANOTHER SECRET
THEY DON'T WANT YOU TO KNOW

The credit card companies want you to be late because there's big money in collecting late fees. Not only can they charge you penalties as high as $39 a month if you're even one day late, they can also hike your interest rate. According to Robert Hammer of R. K. Hammer Investment Bankers, a California credit card advisory firm, the credit card industry earned an estimated $13 billion from late fees and other penalties in 2004. "You've got more fees, charged to more people, triggered more quickly than ever before," Hammer warned.

One woman I recently helped with a money makeover was hit with $295 in late fees in just one month—and her average interest rate was raised to 29%! Her credit card companies love her! And she's more typical than you'd think.

The credit card companies have figured out how to move your due dates around, shrink your payment time from 30 days to as little at 21 days, and generally keep you confused enough to ensure that you'll be late paying—as a result of which they can "get you." It's a great business—and the credit card companies are winning. It's also a numbers game, which is why the industry reportedly mails more than a billion credit card offers each year to homes across America.

AND NOW THE RETAILERS WANT IN ON THE GAME

Of course, it's not just the banks and the credit card companies. These days most big retail chains that offer charge cards do so in conjunction with a bank (or similar financial institution). Why does a store like Banana Republic or the Gap push you so hard to get one of their credit cards? You thought these guys were in business to sell clothes, didn't you? Well, if they can get you to buy your clothes on credit—and if you don't pay off your balance right away—they can make a lot more money.

See if this sounds familiar to you:

You've gone shopping at the local outlet of a national clothing chain and you've picked out $1,100 worth of new clothing. (I know this sounds like a lot of money. I'm just using it as an example to make the math easier.) You're at the register, about to write a check for your purchase, when the cashier, a nice, chipper, good-looking young person, smiles at you and asks, "Wouldn't you like to save 10% on your purchase today? You know, instead of writing that check, you could save $100 by opening one of our charge accounts. It will only take a minute."

A typical shopper, trying to be smart, will think, "Good deal—I save $110! Let's do it!"

Cut to a month later, when the bill arrives. "Total balance," it says, "$990." "Oh, man," you say to yourself, "I totally forgot about that." But then you see a much smaller figure next to it. "Minimum payment due: $24.75."

"Now, that's more like it!" you think—and instead of paying off that painful $990 balance, you make the painless $24.75 minimum payment.

That's exactly what the store hopes will happen. And according to a 2004 study by the Cambridge Consumer Credit Index, it's in fact what nearly half of all Americans do each month when they get their credit card bills.

YOU CAN'T GET OUT OF DEBT PAYING THE MINIMUMS

What's so bad, you ask, about paying less rather than more? The answer is nothing. But if you're trying to deal with your credit card bills by paying the minimum amount due, you're *not* paying less. You're paying more—a *lot* more. If your interest rate is a typical 18% and you make only the minimum payment each month on a $990 charge, it will take you 152 payments—or nearly 13 years—to pay off the balance due. By then, the clothes you bought will be long gone—and because of all the interest you've had to pay, your $1,000 purchase will have cost you more than $2,100.

Not such a good deal, is it? Well, not for you. For the store, it's a great deal.

Again, $1,000 might sound like a ton of clothes. Don't get hung up on that. I'm just using clothing as an example. You could just as easily go to the local big-box hardware retailer right now and finance a new lawn mower or dishwasher or large-screen television. It's all the same game—and in most cases, you lose and they win when you take out a new credit card.

BORROW MONEY TO MAKE MONEY, NOT TO LOSE IT

As of 2004, the average household credit card debt of people who carry balances (that is, typical credit card users who don't pay off their bills in full each month) was roughly $12,000. If you pay just the minimum due each month on a $12,000 credit balance, you will wind up having to make 400 monthly payments before it goes to zero. That's 33 years and four months' worth of payments. And that's assuming you never charge another dime on the card, never get hit with a late charge, and are never billed for an annual service fee.

Take a guess how much it will end up costing you to pay off that $12,000 balance on a credit card that charges 18% interest if you pay only the minimum each month.

The answer is $29,616! And that's for a card that charges 18% annual interest. Many cards charge much higher rates—some as high as 29%.

The conclusion this should lead you to is simple: **You can't finish rich if you're carrying credit card debt.**

Think of debt as a trap that forces you to work longer than you should have to. What puts you into debt are bad habits like running up big balances on your credit cards and then paying them down slowly, if at all. You can be hurt and held down by habits like these, or you can take action to break them.

Here's a simple rule to follow: The only time borrowing makes sense is when you do it to buy something that can go up in value, like a house—and even then, you want to pay off the loan as soon as possible.

IF YOU CAN'T PAY FOR IT IN CASH, DON'T BUY IT

There's an old commonsense saying: "If you don't have cash, don't buy it." Hello! That's a pretty darn simple saying that works really well. You only want to borrow to get rich. **You don't want to borrow to look rich!** You don't want to lease your lifestyle. If you are borrowing to look rich, you are guaranteed to stay poor. Really. No joke.

Think about what you bought with your credit cards recently. Was it a need or a want? Be honest. In order for us to get you out of debt (assuming you're in debt), we have to get you to STOP.

IF YOU'RE IN A HOLE, STOP DIGGING

One more bit of preaching and then we'll jump into the technical "how to" part of getting out of debt. Here it is: If you are in a hole, stop digging.

It's time to cool it with the credit cards.

If this means putting a spending limit on yourself, do it. If it means vowing never to spend more than $100 at any store on anything that you didn't go in already intending to buy, do that. If it means forcing yourself to take a 48-hour "cooling-off period" before you spend $100 on an impulse purchase, do that! (This 48-hour time-out is an approach I discuss in *Smart Women Finish Rich*. It helped me stop being a compulsive shopper, because it forced me to go home and ask myself, "Do I really need this?" Once I really thought about it, I almost never went back to the store and purchased whatever it happened to be. Eventually, I stopped shopping all the time because it got to be boring!)

The fact is, it simply makes no sense these days to run up credit card debt. It's not only too expensive; it's also too dangerous. Do what I do now. Don't run up any bills you can't pay in full every month. Refuse to pay 18% interest for items that are perishable. As those figures I cited earlier make clear, carrying a credit card balance is not a smart investment.

Better yet, pay cash for all your purchases. If you come across an item that is too expensive for you to pay for in cash, *don't buy it*. If you spend only cash, chances are you'll spend less. Spending $200 on clothes seems like a much bigger deal when you're handing over a stack of $20 bills, as opposed to just signing a charge slip.

So now we know what we don't want to do with our credit cards. With that in mind, let's take a look at what we *do* want to do with them.

KEY "START LATE" PRINCIPLES IN CHAPTER FOUR

- Dealing with debt doesn't mean putting the rest of your life on hold.
- Your real enemy isn't the debt; it's the interest.
- You can't finish rich if you're carrying credit card debt, and you'll never get out of credit card debt if you make only the minimum payment.
- The easiest and most effective way to pay off your credit card balance is to get your credit card company to lower the interest rate it charges you.
- Don't run up any bills you can't pay in full every month.

FINISH RICH ACTION STEPS

Reviewing the principles we discussed in Chapter Four, here is what you should be doing right now so you can Start Late and Finish Rich. Check off each step as you accomplish it.

❑ Decide to stop using credit cards to buy things you can't afford to pay off in full the same month you purchase them.

❑ Commit to making more than the minimum payment due.

❑ Commit to *always* paying your credit card bill on time, every time, so you don't get hit with late fees.

CHAPTER FIVE

MANIPULATE THE CREDIT CARD COMPANIES— LEGALLY

When I was a kid in school, the teachers always used to tell me, "David, stop talking." Maybe you got that growing up, too? Well, when it comes to credit card debt and starting late and finishing rich, it's time to *start* talking.

The reality is that if you know what to say and how to say it, you can literally get the credit card companies to lower your interest rates and waive your annual fees or late fees.

How is this possible? Because the credit card companies need you! The credit card industry can't operate without your business. The industry today is all about recruitment. It's like the Army, except instead of saying, "Join Us—Be All You Can Be!" their message is . . .

JOIN US—SPEND ALL YOU CAN SPEND

In order to recruit you, the credit card industry is doing everything it can to make you believe that credit card companies exist to help you. They are your friends, and to prove it they offer all kinds of perks, bonus reward points, frequent-flyer points, college account rebate programs, and on and on.

Unfortunately, for people who are trying to start late and finish rich, credit card companies can be false friends. While their services can make your life easier and more convenient, if you don't use them responsibly, you will end up getting deeper and deeper in debt at higher and higher interest rates.

Even the name of their product—the "credit card"—can mislead you. Credit is such a positive word. Here's what you find when you look it up in Webster's:

> **cred-it** (kred'it), *n.* [Fr. *crédit*; It. *credito*; L. *creditus*, pp of *credere*, see CREED], 1. belief; confidence; trust; faith. 2. the quality of being credible or trustworthy. 3. the favorable estimate of a person's character or reputation; good name. 4. praise or approval to which a person or thing is entitled: as, he deserves *credit* for telling the truth. 5. a person or thing bringing approval or honor: as, he is a *credit* to the team . . .

The dictionary goes on in this vein for a while. Credit means *confidence, trust, praise, approval, good name*—all terrific things. It's not until you get all the way down into the fine print of the definition that Webster's mentions that credit can also imply financial obligations and "one's ability to meet payments when due."

The point is that when we hear the word "credit," most of us tend to think of good things, not obligations. And so, we think, a credit card must also be something good—a kind of ticket to the good life.

THEY SHOULD CALL THEM LIABILITY CARDS

If they wanted to be honest with us, the banks and the credit card industry would call their cards something else. I think labeling them *liability cards* would be much more accurate. After all, what does a credit card do every time we use it? It incurs liabilities—that is, debts—that we have to finance and eventually pay off.

To be fair, credit card companies are no different from any other company in our free-enterprise system. They've been created to make money for their owners. In their case, they do this by providing credit to consumers like you and me. We pay for this credit in the form of interest charges. So obviously the more credit the credit card companies can get us to take on— and the higher the interest they can charge us—the more money they make.

The reality is that credit cards can be a great convenience if you use them responsibly. That's the challenge—and the big "if." What you need to know now is how to fix the problem that your "if" may have created.

YOU ARE NOT AT THE CREDIT CARD COMPANIES' MERCY

Fortunately, we are not totally at the mercy of the credit card companies. As I mentioned earlier, they have spent a fortune to get you as a customer. According to *The Wall Street Journal,* the credit card industry sent out 1.3 billion credit card applications in 2003. That's a lot of direct mail, which cost them a lot of money. As a result, it makes much more economic sense for them to do what they can to keep you happy than to lose you to a competitor that's offering a lower rate or a better deal. *You just have to know how to negotiate with them.*

CREDIT CARD COMPANIES WANT YOUR BUSINESS

As we discussed in Chapter Four, the credit card business is an extremely competitive one. It is also highly regulated by the government. What this means is that rather than your being at their mercy, credit card companies can be at your mercy—if you know what you're doing. The thing to keep in mind is that unless you're a total deadbeat, the credit card companies want and need your business.

This fact—and it *is* a fact—should serve as the basis for all your dealings with credit card companies. As long as you operate on the assumption that they need you at least as much as you need them—and that if they don't treat you right, you'll take your business elsewhere—you will do just fine. You'd be amazed at how accommodating they can be when you remind them of this (politely, of course!).

The key thing is never to let them intimidate you. Yes, you owe them money. And, yes, you are both legally and morally obligated to pay off your debts. But that doesn't mean they are ever entitled to treat you badly, take you for granted, or charge you an unfair rate.

YOU CAN TALK YOUR WAY OUT OF DEBT

The fastest way to save money on your credit card debt is to talk down the costs—that is, to get your credit card company to lower the interest rate it charges you.

Here's how you go about doing this:

1. Find out how much interest you are currently paying.
Pull out your latest credit card statement and read the fine print. Generally speaking, the interest rate you are currently paying is listed on the bottom of the very last page in a table called something like "Finance Charges" or "Rate Summary." Don't blame yourself if you find it difficult to figure this out. These tables can be very confusing, with one rate for purchases, another for cash advances, and a third for special promotions. On top of that, they list both a daily rate (which is usually a tiny fraction of 1%) and an "APR," which stands for Annual Percentage Rate. Is it possible the credit card companies don't really want us to know how much we are paying? Whatever the reason, if you're having trouble telling what your interest rate is, call the company and ask exactly how much your debt is costing you. By law they have to answer truthfully. Don't be confused if they quote a rate "over prime"—as in, "Your rate is only 9% over prime." This doesn't mean your rate is 9%; it means your rate is 9% *plus* whatever the so-called prime lending rate happens to be. As of this writing, the prime is at 4%—which would make your annual rate 13%.

2. Find out what the competition is offering.
Once you know your rate, you need to find out how much better you might be able to do elsewhere. This doesn't mean you should start applying for other credit cards—not yet, at least. All you should do at this point is go online to one of the many web sites that specialize in consumer finance information and see what the prevailing rates are as well as what kind of introductory offers you can find. Among the better ones are **www.bankrate. com**, **www.cardweb.com**, and **www.lowermybills.com**. On these web sites, you'll find credit card offers as well as introductory teaser rates.

In addition to researching rates on the Internet, go through your junk mail and keep all the credit card solicitations you get over the course of a month. Then open them all at once and see what kind of rates they're offering. You'll be able to use the figures to negotiate better with your current credit card company. This week alone, I received seven "preapproved" credit card applications. The average offer was for nine months of zero-percent interest.

3. Talk to someone who can make a difference.

Having armed yourself with some specific information about both the rate you're currently paying and the kind of rates other banks are offering, find the "Customer Service" phone number on your latest credit card statement, then call your credit card company and ask to speak with a supervisor. Do not—I repeat, do not—ever try to negotiate a lower rate with the first person who answers the phone. The people who answer the phones generally don't have the authority to approve changes, so you'd just be wasting your time.

When you are connected to the supervisor, tell him or her that a competing bank is offering you a much lower interest rate than the one you're currently paying—and that unless he can match or beat the competitor's rate, you intend to transfer your balance to that competitor. Don't be vague: Tell the supervisor the name of the competing bank and the actual interest rate it is offering. Chances are that the supervisor will agree to lower your rate on the spot.

I've worked with people who were being charged rates as high as 29%, and with one phone call we were able to get it lowered to below 14%. I've also worked with people who were paying 14% and were able to reduce the rates to below 6%. And in some cases, I've had listeners to my radio shows get their rates lowered to zero percent for a year. One woman who went through my *FinishRich Coaching Program* told me that by following my advice, in less than two hours she was able to get her rates on five credit cards (on which she was carrying a total of $20,000 in debt) lowered from an average of 19% to an average of 4%.

By the way, you should be aware that there are often many levels of supervisors. The departments that handle these calls have on average two to five levels of management. So if the supervisor you get the first time around doesn't give you what you want, ask to speak to that supervisor's manager. And if you don't like what he or she tells you, ask to speak to his or her superior.

One other thing: Make sure you write down the names of everyone you talk to. If you're told company policy forbids giving out last names, ask for an identification number. Not only will this enable you to keep track of all the different supervisors and managers you're bound to wind up dealing with, it will also make the customer service people wary of offending you. Generally speaking, as long as you are polite and reasonable, they will probably try their best to satisfy your request, because ultimately they want to keep your business. If you don't get what you want, apply for an account with a company offering better rates and then transfer your balance to that card.

GET OUT OF DEBT SUCCESS STORY

"I bought *The Automatic Millionaire* after seeing you on *The Oprah Winfrey Show*. The first thing I did was call my credit card company and ask for a rate decrease. I let them know that I had compared rates on bankrate.com and they decreased my apr by more than HALF! Thank you, thank you. I am plowing through the rest of my to do's now and can't wait to get them all rolling. Thank you for sharing this great information with everyone."

Jane Reeder
Santa Clara, CA

4. Get the fees waived.

Yet another secret the credit card companies don't want you to know is that you can get them to waive both late fees and annual fees. How? Exactly the same way as you got your interest rate lowered—by calling and negotiating. In fact, it's often easier for the person on the phone to cancel your late fees than to lower your interest rate. The best time to get a late fee waived is the minute you see it on a bill. Call the company immediately and ask, "Can you please waive this late fee? I'm not normally late and I would really appreciate it." I've never—NOT ONCE—had a late fee not credited back to me. Late fees can cost you as much as $39 a pop. If you get hit with multiple late fees, you can be out hundreds of dollars before you know it. This is your money we're talking about—so if all it takes to get it back is making a few phone calls, why not make the effort? I can't guarantee this will work, but you'll never know unless you try.

IMPORTANT TIP: Don't make one phone call and bumble along uncertainly—mumbling something like, "Uh, can you, umm, waive my fees? Oh, you can't? Okay."—and then decide this advice doesn't work. You have to be prepared to try multiple times—and speak with multiple people. This is a game we're talking about. You have to play to win. And like any game, the more you play, the better you'll get at it. Before you know it, you'll be in the driver's seat.

CONSOLIDATING YOUR DEBT

If you have several credit cards, a really effective way to make it easier to get out of debt is to consolidate all your balances on just one card. If nothing else, it means less paperwork for you, since now you have only one credit card company to deal with (and write checks to), making it that much easier to focus on getting debt-free.

Again, to get what you want, you really don't need to do much more than "just ask." When you're negotiating with the credit card companies to lower your interest rate, make a point of telling them that you're prepared to move all your outstanding credit card balances to the company that offers you the lowest rate. You should have a pretty good idea of what prevailing rates are from your research online. (If you don't have Internet access, check the business section of your local newspaper.) See what the national average is for credit card rates—and ask for half of that.

Even better, ask the credit card company or your local bank what kind of rate it is offering to customers like you who are willing to consolidate their debt. Let them try to sell you!

As I told Tammy and Terry, you may find that in order to get all of your business, one of your credit card companies will offer to waive all interest charges for 6 or 10 or even 12 months. If so, be careful—ask them what the rate will be when the introductory offer expires, and remember it! It may jump to 25%, in which case you will need to move once again to a new card company.

WATCH OUT FOR RETROACTIVE PENALTIES!

Also, make sure you understand the penalties they will impose if you are late on even one payment. Many of these zero-interest-rate offers have very specific disclaimers—in tiny print—to the effect that if you are late paying by even one day, your zero-percent interest rate will be increased to 19.98% retroactively; if you're late twice, your interest rate will jump to 24.95%, and so on. As a rule, the moment you fall behind, you forfeit your zero- or low-interest deal and can wind up getting socked with a hefty interest charge back-dated to when you first opened the account.

And pay attention to the due dates. As I mentioned before, the banks have been shortening what's known as the "grace period"—the time you have to pay a bill before they start charging interest. Back in 1993, grace periods averaged 27.8 days, according to Cardweb.com; by 2003, they had shrunk to just 20.6 days. Of course, the companies are legally required to inform cardholders of changes like this, but the notices are usually so filled with legal gobbledygook that they're easy to miss.

Consolidating your credit card balances—and reducing the interest charges they generate—are both important. But let's not forget that the real goal is to eliminate them. In the next chapter, I'll share with you a proven system that will enable you to get rid of your credit card debt entirely—and do so far more easily and quickly than you probably thought was possible.

KEY "START LATE" PRINCIPLES IN CHAPTER FIVE

- If you know what to say and how to say it, you can get the credit card companies to lower your interest rates and waive your fees.
- The credit card industry is brutally competitive. Credit card companies need you as much as—if not more than—you need them.
- The easiest and most effective way to pay off your credit card balance is to get your credit card company to lower the interest rate it charges you.
- Don't run up any bills you can't pay in full every month.

FINISH RICH ACTION STEPS

Reviewing the principles we discussed in Chapter Five, here is what you should be doing right now so you can Start Late and Finish Rich. Check off each step as you accomplish it.

❑ Find out how much interest you're currently paying.

❑ Find out what the competition is offering.

❑ Call your credit card companies and negotiate lower rates and no fees.

CHAPTER SIX

DOLP®

YOUR DEBT

OUT OF

EXISTENCE

DOLP® stands for "dead on last payment," and the goal is to eliminate your credit card debt. Sounds simple enough, doesn't it? Well, not if you happen to be faced with several good-sized credit card balances on the one hand and a not-huge income on the other. If you're in that position, it can seem impossible. It can seem like it's too late for you. But it's truly not. The good news is that if you organize things properly, paying off your credit card debt can be a lot easier than you think.

Ideally, you should begin the process by consolidating all your balances on one card, as I described in the last chapter—putting everything on a card with as low a rate as possible (ideally, zero). The new consolidated balance may look kind of scary (at least at first), but if you're like most people, you'll find it easier and less anxiety-provoking to deal with one big debt than a whole bunch of medium-sized ones. You'll also appreciate the fact that with fewer separate bills to pay, it's less likely that you'll miss any payment due dates.

Once you've consolidated all your balances into one account, the next question is obvious: How much of your resources should you devote to paying it off? Of course, you're going to make more than the minimum payment. But how much more?

PAYING DOWN YOUR DEBT FIRST DOESN'T ALWAYS MAKE SENSE

An awful lot of experts will tell you the same thing: If you owe credit card debt, paying it off should be your top priority. Once you've done that, *then* you can start saving.

While I know this advice is given with good intentions, I happen to think it represents the single biggest mistake people make when it comes to dealing with credit card debt.

Devoting all your resources to paying off your credit cards means not having anything left over to Pay Yourself First (something we'll cover later on). It also virtually guarantees you will stay in debt and never start saving.

Here's why it doesn't add up from an economic point of view. Because they don't know the system you're about to learn, it takes the average person roughly 10 years to pay off his credit card debt. They focus their energy on their debt, they don't save, and before they know it another decade has gone by and they haven't made any progress toward financial freedom. (Sound familiar?) When people are polled on why they put off saving for the future, paying off debt is always a top factor.

WHAT BAD ADVICE LIKE THIS CAN COST YOU

Let me give you a real-life example. I did a financial makeover show with a couple named Karen and Victor who owed $25,000 in credit card debt. They had seen a television show where an expert had said, "You must pay down your debt before you do anything else with your money. If you don't, you'll never be responsible, and if you're not responsible with your debt, money will be repelled from you."

This shook up Karen and Victor. So they did what they thought they should do. They kept paying down their debt and put off trying to save. Unfortunately, they were paying only a little more than the minimum. Specifically, although they owed $25,000 on their credit cards, they were barely paying $500 a month.

One of the first things I did when I met Karen and Victor was to explain to them that at that rate, it would take them more than 35 years to pay off their credit card debt. Then I showed them what would happen if they increased their debt payment by just $10 a day—and at the same time started adding $10 a day to their savings.

Since they were both in their early thirties, the numbers were great to look at. Putting an extra $10 a day toward their credit card debt would get them out of debt in less than three years. More important, the $10 a day extra contribution to savings would yield them nearly $700,000 at retirement. As I told them, the benefit of this approach is that you get out of debt and start building your financial freedom at the same time!

BUT WHERE DO WE FIND $20 A DAY?

Karen and Victor were earning about $75,000 a year, so coming up with an extra $20 a day (or $600 a month) wasn't easy. We went through their expenses, including both their Latte Factor and their Double Latte Factor, and the only way we could make this work was to cut it to the bone. No one ever said getting out of debt and finishing rich would be easy. All I said was that it was doable! And what mattered to Karen and Victor was that they now had a real plan to DO IT.

If you just focused on slowly paying off your credit card debt—and it wound up taking 10 years before you could start to save—do you know what it would cost you?

Let's say you had $300 a month you could either save or use to pay down credit card debt—or both. Assuming a 10% annual return on your money, if you used it all to pay down credit card debt for 10 years and then, once the debt was paid off, started saving the full $300 a month for the next 20 years, you'd wind up with a nest egg worth $227,811. On the other hand, if you allocated just $150 a month to paying down your debt and at the same time started saving $150 a month, after 30 years you'd have no debt and $339,073. In other words, waiting 10 years to start saving would reduce the size of your potential nest egg by NEARLY A THIRD! It's even worse when the time spans are shorter (which is generally the case when you're older). For example, if you saved $600 a month for 10 years, you'd wind up with $122,907, which is only about half of the $227,811 you'd have if you saved $300 a month for 20 years.

Financially speaking, putting off saving in order to pay off your credit card debt can be a huge mistake.

LOOK AT HOW CORPORATE AMERICA HANDLES DEBT

Think about how corporations handle debt. Most companies borrow money—huge amounts of it—in order to finance their growth. Now, once a company incurs a debt, does it devote all its income to paying it off? Of course not. Any company that did so would see its stock price get crushed—and would more than likely go out of business. What smart companies do is allocate a portion of their resources to debt reduction while at the same time devoting other portions to developing new products, exploring new markets, and generally expanding their business.

What businesses do is grow themselves out of debt. They pay down their debt and invest money in their future at the same time. And that's exactly what you want to do. You want to pay down your debt and save at the same time.

IT'S NOT JUST FINANCIAL— IT'S PSYCHOLOGICAL

There is also an important emotional/psychological reason to save for the future at the same time as you're paying off your debt. By doing both of these things at the same time, you will feel your progress. You'll see money being saved and debt being reduced.

As I said before, if you were to direct all of your available cash flow to debt reduction, with the idea that you wouldn't begin to save until all your credit card bills were paid off, it might be years before you could begin saving for the future. In addition to the phenomenal economic cost of doing this, from an emotional point of view this is way too negative—so negative, in fact, that many people who follow this path get discouraged, give up early, and never get to the saving part. For someone who is starting late, this can be catastrophic.

AND DON'T WAIT TO BUY A HOME, EITHER

Saving is not the only thing you shouldn't put off while you pay down your credit card debt. You shouldn't put off buying a home, either. We'll get into the details of why you need to own your own home—and how you can go about becoming a homeowner—in Chapter Eleven. Right now consider the story of a good friend of mine named Christopher, who moved to Manhattan four years ago.

Christopher arrived in the Big Apple with about $15,000 in credit card debt and just a few thousand in savings. When he told me he was planning to rent an apartment for about $1,200 a month, I suggested to him that instead of renting, he should buy a home.

"Come on, David," he said. "I have $15,000 in credit card debt. No one is going to give me a mortgage. And, anyway, you're supposed to pay off your debts before you take on an obligation like a house."

I told Christopher he was wrong on both counts. To make a long story short, Christopher listened to me and bought a home (using the techniques you'll learn in Chapter Eleven) with a 95% mortgage—meaning he had to put only 5% down—for which he was able to qualify even though he had credit card debt. He purchased a studio apartment in Manhattan for $125,000—and four years later sold it for $365,000!

As a result, Christopher has been able is pay off his credit card debt completely and still pocket more than $225,000 tax-free! Had he waited to pay off his credit cards first and then buy a home, he'd more than likely still be in debt and still be renting.

The point is that if you're starting late, you can't simply accept the conventional wisdom that's been out there for decades. You need to think differently and act differently.

BURY THE PAST AND JUMP TO THE FUTURE

The bottom line here is that while you want to get rid of your credit card debt as quickly as possible, you also need to start building a nest egg for your future as quickly as possible. I call this approach "Bury the past and jump to the future."

We'll deal with the nuts and bolts of "jumping to the future"—that is, how to turbocharge your saving—in Step Three. Right now, let's focus on how you "bury the past"—specifically, how much of your money should be directed to debt repayment. Basically, the most effective way to make sure you'll finish rich, especially if you are starting late, is to divide your resources equally. In other words, you take all the "extra" Latte Factor money you've carved out of your spending and split it 50-50, with half going to your nest egg and half to paying off your credit card bill.

For example, let's say that by determining your Latte Factor, you've managed to cut $15 a day from your normal spending habits. That's $450 a month. What I'm saying is that you take half of that—or $225—and put it toward debt reduction.

THE MAGIC FORMULA FOR PAYING OFF CREDIT CARD DEBT

As I hope I've already made clear, the key to getting out of credit card debt is to pay more than the minimum due each month. How much more? The magic formula for figuring this out is really quite simple. You should aim to pay at least $10 a day more than the minimum payment. If you do that, you can be out of debt in less than five years.

Say, for example, you owe $10,000 on your credit cards, with an average interest rate of 20%. The standard minimum payment for a $10,000 balance is $250. As I noted earlier, if that's all you pay each month, it will be *37 years* (and more than $19,000 in interest charges) before your balance is paid off. On the other hand, if you up that monthly payment by $10 a day (or $300 a month) to $550, you will be out of debt in just 22 months—less than two years! And you'll have paid only about $2,000 in interest.

Need I say more?

DOLP® YOUR DEBT OUT OF EXISTENCE

The process I just described depends on your being able to consolidate all your credit card balances in one account. But what do you do if, for some reason (say, you owe so much that no company will give you a sufficient credit limit), you can't consolidate your debt?

The answer is to DOLP® your way out of debt.

I first described the DOLP system in *The FinishRich Workbook*. The basic idea is to rid yourself of credit card debt once and for all by paying off all your balances and then closing all your credit card accounts.

DOLP STANDS FOR "DEAD ON LAST PAYMENT"

In other words, your credit cards are all going to be Dead On Last Payment—or DOLP, for short.

Of course, when you have a lot of credit cards, figuring out how to pay them all off can be pretty daunting. Do you pay a little on all of them at once? Or should you concentrate on one card at a time? And if so, which one goes first?

This is where the DOLP system comes in.

Here's what you do.

1. Make a list of the current outstanding balances on each of your credit card accounts.

2. Divide each balance by the minimum payment that a particular card company wants from you. The result is that account's DOLP number. For example, say your outstanding Visa balance is $500 and the minimum payment due is $50. Dividing the total debt ($500) by the minimum payment ($50) gives you a DOLP number of 10.

3. Once you've figured out the DOLP number for each account, rank them in reverse order, putting the account with the lowest DOLP number first, the one with the second lowest number second, and so on. The table below shows what your list should look like.

Account	Outstanding Balance	Monthly Minimum Payment	DOLP Number (Balance/Min Payment)	DOLP Ranking
Visa	$500	$50	10	1
MasterCard	$775	$65	12	2
Sears Card	$1,150	$35	39	3

You now know the most efficient order in which you should pay off your various credit card balances. Take half your Latte Factor savings and apply them to the card with the lowest DOLP ranking.

For each of your other cards, you make only the minimum payment.

In the example above, the card with the lowest DOLP ranking is Visa. So each month, you'd devote half your Latte Factor savings to reducing your Visa balance, while making the minimum payments on the other cards. Once you've DOLPed your Visa account (that is, paid it off entirely), you'd close it down and turn your attention to the card with the next-lowest DOLP ranking—in this case, MasterCard.

You should continue doing this until you've DOLPed your way to being debt-free.

Here's a blank table you can fill in to create your own DOLP list.

Account	Outstanding Balance	Monthly Minimum Payment	DOLP Number (Balance/Min Payment)	DOLP Ranking

DOLP DOESN'T HELP IF YOU DON'T CHANGE YOUR HABITS

There's not much point in DOLPing your way out of credit card debt only to fall right back in. And that's really easy to do unless you change your habits.

I know because I did just that in my early twenties. I got out of debt only to tumble back in deeper than ever within two years. What finally saved me was a complete change in attitude. While I still use credit cards, I don't allow myself to carry any credit card debt—which is to say I only charge items I know I can (and will) pay off in full as soon as the bill arrives. I do this because I consider my credit cards a convenience, NOT A LOAN. That's how I suggest you look at them from now on.

Now let's look at what you can do if you've really, really buried yourself in debt . . . to the point where you need professional financial help. Even if your situation isn't that bad, you probably should read this chapter anyway, because (1) you may have a friend who needs this kind of help, and (2) you never know when it may come in handy for yourself.

KEY "START LATE" PRINCIPLES IN CHAPTER SIX

- Devoting all your resources to paying off your credit cards virtually guarantees you will stay in debt and never start saving.
- Putting off saving in order to pay off your credit card debt can cost you big-time in savings down the road.
- You want to pay down your debt and save at the same time. Whatever you can put aside should be split equally between paying off your debt and paying yourself.

FINISH RICH ACTION STEPS

Reviewing the principles we discussed in Chapter Six, here is what you should be doing right now so you can Start Late and Finish Rich. Check off each step as you accomplish it.

❑ Consolidate your credit card debt.

❑ If consolidating isn't possible, start DOLPing your credit card accounts.

❑ As you pay off each balance, close down the account.

CHAPTER SEVEN

BEWARE OF THE "NONPROFIT" PROMISE OF DEBT COUNSELORS

If you are starting late with massive amounts of debt, you may need professional help. Why? Because serious debt problems are the worst. They can cripple your spirit, break your courage, threaten your marriage, and even ruin your health. The good news is that for people who feel overwhelmed, there are places called credit counseling agencies you can turn to for help. The bad news is there are a growing number of companies that try to take advantage of people with debt problems. Not a day goes by that my e-mail inbox doesn't fill up with bogus "get out of debt" or "fix your credit" offers. This chapter is designed to help you better understand whom credit card counseling agencies can really assist, and what they can do to help you or hurt you.

Legitimate credit counseling agencies like the *Consumer Credit Counseling Services* basically do two things. They help you sort out your current problems by negotiating with your creditors to get you lower interest rates and more bearable payment plans. And they try to prevent future problems by teaching you some basic financial management skills.

Depending on your situation, a good credit counseling agency should be able to offer you everything from simple advice about handling your money to (in the worst case) suggesting that maybe you need to talk to a bankruptcy lawyer. One service virtually all of them offer is something called a "debt-management plan," or DMP.

DMPs can be lifesavers when your situation is dire—say, you're incapable of making even your minimum payments or you're unable to renegotiate your interest rates. Under a DMP, the agency works out a payment plan with all your creditors, in the process often getting late fees waived and interest rates lowered. Once the DMP has been set up, you simply make one consolidated monthly payment to the agency, which then parcels out the money to all your creditors.

THE PROBLEM WITH "DEBT MANAGEMENT PLANS"

DMPs can be great things for debt-strapped consumers . . . *if* they're used appropriately and run properly. Unfortunately, the new breed of rip-off artist that has flooded into the credit counseling industry over the last decade rarely does either. To the scammers, DMPs are just another way to separate unwary consumers from their hard-earned dollars.

Legitimate credit counseling agencies cover their expenses by charging clients small fees to set up and administer DMPs. (These fees shouldn't run much more than $50 up front and $25 a month after that.) They also receive what are called "fair share" payments from your creditors, who pay them a percentage of the money the agency collects from you and passes along to them—the idea being that if the agency hadn't set up the DMP for you, your creditor might not be getting anything.*

Unfortunately, because DMPs can generate revenue, unscrupulous credit counseling agencies try to pressure everyone who comes through their doors into enrolling in one—whether it makes sense for them or not.

---

*For many years, credit card companies paid the counseling agencies 15% of the debt payments they passed along from consumers. But lately they've cut back to 8%—largely in response to the influx of bad apples, who not only ripped off unwary debtors but also took advantage of the banks by offering their services to people who weren't behind in their payments but simply wanted lower interest rates.

They also charge unconscionably high fees, pressure clients into making "voluntary" donations, and even deduct money from consumers' payments without letting them know.

In testimony before a U.S. Senate subcommittee in March 2004, Commissioner Thomas Leary of the Federal Trade Commission described the kind of "deceptive and other illegal practices" typical of corrupt credit counseling agencies. They included:

- **Misrepresenting fees or "voluntary contributions."** Some agencies charge excessive fees that are automatically deducted from DMP payments without the client's knowledge. Others trick clients into making a "donation" by hiding in the fine print of their contracts a line that states, "I voluntarily agree to contribute one month's payment ..."
- **Promising results that cannot be delivered.** Some agencies market themselves and their DMPs by insisting they can get creditors to lower interest rates, monthly payments, or overall debt by ridiculously large amounts. They also claim (falsely) that they can eliminate accurate negative information from your credit report, and they exaggerate how much money you will save by signing up for a DMP.
- **"One size fits all" counseling.** Some agencies say they provide money-management advice and education to consumers, when in fact they enroll all clients indiscriminately in DMPs without any actual counseling.
- **Failure to pay creditors quickly—or at all.** The worst agencies take their time forwarding your money to creditors, making money on the "float" (the interest that accrues while your dollars sit in their account). The absolute worst simply pocket your money and disappear. Since you're still responsible for your debts even after you enroll in a DMP, the late fees, interest penalties, and possible defaults that result from this kind of conduct can destroy your already shaky finances, not to mention your credit record.

HOW ONE CREDIT COUNSELING AGENCY TOOK ADVANTAGE OF MILLIONS OF CONSUMERS

One of the worst examples of this kind of fraud involved Maryland-based AmeriDebt, Inc. Until it collapsed in 2004 under a blizzard of lawsuits— including a major action filed by the FTC—AmeriDebt was one of the nation's largest and most aggressively marketed debt-management firms, spending more than $11 million a year on cable TV and Internet advertising. Touting itself as "the friend of consumers in crisis," AmeriDebt claimed to have served upward of 400,000 clients.

In fact, according to the FTC and a variety of other plaintiffs (including law-enforcement officials in Illinois, Minnesota, Missouri, and Texas), AmeriDebt actually bilked hundreds of thousands of people out of tens of millions of dollars by misleading them about fees and pretending to be a nonprofit organization when it was actually being run to make money for its founders.

Specifically, the lawsuits alleged, even though AmeriDebt promised to teach people how to handle credit, it offered no such instruction. Rather, it simply enrolled everyone it could in DMPs that were run by a profit-making company called DebtWorks, which just happened to be owned by AmeriDebt's founder, Andris Pukke. In addition, though AmeriDebt claimed it didn't charge any up-front fees, it typically pocketed a consumer's first monthly payment as a "contribution," instead of forwarding it to creditors.

BEWARE OF THE "QUICK FIX"

To be fair, AmeriDebt was hardly a typical operation. Still, you do need to be extremely careful when picking a credit counseling agency. The thing to remember is that you've got to be realistic about credit card debt. You are not going to be able to solve your problems overnight. It probably took a long time to get into trouble with credit card debt. And chances are it will take you a long time to get out of it.

With this in mind, you should be suspicious of "experts" who claim they can solve all your credit problems with some magical quick fix. In addition, the National Consumer Law Center and the Consumer Federation of America suggest you watch out for the following "red flags" when you're considering signing on with a credit counseling agency:

- **High fees.** If an agency charges more than $50 up front and $25 a month to set up and maintain a debt-management plan, they're probably ripping you off. An equally bad sign is if they're vague or reluctant to talk about specific fees.
- **The hard sell.** The "counselor" who answers the phone should not be

reading from a script. If he or she aggressively pushes the idea of debt "savings" or the possibility of a future "consolidation" loan, hang up.

- **Commission-paid employees.** The best credit counseling agencies are nonprofit organizations whose only motivation is supposed to be what's best for you. Employees who earn commissions for signing up clients are likely to care more about their own paychecks than your debt problems.

- **The 20-minute test.** Whether you do it in person or over the phone, an effective credit counseling session generally takes a fair amount of time—at least 30 minutes, and often as much as an hour and a half. An agency that offers you a debt-management plan after a consultation of just 20 minutes or less can't possibly know enough about you and your situation to be making an informed recommendation.

- **Aggressive ads.** Don't be fooled by hard-sell pitches on television or the Internet that promise to solve all your debt problems. Before you sign up with any credit counseling agency, get referrals from friends or family, and check with consumer groups like the Better Business Bureau to see if they've had any complaints lodged against them.

HOW TO FIND A CREDIT COUNSELOR YOU CAN TRUST

Consumers looking for a counselor to help them solve their debt problems face a real challenge. As the Consumer Federation of America points out, it is virtually impossible to tell the honest, caring agencies from the rip-off artists simply by looking at a TV ad or making a quick phone call. So how do you find a good one?

By far, the best way to find a trustworthy credit counseling agency is through a referral. As I noted above, if you know any friends or relatives who've used a credit counseling agency, ask them how they fared. Nothing beats personal experience, and a satisfied client is a pretty strong recommendation. (All the same, you should still double-check with the Better Business Bureau before you sign up with anyone.)

If you don't know anyone who's used a credit counseling agency—or if the people you know who did had a bad experience—you should try a referral service. Probably the most highly regarded referral service in the country is Consumer Credit Counseling Services.

As I noted at the beginning of this chapter, CCCS is an offshoot of the National Foundation for Credit Counseling, the nation's oldest national nonprofit organization for consumer counseling and education on budgeting, credit, and debt resolution. You can find an affiliate near you by telephoning (toll-free) 800-388-2227 or by going online to **www.nfcc.org**.

When you contact CCCS, you will be referred to a nonprofit credit counseling group in your area that can help you. When you call to arrange a meeting with this group, try to find out as much as you can about what they can and can't do to help you.

Though CCCS is extremely reliable, that doesn't mean you shouldn't do some research of your own. Among other things, you should:

- Carefully read through any written agreement that an agency asks you to sign. The agreement should describe in detail what services will be performed, how much you will have to pay for these services, how long it will take to achieve results, the exact nature of any guarantees that may be offered, and the organization's legal business name and address.
- Make sure your creditors are willing to work with the agency. If they are, follow up with them regularly to make sure your debt is being paid off.
- Check with state agencies and the local Better Business Bureau to find out about the agency's record.

In addition, as the CEO of Bankrate.com, a leading financial information web site, pointed out, "It's a good idea to go and visit the agency to make sure it actually exists."

Finally, if you think you've been victimized by a fraudulent or unethical credit counseling agency, you can file a complaint with the Federal Trade Commission by calling toll-free 1-877-FTCHELP or by going to the FTC's web site at **www.ftc.gov**.

KEY "START LATE" PRINCIPLES IN CHAPTER SEVEN

- While legitimate credit counseling agencies can be enormously helpful, the industry has been invaded by a "new breed" of scam artists.
- Debt-management plans can be lifesavers, but they are not necessarily the right solution for everyone.

- Beware of "experts" who claim they can solve all your credit problems with some quick fix.
- The best way to find a trustworthy credit counseling agency is through a referral, whether from someone you know or the National Foundation for Credit Counseling.
- Always check with the Better Business Bureau and state agencies before you sign up with any agency.

FINISH RICH ACTION STEPS

Reviewing the principles we discussed in Chapter Seven, here is what you should be doing right now so you can Start Late and Finish Rich. Check off each step as you accomplish it.

❑ If you decide to use a credit counseling agency, watch out for the red flags described on pages 80–81.

❑ Ask friends and relatives for a referral.

❑ Check out an agency's record with the Better Business Bureau.

NOW LET'S GET YOUR START LATE SAVINGS PLAN GOING

You've come a long way. Congratulations! At this point, your Latte Factor should be truly turbocharged—which means you've taken control of your spending and are in the process of transforming your past debts into future wealth. With this as a rock-solid foundation, it's time to learn how to turbocharge your saving by learning how to Pay Yourself First . . . Fast.

PART THREE

SAVE MORE

CHAPTER EIGHT

PAY YOURSELF
FIRST . . .
FASTER!

When it comes down to it, finishing rich is simple. All you have to do is make a decision to do something that most people don't do—to Pay Yourself First. And if you're starting late, you have to *Pay Yourself First . . . Faster!*

It really is that simple. The catch is that you have to know what Pay Yourself First means and then you have to do it. And if you're not where you'd like to be financially at this point in your life, chances are you don't and you're not.

The idea that you should Pay Yourself First is not new. I've been teaching and writing about it for years, and it had already been around for a long time when I started. So I don't expect this is the first time you've heard of it. But hearing about a concept and using it to change your life are two different things.

Paying yourself first is one of those concepts like the Latte Factor that most of us think we know but few of us actually put into practice. Everyone says they have heard of Pay Yourself First and yet most Americans are not doing it. Most Americans—and maybe you're one of them—actually pay everyone else first when they get their paychecks. For starters, most of us pay the government first through taxes. Do that—pay your taxes before you put some of your earnings into savings—and you've pretty much guaranteed yourself a hard time starting late and finishing rich.

HOW TO GET OUT OF PAYING THE GOVERNMENT FIRST

There is a perfectly legal way to avoid paying the government first. You do it by funding a PRETAX retirement account. These accounts come in all sorts of shapes and sizes, with names like 401(k) or 403(b) plans, IRAs, and SEP IRAs. We'll cover them in detail later on. All you need to know right now is that a pretax retirement account is TAX-DEDUCTIBLE—meaning it's the only legal way for most of us to get out of having to pay the government its federal and state taxes before we pay ourselves.

This is a crucially important benefit for working people who want to finish rich—especially those who've started late. Unfortunately, too many of us are not taking advantage of it. According to the Employee Benefit Research Institute, a nonprofit group that studies this sort of thing, fewer than one out of four working-age Americans contribute to 401(k) plans—and only 15% have Individual Retirement Accounts (better known as IRAs).

The fact is, when most of us earn a dollar, the first person who gets paid isn't us. It's Uncle Sam. Even before that dollar makes it onto our paycheck, the government grabs something like 27 cents in federal income withholding taxes (often more). On top of that, local governments may grab another five cents in city and state withholding. (Exactly how much depends on where you live.) And then there are Social Security taxes, Medicaid, and unemployment.

IF YOU PAY THE GOVERNMENT FIRST, YOU CANNOT START LATE AND FINISH RICH

When all is said and done, most of us wind up losing 30 to 40 cents out of every dollar we make *before we ever have a chance to spend—or invest—a penny of it.*

Under the best of circumstances, this can make life tough. For people who are starting late—in other words, people who have a lot of catching up to do on saving and investing—it makes it impossible.

I'm going to be blunt here. There is absolutely no way to start late and finish rich if you let Uncle Sam get his hands on your paycheck before you do. And unless you're putting as much of your income as you possibly can into a tax-deferred retirement account, that's exactly what you're allowing the government to do.

YOU'VE GOT TO GET YOUR MONEY BEFORE UNCLE SAM DOES

The reason you need to get to your money before the government gets to it isn't just so you can reduce your tax bill. It's also so you can grow your nest egg as fast as you possibly can. And if you're starting late, believe me, that's what you need to do.

Fortunately, there is a way—and it's amazingly easy. All you have to do is open a pretax retirement account and start putting a portion of your salary into it. Every dollar of your income that you deposit (up to certain limits that we'll discuss later), as long as it stays in the account, is not subject to any taxes. And neither is any of the interest (or capital gains) that you earn on it.

I know what the skeptics are thinking. Big deal. So the money is tax-free *as long as it stays in the account.* All you're doing is deferring the taxes. Once you take the money out, don't you have to pay taxes on it then? What good is that?

JUST LOOK AT HOW SIMPLE THE MATH IS

The answer is that it's huge. For one thing, because you're not sharing your hard-earned dollars with the government, you can invest more of them in your retirement account to begin with. For another, because you don't have to pay taxes each year on whatever returns your investment happens to achieve, your nest egg is able to grow much, much faster.

The table that follows shows just how this works. It compares two investments that offer the same 10% annual return—in a tax-deferred account versus a regular one.

	Tax-deferred Account (Pretax)	Regular Account (Taxable)
Gross income	$1.00	$1.00
Taxes deducted	–0	–30%
Amount available to invest	$1.00	$0.70
Annual return	+10%	+10%
Balance after one year	$1.10	$0.77
Are gains taxable?	No	Yes

The tax-deferred advantage is clear. At the end of a year, the tax-deferred investment is worth nearly 43% more than the regular one. And if you happen to work for one of the many companies that match a percentage of employee retirement contributions, you could do even better. The table below shows the kind of return you get if your employer offers a 25% match.

	Tax-Deferred Retirement Plan (with Employer Match)	Regular Investment
Gross income	$1.00	$1.00
Taxes deducted	–0	–30%
Amount available to invest	$1.00	$0.70
Typical Employer match	+ 25%	0
Amount invested	$1.25	$0.70
Annual return	+ 10%	+ 10%
Balance after one year	$1.38	$0.77
Are gains taxable?	No	Yes

Amazing, isn't it? After just one year, you're 100% ahead with a pretax retirement account! And that's just the beginning. The advantage only gets wider over time.

Just to give you an idea of how much this can mean if you do it over time with real money, say you put $100,000 in an investment that generates an annual return of 10%. If it's a regular taxable investment and you're in the 35% tax bracket, after 30 years your nest egg will have grown to a little over $661,000.

Not too shabby, you say. Well, maybe not, but consider how much the same investment would be worth after 30 years if it were tax-deferred. *The answer is nearly three times as much—more than $1.7 million!*

To put it simply, if you pay the government first, you're trying to finish rich with one hand tied behind your back.

Well, now you're going to untie that hand.

WHAT "PAY YOURSELF FIRST" REALLY MEANS

When people tell me they know all about Pay Yourself First, I generally ask them four questions. Based on their answers, I can immediately tell if they have a realistic plan to become rich. Most people don't.

These are the questions:

• Do you know how much you should Pay Yourself First?
• Do you know where to put the money you Pay Yourself First?
• Are you actually doing it?
• Is your Pay Yourself First plan automatic?

Anyone who can answer all these questions with an unequivocal "yes" deserves congratulations. That's because they are doing more than most people ever will to attain financial freedom.

But most people aren't in that position. Most people don't pay themselves first, nor do they have an automatic plan. In fact, most people don't have any kind of plan at all. That's why most people don't finish rich.

You know, the good things in life don't just happen to people. Sure, people occasionally get lucky. They win the lottery or inherit a bundle from a rich uncle they never knew they had. But those are the exceptions—the rare exceptions. As a rule, the good things in life happen to people only when they make them happen.

Maybe you used to believe that something good would just happen in your life and your future would all of a sudden be taken care of. By now, you've probably realized that life doesn't work like that. (Perhaps this is why you bought this book.) If you want a future of security and independence, you've got to build it for yourself. And whether you're talking about a future or a family room, you can't expect to build anything worthwhile without a plan.

So let's get started on your plan.

YOU'VE GOT TO SAVE AT LEAST AN HOUR A DAY OF YOUR INCOME

The question I'm asked most often about Pay Yourself First is, "How much?" I've always believed that to be fair to yourself and your future, you should Pay Yourself First at least one hour's worth of income every day.

(Another way to put that is to say you should Pay Yourself First 12½% of your gross income; but an hour a day is easier to remember.)

Say you make $50,000 a year. That works out to roughly $1,000 a week (figuring 50 working weeks a year), or $25 an hour (figuring a 40-hour workweek). So paying yourself first an hour's worth of income every day means saving $25 per workday, or $125 a week, or $6,250 a year.

Paying yourself first this much makes a lot of sense if you start relatively young. Begin putting $6,250 a year into a tax-deferred retirement account when you're 25 or 30, and you'll be a multimillionaire by the time you're 65. In case you're wondering, if you were to begin at 25 and got a 10% average annual return on your money, by the time you reached retirement age, your nest egg would be worth nearly $3.3 million. Begin at 30, and you'd end up with just under $2 million.

BUT WHAT IF I'M STARTING LATE?

The picture is a bit less rosy, however, for people in their forties or fifties who are just getting started. If you're over 40 and looking to retire at 65, paying yourself first just one hour's worth of income every day isn't going to be enough. Of course, it's quite possible you'll choose to put off your retirement past 65, and later on in Step Four we'll talk about the many alternatives available to people who may want (or need) to keep earning money into their seventies and beyond. But if your plan is to stop working in your mid-sixties, and you're already past 40, there's no getting around it: *You're going to have to Pay Yourself First . . . Faster!*

While you can do fine working the first hour of every working day for yourself if you start in your twenties, as a late starter your goal should be to work the first and the last hour for yourself. In other words, you should strive to Pay Yourself First two hours' worth of income every day.

Now, I know what you're going to say. "Two hours! Are you crazy? That's a quarter of my gross income! How can I possibly save that much?"

Hey, don't shoot the messenger. Nobody said starting late would be easy. And I'm not saying that you should start out trying to pay yourself first that much. But in a perfect world, that is where you'd like to end up.

The sad fact is that most people don't even come close to saving that much. According to the federal government's Bureau of Economic Analysis, in the first quarter of 2004, the average American barely saved more than 2%

of his or her disposable income. And that represented an increase over the previous year, when the saving rate was 1.9%. In other words, most of us work barely 10 minutes a day for ourselves. And one out of five workers don't put in any time at all for themselves—meaning they don't save anything.

SO LET'S GET STARTED!

In general, I find this truly sad. Why should you get out of bed, leave your family, spend most of your waking hours taking care of business for someone else, and NOT work at least one hour (and, ideally, two) for yourself? As a late starter, you know that in order to retire comfortably, you're going to need more money than you have right now—probably a lot more. So for you there should only be one question: Where is that money going to come from?

As of right now, today, this very minute, your goal should be to get to the point where you are working the first and last hours of every day for yourself (especially if you're over 50 and are just starting to save). This means paying yourself first by putting 25% of your gross income into a pretax retirement account.* I know this probably seems like an impossibly ambitious goal, but remember what I told Harriet, the woman I talked about in the Introduction who was shocked when a financial planner ordered her to start saving $2,700 a month: You don't prepare for a marathon by trying to run 26 miles the first day of training. You build up to it gradually.

Same thing here. While your goal should be to Pay Yourself First two hours' worth of income a day, I'm a realist. You may want to start by paying yourself first just 30 minutes a day of your income (that's about 6%). Then, in six months, go to one hour a day of your income (around 12%). Then, six months after that, to an hour and a half of your income—and so on until you get to the point where you are saving two hours a day. I've also coached people to gradually increase their savings by 1% a month for two years (at which point they are saving more than 25% of their income).

Here is all you need to do right now (details on how to do this follow in the next two chapters):

• Decide to Pay Yourself First . . . Faster! For your future.

• Open a retirement account.

---

*The maximum amount you can contribute to a qualified retirement account is determined by your company as well as by government regulations.

- Start funding it with at least one hour's worth (12½%) of your gross income.
- Make it automatic.

Now, when I say it's time to get started, I really mean it. You can regard this book as interesting reading or you can use the ideas I'm coaching you on to change your life. The difference is your willingness to act. You can take a few days to think about whether you really need to start paying yourself first automatically, and wind up never quite getting around to it. Or you can make the commitment now to begin—today—to guarantee yourself the future you want and deserve.

So please don't hesitate. This really should be a no-brainer. Decide TODAY to do something, save something, save more than you think you can save.

IT MAY SEEM IMPOSSIBLE, BUT PEOPLE DO IT EVERY DAY!

I've had people who never saved a dime go through my coaching programs, and in a matter of weeks they were saving 25% of their income. How did they do it? They *decided* to do it. They simply acted on our advice and got going.

Trust me—it may not be easy, but once you start you'll find it's easier than you think.

Let's say you make $50,000 a year and you started having 12½% of your gross income automatically taken out of your paycheck and put in a pretax retirement account. (Don't worry how; we'll get to that soon enough.) An annual income of $50,000 amounts to roughly $4,167 a month before taxes—and 12½% of that comes to a little more than $520. So that's what you'd be paying into your retirement account each month: $520.

Are your eyes rolling now? "Put aside $520 a month! Are you nuts? There's no way I could save $520 a month."

Don't worry. This is a perfectly normal reaction. It just happens to be totally wrong.

IT'S ACTUALLY EASIER TO SAVE WHEN YOU PAY YOURSELF FIRST

For one thing, don't forget the Latte Factor. There is a lot more "give" in your monthly spending habits than you're willing to admit.

A PAY-YOURSELF-FIRST SUCCESS STORY

Hey David,

I saw you on television and wanted to share our story. About 3 years ago, I heard about your phrase "Pay Yourself First." My husband and I were contributing to our retirement plans, but not as much as we could have been.

Our first step was to increase my husband's contributions to his 401(k) plan to the maximum his company allowed. As a small business owner, I also started my IRA plan.

Then came the Latte Factor. Mine was a little different—it was a Wal-Mart factor!! I would walk out of Wal-Mart with $200 worth of junk—things I certainly didn't need. You know, a box of candles here, a fake plant there. So I started to go shopping with a list. That went for the grocery store as well.

I absolutely could not believe how much money I had left over at the end of the month. I opened a money market account and, within 6 months, I had so much money just sitting there that my financial advisor advised me to purchase stocks and bonds. Three years later my account is over $150,000!!!!!!

Our 401(k) and IRA accounts keep growing as well. Now, I must admit this has almost become an obsession. I am addicted to saving!!! I actually write my savings check first and go grocery shopping with the money that's left over!!

As a result, our retirement plans have changed. My husband is 43 and I am 40, and we thought we'd both have to work until we were 65, but now we've bumped that down to 55!!! If I keep going at this rate, we might actually retire even earlier.

The best feeling in the world is when my husband tells me how proud he is of me and how well I have handled our money. (He wants to retire ASAP.)

Thanks for all the wonderful advice!

Lisa Gros
Houston, TX

For another, keep in mind that when you Pay Yourself First correctly, the money is taken out of your paycheck and automatically invested for you before you ever see it. You can't spend what you don't have, right?

But most important of all, you should be aware that saving $520 a month in a tax-deferred retirement account does NOT reduce your take-home pay by $520 a month. Try $336.

HERE'S HOW IT WORKS

If you earn an annual salary of $50,000, your overall tax rate is probably around 30%, which means that, after withholding, you take home something like $35,000 a year—or roughly $2,917 a month. Now, you may think that paying yourself first $520 a month will reduce your monthly take-home by $520, from $2,917 to $2,397. In fact, it doesn't. Remember, you're paying yourself first—*before* you pay the government. In other words, the $520 you're putting into your retirement account comes off the top. What gets reduced is your gross taxable income, which will drop from $4,167 a month to $3,647.

Now let's do the math: $3,647 taxed at 30 percent leaves you with a take-home income of $2,553. Before, you were taking home $2,917 a month. Now you're taking home $2,553. The difference is $336 a month. NOT $520.

In other words, you put $520 a month into your retirement account, but your take-home pay goes down by only $336.

This is what we call a good deal.

A GOOD DEAL GETS EVEN BETTER

So how much is this $520 a month—which actually costs you only $336 a month—worth to you in the long run?

The answer is quite a lot—even if you're starting late.

Let's say you're 40 and you start putting $520 a month into a tax-deferred retirement account that earns an average annual return of 10%. Do you know how much you'd have in the account by the time you were 65? Keep in mind that over the course of 25 years, your total contributions would have cost you just over $100,000 in terms of reduced take-home pay.

The exact figure is $689,953.

That's right. Even though you didn't get started until you were 40, you would effectively wind up with nearly seven times as much money as you put in.

This is more than just a good deal. This is a phenomenal deal.

KEY "START LATE" PRINCIPLES IN CHAPTER EIGHT

- You can't start late and finish rich unless you Pay Yourself First . . . Faster!
- There is a perfectly legal—and amazingly easy—way to get to your money before the government does: Put a portion of your salary into a pretax retirement account.
- Because you're not sharing your gains with the government, money in tax-deferred accounts can grow much faster than money in regular accounts.
- The good things in life don't just happen. You have to make them happen.
- As a late starter, your goal should be to work the first and the last hour of every workday for yourself.
- Because the money is taken out of your paycheck before you see it—and because tax-deferred dollars go farther than regular dollars—it's actually easier to save when you Pay Yourself First.

FINISH RICH ACTION STEPS

Reviewing the principles we discussed in Chapter Eight, here is what you should be doing right now so you can Start Late and Finish Rich. Check off each step as you accomplish it.

❑ Calculate how much paying yourself first two hours' worth of income every day would actually reduce your take-home pay.

❑ Commit to paying yourself first at least one hour's worth of income every day, with an ultimate goal of two hours' worth of income.

You are doing great. Give yourself a pat on the back for getting this far. Remember, you'll hardly miss the money that is deducted from your paycheck. And think how exciting it will be to watch the balance in your retirement account climb.

With this in mind, let's look at some specifics. In the next two chapters, we'll tackle exactly how you Pay Yourself First . . . Fast, and what exactly you will do with the money you're saving.

CHAPTER NINE

TOSS OUT
THE BUDGET
AND MAKE IT
AUTOMATIC

You can't start late and finish rich by budgeting. Why? The fact is, budgets simply don't work—at least not in the real world.

Wait a minute. Did David just say, "Don't budget"?

Yes—that's exactly what I'm saying.

Think about it. Do you know anyone who budgets? I don't. The few people I know who tried couldn't stick to it. If you're starting late and you begin your catch-up process with a budget, you may never get truly started.

If budgeting worked, then everyone would be doing it and we'd all be rich. This advice has been around forever. And the problem with it is simple— budgeting takes time, requires discipline, and pretty much goes against human nature, not to mention the 3,000 marketing messages we're bombarded with every day urging us to spend our money.

So forget about budgets. Not only are they enormously time-consuming (which is why most people never do them), but they can also be counterproductive. Think about all the people you've known who've tried to lose weight by going on some strict diet. In the end, don't most of them get tired of counting calories? And then what happens? That's right, they get sick of depriving themselves, go off on an eating binge, and wind up heavier than ever.

The same thing happens with people on financial diets. For a while, they track every penny that comes in and goes out. But then, one day, they can't take it anymore, and they go off on a shopping binge. And then there's the unfortunate fact of life that we almost always fall in love with our financial opposite. So if you like to budget, chances are you fell (or will fall) in love with someone who loves to shop, and so much for the budget. Right?

OKAY, THEN WHAT *IS* THE ANSWER?

Because you're starting late, your saving goals have to be ambitious. And if you have ambitious goals, you can't afford any slipups. You can't afford to "forget" to Pay Yourself First one month. You can't afford to "temporarily" switch your priorities because there's this amazing pair of shoes on sale or because a buddy just offered you a great deal on a new set of golf clubs. And you certainly can't afford to get so burned out by budgeting that you wind up going nuts at the mall.

So what can you do? How do you make your plan to Pay Yourself First both reliable and fail-safe? The answer is amazingly simple. All you need to do is imitate the government.

THE GOVERNMENT FIGURED OUT
YEARS AGO THAT BUDGETS DON'T WORK

The government knows for a fact that you can't budget. It figured this out more than 70 years ago. That's why it doesn't give you the option of taking home all of your pay in the hope that you'll budget intelligently and be able to pay your taxes when they come due the following April. Instead, what the government does is take your money from you AUTOMATICALLY (through withholding taxes). It does this because it figured out that the best way to get your money is to take it before you can spend it.

PRETTY DARN SMART—IF YOU THINK ABOUT IT

When you think about it, this is pretty darn smart. In order to make sure it got paid, the government came up with a system that took human nature into account. Sure, we'd all like to be prudent and disciplined and thrifty. But how many of us actually are? The government's withholding system was designed with this in mind.

This is a strategy worth imitating. You need to do for yourself what the government did for itself: set up a system that guarantees you won't have spent all your money on other things before you get around to paying yourself—a system where you Pay Yourself First automatically.

AND NOW CORPORATE AMERICA IS DOING IT TO US

And by the way, corporate America has learned to do the exact same thing. Think about it. When you join a health club, the first thing it does is to set up an automatic debit of your checking account or credit card to pay your monthly bill. The same goes for countless other businesses that depend on regular payments. They do it because they know the best way to get you to pay them on time all the time is to *make it automatic!*

YOUR DO-IT-YOURSELF WITHHOLDING PROGRAM

It took the government years to create and establish the withholding tax system. You should be able to launch your own personal do-it-yourself withholding program in less than an hour. Basically, it involves setting up a simple system that will automatically fund your own personal retirement account. Over the next few pages, I will explain exactly how you can do this.

Before we get started, though, I want to emphasize the importance of making the process automatic. One of the things I've learned from working with hundreds of clients as a financial advisor is that the only plans that work are the ones that are automatic. Over the years, I have had countless clients who insisted they were disciplined enough to do it themselves. In fact, there was only one who was actually able to keep paying himself first manually (that is, by sitting down and writing checks to himself every month) for any length of time.

So even if you think you're the most disciplined person in the world, don't regard the automatic part as an optional extra. If you are serious about starting late and finishing rich, it's not enough to arrange to Pay Yourself First. *You've also got to make the process automatic.*

WHERE YOUR MONEY SHOULD GO

Okay, so you've bitten the bullet and you've decided to deduct at least one-eighth of your gross income from your paycheck. How do you do this? If you work for a company, big or small, the answer is simple. You do it by signing up for what's known as a self-directed retirement account.

The reason I say doing this is simple is that most companies in the United States now offer employees self-directed retirement accounts. (They are called self-directed because the employee who sets up and contributes to the account gets to direct how his money will be invested.) The most important aspect of these plans is that you make your contributions to them with pre-tax dollars, as we discussed in Chapter Eight. That is, you don't pay any income taxes on the earnings you use to fund your account. Nor do you pay any capital gains taxes on the returns your account may generate.

The best-known and most popular self-directed retirement account is called a 401(k) plan. If you work for a nonprofit organization such as a school or a hospital, you will likely be offered a similar account called a 403(b) plan. (The numbers and letters refer to the parts of the tax code that established these various retirement plans.) In essence, both plans offer the same opportunities, so everything I say about 401(k) plans from here on also applies to 403(b) plans.

Anyone who is eligible for a 401(k) plan should definitely take advantage of the opportunity. Not only are these plans generally free (that is, most employers offer them to employees without charge), but they often also make you eligible for FREE MONEY (since many companies offer to match a percentage of employee contributions).

There are three simple reasons why late starters shouldn't pass up the chance to enroll in a 401(k) or 403(b) plan if they are eligible.

REASON NO. 1: YOU CUT OUT UNCLE SAM

As I noted earlier, you don't pay a cent in taxes on the earnings you put into the plan or on any of the returns your money generates over the years. Uncle Sam doesn't ask for his cut until you start taking the money out of the account, which is something you presumably won't do until after you reach retirement age—by which time your contributions will have had the opportunity to make full use of the miracle of compound interest. (The catch, to the extent that there is one, is that if you take out any money before you're 59½, you have to pay a 10% penalty on top of whatever taxes you might owe.)

REASON NO. 2: YOU CAN MAKE IT AUTOMATIC

Most 401(k) plans make it extremely easy for you to make the Pay Yourself First process fully automatic. Since payroll deduction is a standard feature of most plans, there's only one thing you need to do to have your contributions automatically withheld from your paycheck. You simply have to sign up. That's all it takes, and your money will be funneled straight into your retirement account before you ever see it—just like the government does with your withholding taxes, except now instead of Uncle Sam getting priority, you're paying yourself first.

REASON NO. 3: YOU CAN USE THE CATCH-UP PROVISIONS

If you are over the age of 50, you can save even more money tax-free because of what's called a "catch-up provision" created by the government (something we'll cover in a bit).

DON'T ASSUME YOU'RE ALREADY IN THE PLAN

Just because your company offers employees a 401(k) retirement plan, don't assume you're automatically enrolled. As a rule, you've got to sign up for it. So if you don't recall ever enrolling, contact the benefits office at your employer today and ask them for a retirement account sign-up package. You were probably given one when you first started work—and because it was so thick and boring-looking, you probably stuck it in a drawer somewhere and haven't seen it since.

If that's what you did, by all means go get yourself a new package—and this time fill it out and send it in. (If you work for a big corporation, you may be able to download all the necessary forms from the company web site.)

AIM TO "MAX IT OUT"

The first decision you have to make when you get your sign-up package is how much of your income you're going to contribute to your retirement account every pay period. Every sign-up package contains a form for you to sign authorizing your employer to deduct money from your paycheck to fund your retirement account. Most plans will ask you whether you want the amount deducted from your paycheck to be a set percentage of your income or a specific dollar amount. I always recommend that you go with the percentage. If you pick a specific amount, you'll need to readjust it every time you get a raise. Not only is this a bother, but it also creates the possibility that you might forget and, as a result, wind up underpaying yourself.

Most people who sign up for 401(k) plans contribute around 4% of their income. Most people also retire poor, dependent on Social Security or family to survive. So this is not a model you want to follow.

As we've already discussed, if you're starting late and want to finish rich, you should aim to save the first and last hours' worth of income each day. On a percentage basis, that would come to 25% of your gross pay.

Of course, as we've also discussed, it's not likely you'll be able to start saving that much right off the bat. It's okay to begin slowly, saving a smaller percentage at first, and working your way up to where you need to be. Still, as a late starter, your back is against the wall. What this means is that you can't really afford to begin any lower than the equivalent of one hour's worth of pay a day—which is to say you should contribute at least 12½% of your gross income.

I realize this is ambitious. But it *is* your future we're talking about. Keep in mind that most of us tend to underestimate how much we think we can manage. As a result, we wind up lowballing ourselves . . . and our futures. If you're skeptical of your ability to do this, go back to Chapter Three and reread about turbocharging your Latte Factor. You *can* find the money, and you will be amazed and excited about how fast it will pile up—especially if you're one of the millions of Americans whose employers contribute matching funds to their retirement accounts.

In any case, your real goal should be to "max out the plan." This means making the maximum contribution your company's plan allows. As of 2005, you can put up to $14,000 a year into a 401(k) plan. If you are over age 50, you can contribute up to $18,000 a year. (This is the catch-up provision I was talking about before.) In 2006, the ceilings will rise to $15,000 and $20,000, respectively. After that, they will be adjusted annually in $500 increments to keep up with inflation.

While you can use these figures as a guide, you should double-check them with your employer's benefits office. If your company has a poor participation rate (meaning not enough of your fellow workers are paying themselves first), your maximum allowable contribution may be lower. Don't guess at this. Check with your benefits office *today*. And recheck the maximums every January, so you can take full advantage of any increases that may have been made. The reason you need to recheck is that many plans won't allow you to save more than 15% of your gross income.

WHAT IF YOU'RE *NOT* ELIGIBLE FOR A 401(K) PLAN?

Lots of workers aren't eligible for 401(k) plans—some because their employers don't offer them, others because they're not considered full-time staff. If you're in this boat, don't despair. The fact that you can't enroll in a company retirement plan doesn't mean you'll never finish rich. It simply means that you're going to have to be a bit more proactive and get yourself an Individual Retirement Account, or IRA.

As the name suggests, an Individual Retirement Account is a personal retirement plan that you open and maintain for yourself. Most anyone who earns an income can set one up at a bank, a brokerage firm, or even online. As with a 401(k) plan, when you open an IRA, you first decide how much to put in, then how to invest it. (We'll cover investment choices in the next chapter.) Also, like a 401(k), the money you put into an IRA is tax-deferred. The most obvious difference between an IRA and a 401(k) account is that the contribution limits on IRAs are much lower.

TRADITIONAL AND ROTH IRA CONTRIBUTION LIMITS		
Year	Maximum Allowable (if age 49 or younger)	Maximum Allowable (if age 50 or older)
2005	$4,000	$4,500
2006	$4,000	$5,000
2007	$4,000	$5,000
2008	$5,000	$6,000

Note: After 2008, increases will be adjusted for inflation in $500 increments.

HALF A MILLION IS
BETTER THAN NOTHING!

Putting aside $4,000 a year (or $333 a month) may not sound like much, but don't forget the power of compound interest, especially when your money grows tax-deferred. Even if you waited until you were 40 to get started, if you put $333 a month into an IRA that earned an annual return of 10%, by the time you were 65, you'd have a nest egg worth nearly $442,000.

THE TRADITIONAL IRA
VS. THE ROTH IRA

There are many different kinds of IRAs, but for working people who are not self-employed, there are basically only two worth considering: the traditional IRA and the Roth IRA. (The Roth is named after former Sen. William Roth of Delaware, who introduced the legislation that made it possible.) The biggest difference between them involves when you pay income tax on your retirement money.

Except for the difference in contribution limits, traditional IRAs are very much like 401(k) plans. You contribute pretax dollars, which is to say that you don't pay any taxes—either income or capital gains—on the money you contribute as long as it remains in the account.* And if you try to take it out early (i.e., before you're 59½), you get hit with a penalty. But eventually you do have to take it out. The law requires you to start withdrawing your money from an IRA by the time you reach the age of 70½— and your withdrawals are subject to income taxes.

The opposite is true of Roth IRAs. Contributions to a Roth are not tax-deductible—which is to say you make them with after-tax dollars. On the other hand, as long as your money has been in the account for at least five years and you are older than 59½, there's no tax to pay when you take it out. And unlike the traditional IRA, you are not forced by the government

---

*A traditional IRA may not be tax-deductible if you are covered by an employer plan. Check IRS Publication #590, page 112, for details.

to start taking money out at age 70½. The only real catch here is that there are income limits on who can use a Roth IRA.*

SO WHICH ONE IS RIGHT FOR ME?

Whether you should go with a traditional IRA or a Roth IRA really depends on when you want your tax breaks: right now or after you retire. There's a commonsense argument that favors the traditional IRA, on the grounds that tax breaks are worth more to you now than they will be later. That's because you're probably in a higher tax bracket now than you will be after you retire. On the other hand, once you reach retirement age, a Roth IRA can provide you with tax-free income for the rest of your life.

Many experts are now pushing the Roth IRA over the deductible IRA. I'm not as convinced of the Roth's superiority.

For one thing, I'd rather have my money in my retirement account than in the government's hands. If I fund a deductible retirement account, I've got the use of all my money and am earning interest on all of it without paying taxes first—not sharing 30% with the government.

For another, no one really knows what taxes will be like 20 years from now. They could be much higher; they could also be lower. There could be a voter revolt led by the more than 80 million baby boomers in which a presidential candidate gets elected by promising to waive taxes on IRA distributions. When it comes to taxes, ANYTHING is possible. I personally think we are going to see a lot of changes in the retirement tax laws over the next 20 years because of those 80 million baby boomers who are heading into retirement. So I want my money in a place where I can keep my options open—and that means keeping it under my control.

Finally, and this is not a small point, it's harder to fund a Roth IRA than a deductible retirement account. That's because you have to fund it with after-tax dollars—meaning you have to earn more to fund the same amount. For example, you've got to earn roughly $6,000 in order to come up with the $4,000 maximum contribution.

---

*If you earn less than $95,000 a year ($150,000 for married couples), you can contribute up to $4,000 a year. If you earn more than that, the amount you can put in is reduced. If your earnings top $110,000 a year ($160,000 for married couples), you can't use a Roth IRA at all.

MAKING YOUR IRA AUTOMATIC

Unlike 401(k) plans, IRAs do not offer payroll deduction as a standard feature. But this doesn't mean you can't make an IRA-based Pay Yourself First program automatic. It just means you'll have to put in a little effort to set it up yourself. And when I say little, I mean it shouldn't take you more than an hour to open an IRA and make it automatic—probably a lot less. In fact, the process is really not any more complicated than opening a checking account.

When you go into a bank or brokerage to open your IRA, make a point of telling the banker or broker assisting you (or the telephone representative, if you're opening your account online) that you want to set up a *systematic investment plan*. This is a plan under which money is automatically transferred on a regular basis into your IRA from some other account of yours (usually your regular checking account).

OPTION NO. 1: PAYROLL DEDUCTION

The best way to set up this sort of plan is to ask your employer to do a payroll deduction for you, in which money is automatically taken out of your paycheck and transferred directly to your IRA. Virtually every large company and many small ones offer this service. Most likely, they will give you a form to fill out that asks you to provide the account information they will need to be able to make the transfer—meaning you will need to open an IRA account first so you will be able to provide your employer with the account number and routing information. Some banks and brokerage firms will handle all this for you, contacting your employer's payroll department on your behalf and dealing with all the paperwork.

OPTION NO. 2: DEDUCTING FROM YOUR CHECKING ACCOUNT

If your employer doesn't offer payroll deduction, find out if he provides direct deposit, which means you can have your paychecks automatically deposited directly into your bank account. Direct deposit will spare you the hassle of actually having to go to the bank or ATM and deposit the check yourself—and more important, protect you from the temptation of cashing your check, instead of paying yourself first. You can then arrange with your bank to have your retirement-plan contribution automatically moved from your checking account to your IRA—ideally, the day after your paycheck clears. Most banks now offer free online bill payment programs that allow you to schedule regular automatic payments of specified amounts to anyone you want. (If your employer doesn't do direct deposit, you will need to make a point of depositing your entire paycheck into your checking account as soon as you get it.)

This is all actually a lot simpler than it sounds. Most likely, you won't have to do much more than ask the bank or brokerage where you're opening your IRA to make the arrangements for you. And if you decide you want to change your payment schedule or amount, a simple phone call or written request is usually all that's necessary.

WHERE TO GO TO OPEN AN IRA ACCOUNT

These days, virtually every financial service institution imaginable—banks, brokerages, mutual fund companies, you name it—offer Roth or traditional IRA accounts. Since the rules are the same everywhere, your choice of where to go should be based on the kind of service the institution provides. Do they make it easy to sign up? Do they have user-friendly, informative web sites? Do they provide good advice and solid, easy-to-understand research?

IF YOU LIKE TO DO THINGS ONLINE . . .

Here are six reputable firms that get high marks in all these areas, plus they make the process really easy by allowing you to open an IRA online.

ONLINE BROKERAGE FIRMS

Sharebuilder
1-866-747-2537
www.sharebuilder.com

Fidelity Investments
1-800-FIDELITY
www.fidelity.com

INGDirect.com
1-800-ING-DIRECT
www.ingdirect.com

Charles Schwab
1-866-855-6770
www.schwab.com

TD Waterhouse
1-800-934-4448
www.tdwaterhouse.com

Vanguard
1-877-662-7447
www.vanguard.com

DOING BUSINESS THE OLD-FASHIONED WAY: FACE-TO-FACE

Then again, you may prefer to do business the old-fashioned way: by walking into a real office and looking a real person in the eye. If so, here is a list of top-notch places to try. Telephone or go online to find the office nearest you.

FULL-SERVICE BROKERAGE FIRMS

American Express
1-800-297-7378
www.americanexpress.com

AG Edwards
1-877-835-7877
www.agedwards.com

Edward Jones
1-314-515-2000
www.edwardjones.com

Merrill Lynch
1-800-MERRILL
www.ml.com

Morgan Stanley
1-212-761-4000
www.morganstanley.com

Salomon Smith Barney
1-212-428-5200
www.smithbarney.com

NATIONAL BANKS

Bank of America
www.bankofamerica.com

Citibank
1-800-248-4472
www.citibank.com

Washington Mutual
1-800-788-7000
www.wamu.com

IT'S EVEN BETTER IF YOU'RE SELF-EMPLOYED

If you are self-employed, I've got two words to say to you: WELL DONE— you're in a much better position than most late starters to finish rich. That's because the government gives business owners the best tax breaks when it comes to retirement accounts.

There are numerous types of retirement accounts business owners can select. Because you need to take action quickly, I'm going to discuss only two of them—the SEP IRA, which I regard as the most straightforward and uncomplicated retirement account there is for self-employed people, and the relatively new One-Person 401(k) Profit-Sharing Account, which offers some tremendous benefits.*

SEP IRAS: THE FASTEST WAY TO GET RICH

The SEP in SEP IRA stands for Simplified Employee Pension, otherwise known as a "self-employed retirement account." If you are self-employed

---

*If you're interested in other retirement accounts for business owners, such as Money Purchase Plans, Profit-Sharing Plans, Defined Benefits Plans, and SIMPLE plans, you can read all about them in detail in any of my three previous books—*Smart Women Finish Rich, Smart Couples Finish Rich,* and *The Finish Rich Workbook.* You can also visit my web site at www.finishrich.com to read a free excerpt on this topic.

and don't have any employees, a SEP IRA can make it amazingly easy to finish rich, even if you're starting late. As of 2004, you could contribute as much as 25% of your pretax income to a SEP IRA up to a maximum of $41,000 (the amount is adjusted for inflation every year). How's that for Paying Yourself First . . . Fast?

The only slightly complicated part of paying yourself first with a SEP IRA is setting it up to work automatically. That's because as a self-employed person, you probably don't draw a regular salary. If you do pay yourself regularly, all you need to do is program your payroll system to automatically transfer contributions to your SEP IRA. If you don't, however, you simply must be disciplined enough to make sure that every time you take money out of your business, you immediately deposit your Pay Yourself First percentage (i.e., somewhere between 12½% and 25%) to your SEP IRA.

THE AMAZING ONE-PERSON 401(K)/ PROFIT-SHARING PLAN

This plan offers people who operate one-person businesses some of the most generous advantages of any tax-deferred retirement account. Unfortunately, even though it's been around for a few years now, not many people seem to know about it.

As the name suggests, it combines a 401(k) account with a profit-sharing plan. As of 2004, you could fund it with up to 100% of the first $14,000 in salary you pay yourself, $18,000 if you're over 50. (These ceilings will rise along with the 401(k) ceilings.) You can then use the profit-sharing portion of the plan to contribute as much as another 25% of your remaining profits for the year. The combined total you could contribute in 2004 was $41,000—and every penny is tax-deductible. (This figure will be ratcheted up to account for inflation in future years.)

Most financial-services firms can provide you with details on these exciting new plans. You can also check with your bank or payroll company.

KEY "START LATE" PRINCIPLES IN CHAPTER NINE

• Budgeting doesn't work; the simplest and most effective way to Pay Yourself First . . . Fast is to imitate the government and automate the process.

• The simplest way to do this is to open a self-directed retirement account.
• If you're eligible for a 401(k) or 403(b) plan, make sure you're signed up. If you're not, open an IRA.
• Your goal should be to "max out the plan"—that is, to make the maximum contribution allowed.

FINISH RICH ACTION STEPS

Reviewing the principles we discussed in Chapter Nine, here is what you should be doing right now so you can Start Late and Finish Rich. Check off each step as you accomplish it.

❑ Depending on your employment status, make sure you're signed up for a 401(k) or 403(b) plan or an IRA.

❑ Arrange to fund your retirement account with contributions automatically deducted from your paycheck.

So now you know how to Pay Yourself First and Make It Automatic. So what are you going to do with all this money that will soon be pouring into your retirement account? We'll answer this key question in the next chapter, as we detail exactly how and where you should invest your newfound savings.

CHAPTER TEN

YOUR LIFE SHOULD BE INTERESTING— YOUR INVESTMENTS SHOULD BE BORING

Many people think the secret to starting late and finishing rich is obvious: "I've got to really be smart in the stock market and 'Buy low, sell high.'"

Well, not exactly—at least not in the real world.

There is a widespread notion that the way to do well as an investor is to buy when the market is low and sell when it is high—what's known as timing the market. It would be great if there really was a system you could use to make this work. Unfortunately, no one seems to have found it yet.

TIMING THE MARKET RARELY WORKS

Between 1992 and 2002, the stock market produced an average annual return of 9.34%. This was a period that began with one of the most roaring bull markets in memory—and then ended with one of the most brutal busts in half a century. And yet, for all the turmoil, stock prices still managed to grow by an average of nearly 10% a year—which means that if you put money in the market in 1992 and then just let it ride, your investments would have more than doubled in value by 2002. (In fact, for the entire period, stocks were up more than 150%.)

What if you had tried to time the market? Consider this:

THE DANGERS OF TRYING TO TIME THE MARKET

This chart compares the average annual return of the S&P 500 Index over ten years for those investors who were continually in the market versus those who missed the top 10, 20, and 30 days of returns. The moral is that investing steadily is a lot safer than trying to time the market. Missing out on even a few of the top days of returns can mean big losses. (The S&P 500 index tracks the stock of 500 leading U.S. corporations believed to be representative of the U.S. stock market as a whole.)

TIMING THE MARKET IS RISKY	
The S&P 500 Index, December 31, 1992–December 31, 2002	Average Annual Return
Staying in the market	9.34%
Missed Top Ten Days	4.60%
Missed Top 20 Days	.77%
Missed Top 30 Days	−2.66%
Source: Bloomberg Calculations by Van Kampen Investments, Inc.	

BUY HIGH, SELL LOW!

Yes, I know. It's supposed to be the other way around.

The thing is, in the real world almost no one actually manages to buy low and sell high. At least not consistently.

So why don't more "experts" talk about the fact that investors can't time the market? Because timing the market is an industry unto itself. Imagine that you publish a magazine about financial planning and investing. What exciting new strategies are you going to promote on the cover of your next issue? If you were honest, your cover line would read something like this: "Nothing new to suggest this month—just keep investing in a well-diversified portfolio and over time you'll do fine!"

Not very sexy, is it? I mean, who'd buy that?

BEWARE OF "FINANCIAL PORNOGRAPHY"

Whether you're looking at newspapers, magazines, newsletters, or radio and TV news programs, one fact is inescapable—a huge part of the media's approach to financial news is about scaring you. Why? Because fear makes you pay attention. Scaring you sells.

Unfortunately, scaring you can also cause you to make rash decisions about when to invest and when not to invest. One minute you're investing for the long term. Then the daily news turns bad, and before you know it you're convinced that the world really is falling apart and you'd be best off "doing nothing" with your money until sanity returns. But when will that be?

HISTORY PROVES IT—
THE WORLD IS NEVER SANE

Look back at history. Before the Iraq War there were the Clinton scandals. And before the Clinton scandals there was the first Gulf War. And before the first Gulf War there was Iran-Contra. And before Iran-Contra there was the Carter inflation. And before the Carter inflation there was the Energy Crisis. And before the Energy Crisis there was Watergate. And before Watergate there was Vietnam. And on and on all the way back to the Panic of 1839.

Take a look at the chart on page 117, which puts history and the stock market in context. One thing you'll notice is that following a historical crisis, the market recovers—and recovers fast.

GOOD NEWS USUALLY FOLLOWS BAD NEWS

If you look closely at this chart, you'll notice that uncertainty often affects the judgment of investors—leading many to sell low in a panic. There has never been a time where things were fine. Things are always a little crazy. So knowing that you live in an insane world, what should you do with your money?

The answer is simple. If the world is complicated and crazy, you create an investment plan that is simple and sane. In short, you create an INCREDIBLY BORING INVESTMENT PLAN.

By boring, I mean totally straightforward—something that can be explained with a crayon and one piece of paper.

HISTORY IS FILLED WITH DISASTERS— AND STILL THE MARKETS RECOVER

If you look closely at this chart, you will notice that history is filled with times of trouble. Following difficult times, the markets drop, only to recover, often quickly. While no one can predict that the future will mirror the past, this chart shows that over 88 years, stock markets have rallied within months of a disaster. The moral—don't panic next time something terrible happens. Regardless of what happens, things tend to improve.

Event	Reaction Dates	% Gain/ Loss	22 Days Later	63 Days Later	126 Days Later
Stock Exchange Closed (World War 1)	07/22/14–12/24/14	−10.2%	10.0%	6.6%	21.2%
Bombing at JP Morgan Office	09/15/20–09/30/20	−5.5	2.4	−14.9	−9.5
Fall of France	05/09/40–06/22/40	−17.1	−0.5	8.4	7.0
Pearl Harbor	12/06/41–12/10/41	−6.5	3.8	−2.9	−9.6
Korean War	06/23/50–07/13/50	−12.0	9.1	15.3	19.2
Suez Canal Crisis	10/30/56–10/31/56	−1.4	0.3	-0.6	3.4
Sputnik	10/03/57–10/22/57	−9.9	5.5	6.7	7.2
Cuban Missile Crisis	10/19/62–10/27/62	1.1	12.1	17.1	24.2
JFK Assassination	11/21/63–11/22/63	−2.9	7.2	12.4	15.1
Martin Luther King Assassination	04/03/68–04/05/68	−0.4	5.3	6.4	9.3
United States Bombs Cambodia	04/29/70–05/26/70	−14.4	9.9	20.3	20.7
Arab Oil Embargo	10/18/73–12/05/73	−18.5	9.3	10.2	7.2
Nixon Resigns	08/09/74–08/29/74	−17.6	−7.9	−5.7	12.5
Iranian Hostage Crisis	11/02/79–11/07/79	−2.7	4.7	11.1	2.3
U.S.S.R. in Afghanistan	12/24/79–01/03/80	−2.2	6.7	−4.0	6.8
United States Invades Grenada	10/24/83–11/ 07/83	−2.7	3.9	−2.8	−3.2
Stock Market Crash of 1987	10/02/87–10/19/87	−34.2	11.5	11.4	15.0
Invasion of Panama	12/15/89–12/20/89	−1.9	−2.7	0.3	8.0
Iraq Invades Kuwait	08/02/90–08/23/90	−13.3	0.1	2.3	16.3
Persian Gulf War	01/16/91–01/17/91	4.6	11.8	14.3	15.0
Gorbachev Coup	08/16/91–08/19/91	−2.4	4.4	1.6	11.3
World Trade Center Bombing	02/26/93–02/27/93	−0.3	2.4	5.1	8.5
Oklahoma City Bombing	04/19/95–04/20/95	1.2	3.9	9.7	12.9
Asian Stock Market Crisis	10/07/97–10/27/97	−12-4	8.8	10.5	25.0
United States Embassy Bombings in Africa	08/07/98–08/10/98	0.0	−11.2	4.7	6.5
Sept. 11 Terrorist Attacks	09/11/01–09/21/01	−14.3	13.4	21.2	24.8
Enron Testifies Before Congress	01/31/02–02/07/02	−3.0	10.5	4.3	−9.5
Median		**−3.0**	**5.3**	**6.6**	**9.3**

Source: Ned Davis Research Inc. and AIM Investment

THE PERFECT PIE APPROACH

I created the **Perfect Pie Approach**™ years ago to make managing money simple. I've taught this approach to thousands of people, and now I'm going to share it with you.

Imagine I'm in a classroom with you right now, coaching you one-on-one. In front of us is a chalkboard. Here's my boring approach:

I step up to the chalkboard and draw a circle. Then I divide the circle into three equal slices. One slice is labeled "Stocks," one slice is labeled "Bonds," and one slice is labeled "Real Estate."

Look closely at this picture. I call it my "Perfect Pie" investment plan.

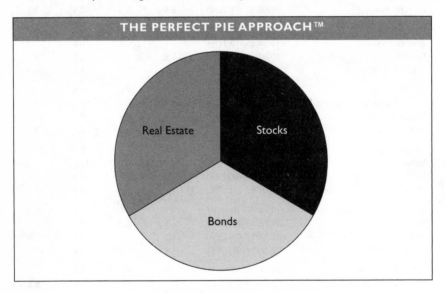

THE PERFECT PIE APPROACH™

Real Estate

Stocks

Bonds

COULD IT BE ANY SIMPLER?

There is one old saying about investing that happens to be true: Don't put all your eggs in one basket. In other words, you've got to diversify—which means that instead of investing all of your money in just one or two places, you spread it around. Now, spreading your money around does not mean opening up a lot of different retirement accounts in different places. If you do that and then make the same kinds of investments with each of them, all you've done is complicate your life. Spreading your money around means making a variety of different investments. Many people make this complicated. It doesn't need to be.

HOW IT WORKS

Let's stay with my concept of keeping it simple.

Your money gets divided up into three equal parts:

- Real Estate
- Stocks
- Bonds

WHY THIS IS THE COMPLETE "START LATE" SOLUTION TO INVESTING

Here's why the Perfect Pie Approach is perfect:

- You get complete diversification.
- You won't be overinvested in the stock market—and be forced to buy and pray.
- You won't have too much money in bonds and be too conservative.
- You *will* be exposed to the real estate market beyond the investment you make in your own home.
- It's amazingly inexpensive.

HERE'S EXACTLY HOW TO DO IT

STEP 1
BUY REAL ESTATE

One-third of your assets should be in real estate. If you own your home, the equity you have in it IS INCLUDED in this piece of the pie. So if your house is worth, say, $250,000 and your mortgage balance currently totals $150,000, then you already have $100,000 in the real estate slice of your pie. Now, if that happens to represent more than one-third of your total assets, don't think you need to rush off and sell your house. All it means is that you don't need to invest any more money in the real estate piece of the pie just now.

If you don't own a home—or the equity in your home doesn't equal one-third of your total assets—then you need to have real estate added to your portfolio.

HOW TO ADD REAL ESTATE TO YOUR PORTFOLIO IN 5 MINUTES!

The single easiest way to add real estate to your portfolio is to invest in REITs. To be technical about it, a REIT (or Real Estate Investment Trust) is a company that happens to be in the business of owning and operating real estate. REITs are generally publicly traded (though some are privately held), and they usually own income-producing properties such as office buildings, stores, apartment buildings, and shopping centers. There are also REITS that own hospitals and nursing care facilities, and some even own real estate loan portfolios.

REITS HAVE OUTPERFORMED STOCKS FOR 25 YEARS!

The great thing about REITs* from an investment point of view is their "yield," or dividend payout. The average REIT offers an annual dividend of around 7%—often higher. And that's apart from any appreciation you may enjoy in the price of your shares.

Why do REITs pay such generous dividends? That's a direct result of the 1960 Real Estate Investment Trust Act, which created the REIT. Among the act's provisions was a section that said that if a REIT paid out 90% of its income to shareholders in the form of dividends, it didn't have to pay corporate income tax. This rule not only made REITs very attractive to run, it also made them a great investment.

How great an investment? *How about the perfect START LATE investment!* Consider the following:

- REITs have outperformed the stock, bond, and gold markets, generating an average annual return of 14.7% over the last 25 years (compared to the S&P 500's 13.4% and the bond market's 10.1%).
- REITs outperform other investments not just in terms of annual returns but also in terms of dividend yield, dividend contribution to total return, correlation with other investments, and risk.
- REITS offer huge dividend yields, historically around 7%. As of this writing (in August 2004), the average REIT yield is 5.6%, compared to 1.6% for stocks in the S&P 500 and 4.7% for Treasury bonds.

---

*National Association of Real Estate Investment Trusts.

THE PERFECT WAY TO BUY REITS

I don't recommend that you buy individual REITs, because it's too easy to pick the wrong one. For example, you might invest in a REIT that focuses on buying apartment buildings (or retail real estate or whatever), only to see that sector turn cold.

START WITH A REIT INDEX FUND

The solution is simple: You should buy an index fund of REITs. (An index fund is a mutual fund that is designed to mirror the performance of a particular market indicator such as the Dow Jones Industrial Average or the S&P 500.)

There are two specific REIT index funds I would consider, detailed below. Both are Exchange-Traded Mutual Funds, or ETFs, and both are managed by Barclay's Global Investors. (ETFs are amazing investment vehicles; I'll describe what they are and their many advantages a bit later in this chapter.) These REIT funds can be purchased through any brokerage and put into your IRA; details are available at www.ishares.com or by calling 800-474-2737.

iShares Cohen & Steers Realty Majors Index Fund (ticker symbol: ICF). This fund's goal is to seek investment results that echo the performance of large, actively traded U.S. REITs, as represented by the Cohen & Steers Realty Majors Index. The expense ratio of this fund is .35%—just one-fifth the cost of a typical mutual fund. To put this in perspective, if you invested $10,000 in the fund, annual management fees would run you just $35. As of this writing, the fund has generated an average annual return of 16.11%.

iShares Dow Jones U.S. Real Estate Index Fund (IYR). The goal of this fund is to seek investment results that match the real estate sector of the U.S. equity market, as represented by the Dow Jones U.S. Real Estate Index. The expense ratio of this fund is .60%—higher than the Cohen & Steers fund but still half the cost of a typical mutual fund. As of July 2004, the fund has generated an average return of 16.35% a year.

YOU CAN ALSO BUY REITS BY
INVESTING IN A REAL ESTATE FUND

If your 401(k) plan is not yet among those that offer ETFs, you can substitute a basic real estate fund. If your plan doesn't offer a real estate fund, contact your plan administrator and ask why, since more and more plans are adding them every year. Here is a list of the top 15 real estate funds, ranked by performance.

TOP 15 REAL ESTATE FUNDS
RANKED BY 10-YEAR RATE OF RETURN

Fund Name	Ticker Symbol	Net Assets ($M)*	10-Year Return (%)	Contact Info.
CGM Realty	CGMRX	620	17.20	www.cgmfunds.com 1-800-345-4048
Alpine U.S. Real Estate Equity	EUEYX	188	17.15	www.alpinefunds.com 1-888-785-5578
Columbia Real Estate Equity Z	CREEX	898	13.30	www.columbiafunds.com 1-800-345-6611
Van Kampen Real Estate Secs A	ACREX	409	12.57	www.vankampen.com 1-800-847-2424
Frank Russell Real Estate Secs	RRESX	1108	12.52	www.russell.com 1-253-572-9500
Cohen & Steers Realty Shares	CSRSX	1255	12.44	www.cohenandsteers.com 1-800-330-7348
Dimensional Real Estate Securites	DFREX	992	12.27	www.dfaus.com 1-310-395-8005
Davis Real Estate A	RPFRX	443	12.24	www.davisfunds.com 1-800-279-0279
PBHG REIT PBHG	PBRTX	126	12.24	www.pbhgfunds.com 1-800-433-0051
Fidelity Real Estate Investments	FRESX	3116	12.23	www.fidelity.com 1-800-544-6666
Franklin Real Estate Securities	FREEX	832	12.08	www.franklintempleton.com 1-800-632-2301
Van Kampen Real Estate Secs C	ACRCX	409	11.76	www.vankampen.com 1-800-847-2424
Van Kampen Real Estate Secs B	ACRBX	409	11.73	www.vankampen.com 1-800-847-2424
Stratton Monthly Dividend REIT	STMDX	190	11.05	www.strattonfunds.com 1-800-634-5726
Pioneer Real Estate A	PWREX	121	10.91	www.pioneerfunds.com 1-800-225-6292

*Assets as of May 31, 2004. All other data updated through July 12, 2004.

STEP 2
BUY STOCKS

One-third of your assets are going to be in stocks. But rather than investing in individual stocks or bonds, you probably should invest in mutual funds. There are a lot of good reasons for this, which I'll list in a minute. But before I do, it probably would be a good idea to explain just what we're talking about here.

WHAT EXACTLY IS A MUTUAL FUND?

One of the more frightening discoveries I've made over the years is that there are a lot of people who invest in mutual funds without having any idea what they are. For the record, a mutual fund is an investment vehicle that sells shares to a large group of investors (often tens or even hundreds of thousands of people). The fund then pools the investors' money and uses it to buy various securities (such as stocks or bonds).

The nature of the various securities determines the character of the fund—for example, whether it's considered a growth fund (which takes chances for the sake of high returns) or an income fund (which earns more modest returns but is much less risky). The combined performance of all the various securities that are in the fund's portfolio determines how much shares in the fund are worth.

The advantage of a mutual fund is that investors who own shares in one automatically achieve the benefit of a diversified portfolio without having to buy individual investments themselves.

DO MUTUAL FUNDS STILL MAKE SENSE
AFTER THE SCANDALS?

Every day, people ask me if I still think mutual funds make sense, given the mutual fund scandals of the last few years. My answer is yes. The "after-hours trading" scandals—in which some mutual fund companies allowed hedge funds to trade shares after normal market hours—gave the industry a black eye, but at the end of the day the financial impact on the average investor was small.

More important for investors is that the mutual fund scandal has forced mutual fund companies to return some of their improper profits to shareholders in the form of reduced fees. As I write this, many mutual fund companies are negotiating settlements with the SEC that include lowering their fund fees by as much as 20% and more.

At the same time, the traditional fund industry is facing increasing competition from ETFs, and that is also forcing fees down.

If that's not enough to convince you that mutual funds are still worth selecting over individual investments, here are five more reasons.

FIVE REASONS MUTUAL FUNDS
STILL MAKE SENSE FOR YOU

1. **Instant diversification.** Even though you may be putting in only a few hundred dollars a month to start, you immediately enjoy a stake in a portfolio that could include hundreds of stocks and bonds.
2. **Professional money management.** Do you feel equipped to analyze the countless number of stocks and bonds that are available on the market today and decide which make the most sense for you? Me neither. The people who run mutual funds are full-time professionals who bring incredible expertise and experience to the job. This includes professional research and trading execution.
3. **Efficiency.** You can make more money investing in the same stocks and bonds through a mutual fund than you would if you bought them separately by yourself. According to the Morningstar rating service, the average internal mutual fund management fee is about 1.40% of the assets managed. If you invest in an ETF, you can get the fees down to as low as 0.20%, which is one-seventh the cost of a mutual fund. In either case, this is almost certainly a lot less than you would pay in brokers' fees managing a portfolio of individual stocks and bonds on your own.
4. **Liquidity.** You can buy and sell shares in most mutual funds as easily as you can in most stocks and bonds. And as with stocks and bonds, you can look up the price of your mutual fund shares every day in the newspaper.
5. **Lack of excitement.** Because they are so diversified, mutual funds don't fluctuate in price as much as individual stocks or bonds. Many people consider this lack of volatility boring. Of course, we know that boring is good.

THE PROOF IS IN THE RETURNS—
WHO SAYS YOU CAN'T EARN 10% A YEAR?

Throughout this book, I've based all the calculations we've done to show you what your savings could be worth in the future on the assumption that your investments will generate an average return of 10% a year. This assumption is based on the average annual return generated by the stock market since 1926.

Despite this 80-year track record, many people say, "No way!" They insist you simply can't earn 10% a year anymore from your investments.

I say, "Really? Who says you can't?"

Take a look at the table on page 126, compiled by using the Premium Fund Screening tool on **Morningstar.com**. This is only a partial list of funds that have produced annualized returns of more than 10% over the last 15 years. *I'm not recommending any of these funds specifically,* but I want you to see that there are a lot of great mutual funds out there that continue to turn in really strong performances, even after the 2000–2002 downturn in the stock market.

One of the most basic rules of investing is that before you put any money in a fund, you should always read the prospectus. And every investment prospectus contains some variation of the same warning: Past performance does not guarantee future results. Still, a consistent track record over a relatively long period of time is nothing to sneeze at. So take a look at some of these funds; *they may be able to help you start late and finish rich.*

FOUR GREAT INDEX FUNDS TO START WITH

Many people have given up on trying to select mutual funds. While the list on page 126 is a good place to start, you may NOT want to invest in an actively managed mutual fund, which tries to pick stocks that are likely to go up in value (a relatively risky endeavor). Instead, you may prefer an index fund, which is designed to match the performance of some broad market indicator (a much easier goal). If I were building a portfolio from scratch and implementing the Perfect Pie Approach, this is what I'd do. Specifically, I'd recommend that you fill your stock slice with equal amounts of the following four exchange-traded index funds:

Diamonds Trust (DIA). Known as the Diamonds, this fund tracks the Dow Jones Industrial Average. For details, go to www.amex.com.

Standard & Poor's Depositary Receipts (SPY). Often referred to as the "Spiders," this fund tracks the S&P 500. For details, go to www.amex.com.

Nasdaq-100 Index Tracking Stock (QQQ). This ETF tracks the Nasdaq 100. For details, go to www.amex.com.

iShares Dow Jones Select Dividend Index Fund (DVY). This ETF tracks the Dow Jones Select Dividend Index, which consists of 50 of the highest

TOP 25 DOMESTIC STOCK FUNDS
RANKED BY 15-YEAR ANNUALIZED RETURN

Fund Name	Net Assets ($M)*	15-Year Return Annualized(%)	Contact Info.
Fidelity Select Electronics	3,561	19.70	www.fidelity.com 1-800-544-6666
Vanguard Health Care	21,600	19.44	www.vanguard.com 1-877-662-7447
Fidelity Select Software & Comp	784	18.50	www.fidelity.com 1-800-544-6666
Eaton Vance Worldwide Health Sci A	2,640	18.43	www.eatonvance.com 1-800-262-1122
Fidelity Select Home Finance	402	17.89	www.fidelity.com 1-800-544-6666
FPA Capital	1,540	17.55	www.fpafunds.com 1-800-982-4372
Mairs & Power Growth	1,677	16.97	www.mairsandpower.com 1-800-304-7404
Wasatch Core Growth	1,557	16.71	www.wasatchfunds.com 1-800-551-1700
Fidelity Select Health Care	2,045	16.60	www.fidelity.com 1-800-544-6666
Fidelity Select Technology	2,370	16.49	www.fidelity.com 1-800-544-6666
Wasatch Small Cap Growth	1,274	16.41	www.wasatchfunds.com 1-800-551-1700
INVESCO Financial Services Inv	993	16.37	www.aiminvestments.com 1-800-959-4246
Fidelity Select Brokerage & Investment	369	16.35	www.fidelity.com 1-800-544-6666
Fidelity Select Biotechnology	2,154	16.33	www.fidelity.com 1-800-544-6666
Fidelity Select Computers	814	16.31	www.fidelity.com 1-800-544-6666
Fidelity Select Insurance	171	16.27	www.fidelity.com 1-800-544-6666
Federated Kaufmann K	6,871	16.11	www.federatedinvestors.com 1-800-341-7400
Seligman Comm & Info A	4,151	15.98	www.seligman.com 1-800-221-2450
Fidelity Select Banking	460	15.96	www.fidelity.com 1-800-544-6666
Heartland Value	2,050	15.85	www.americasvalueinvestor.com 1-800-432-7856
John Hancock Regional Bank B	2,467	15.78	www.jhfunds.com 1-800-225-5291
Waddell & Reed Adv Science & Tech A	2,170	15.76	www.waddell.com 1-888-923-3355
ICM Small Company	1,315	15.61	www.icmfunds.com 1-800-472-6114
INVESCO Leisure Inv	914	15.52	www.aiminvestments.com 1-800-959-4246
Fidelity Contrafund	39,080	15.50	www.fidelity.com 1-800-544-6666

*Assets as of May 31, 2004. All other data updated through July 9, 2004.

© 2004 Morningstar, Inc. All Rights Reserved. The information contained herein: (1) is proprietary to Morningstar and/or its content providers; (2) may not be copied or distributed; and (3) is not warranted to be accurate, complete, or timely. Neither Morningstar nor its content providers are responsible for any damages or losses arising from any use of this information. Past performance is no guarantee of future results.

dividend-yielding securities (excluding REITs) in the Dow Jones U.S. Total Market Index. For details, go to www.ishares.com.

As with the REIT investments I suggested earlier, if your 401(k) plan doesn't yet offer ETFs (more than likely they don't), check to see if your plan offers a regular stock market index fund that will accomplish much the same thing as spreading your money among the four I recommended. And if you're using an IRA, you will find that nearly every bank or brokerage that provides IRAs makes it easy to purchase shares in a wide variety of index funds. (If you're confused, don't worry. In a few pages, I'll share an approach to managing your retirement account that involves making only one simple investment.)

STEP 3
BUY BONDS

And, finally, one-third of your assets are going to be in bonds. As with stocks, I would recommend constructing your bond portfolio out of bond mutual funds—specifically, equal amounts of the following exchange-traded bond index funds (keeping in mind that if you can't get them, regular bond index funds will do nearly as well).

iShares Lehman 1–3 Year Treasury Bond Fund (SHY). This ETF mirrors U.S. Treasury bonds with maturities of between 1 and 3 years. For details, go to www.ishares.com.

iShares Lehman 7–10 Year Treasury Bond Fund (ticker symbol IEF). This fund tracks U.S. Treasury bonds with maturities of between 7 and 10 years. For details, go to www.ishares.com.

iShares Lehman Tips (TIP). This fund mirrors U.S. Treasury Inflation Protected Securities ("TIPS"), all of which have at least 1 year to maturity. For details, go to www.ishares.com.

iShares GS $ InvesTop™ Corporate Bond Fund (LQD). This fund seeks to mirror the GS $ InvesTop™ Corporate Bond Fund Index of 100 investment-grade corporate bonds. For details, go to www.ishares.com.

WHAT IS AN EXCHANGE-TRADED FUND?

In the last few pages I've been referring to Exchange-Traded Funds, or ETFs for short. Exchange-Traded Funds have been around for about a decade. I started recommending them back in 2001 in *Smart Women Finish Rich*. Today, they are becoming increasingly popular. A new class of index fund, the ETF is basically a mutual fund designed to mirror a particular market index. ETFs have two major advantages over traditional mutual funds. First, they trade like individual stocks—which means that unlike traditional mutual funds, they can be traded during market hours. Second, since they are not actively managed, their expense ratios are much lower (an average of *seven times lower*) than those of traditional mutual funds.

As a result, the market for these funds is exploding. As of this writing, there are 134 ETF funds with more than $166 billion in assets. That's not much compared with the more than $7 trillion in traditional funds, but the ETF sector is growing dramatically.

AN APPROACH SO SIMPLE
IT'S MIND-BOGGLING

If you bought all the real estate, stock, and bond funds I just listed, you would be incredibly well diversified. Your money would be invested in the Dow Jones Industrials, the S&P 500, and the Nasdaq's top 100 stocks as well as in the stock market's top 50 dividend producers—not to mention a broad range of the real estate and bond markets—all by purchasing shares in fewer than a dozen funds.

What's the downside? Well, that's still 10 or so funds to buy and track. And if you're starting off with very small amounts of money, the commissions you'd have to pay on so many separate purchases could offset one of the benefits of ETFs, which is their low expenses.

That said, I have to tell you that this is about as easy as it gets when it comes to doing your own asset allocation. You don't need to do any research, the cost is unbelievably low, the funds are tax efficient—and, basically, they require zero management, because with one exception every fund I've recommended aims to do nothing more or less than match the performances of the broad market indexes they're named after. (The exception is the Dow Jones Select Dividend Fund; its goal is to outperform the Dow Jones Select Dividend Index—which, by the way, it's done.)

You now have an investment portfolio that, based on historical averages, should double in value every seven to ten years. *Does that work for you?*

THE ONE-STOP SOLUTION TO INVESTING

Actually, there is one even simpler alternative.

For people who like to keep things really simple, there is a truly one-stop solution that makes investing in retirement accounts (especially IRAs or 401(k) plans) really easy. It involves using either a Balanced Fund or an Asset Allocation Fund, a strategy I talk about in *The Automatic Millionaire*. I like these funds a lot, because they make the complicated both simple and automatic.

WHAT ASSET-ALLOCATION AND BALANCED FUNDS DO

Asset-allocation funds or balanced funds essentially do all of the work of diversification for you by offering an appropriate mix of stocks, bonds, and cash in one fund. More and more of these funds are available these days for the most basic of reasons: The investing public really likes their simplified approach. Among their advantages:

- They provide professional diversification among mutual funds and asset classes.
- They provide automatic rebalancing of investments.
- They can be conservative, moderate, or aggressive.
- They are easy to invest in monthly.
- They are easy to select.
- They can be boring.
- They can work.

MANY NAMES, ONE CONCEPT

Who says you can't get rich being boring? The boring investments listed on the following pages have all generated returns of more than 10% a year for 15 years! Again, so much for the naysayers who claim you can't earn 10% a year anymore. Maybe, maybe not!

There are now hundreds of asset-allocation funds, and they go by a variety of names. Depending on the particular plan, it might be called an Asset-Allocation Fund or a Fund of Funds or a Life Stage Fund. Some of these funds have a specific year in their name (for example, the 2020 Fund or the 2030 Fund), the idea being that you select the fund closest to your projected retirement date. The particular mix of bonds and stocks in one of these funds depends on whether that date is near-term or a long way off.

On the next page is a list of some of the top-performing asset-allocation and balanced funds over the last 15 years.

When you open a 401(k) account, your plan will probably offer you a laundry list of investment choices. Look for an asset-allocation fund or something similar if you like the idea of one-stop shopping for mutual funds. Same thing if your main investment vehicle is an IRA. You can invest in preselected and professionally managed asset-allocation funds through a traditional IRA, Roth IRA, or SEP IRA. Just tell your bank or brokerage that you'd like to look at asset-allocation fund or balanced-fund options.

Below is a *partial* list of companies that offer these types of funds. The companies listed below offer "no-load" funds, meaning you can buy them yourself directly without working through a financial advisor and paying a commission. You can also purchase this type of fund through a professional financial advisor at any major brokerage firm. The firms listed on pages 109–111 can help you. If you contact a full-service brokerage firm or bank, simply tell them you are interested in looking at mutual funds—specifically, asset-allocation funds and balanced funds—and they will be able to assist you.

THE DO-IT-YOURSELF OPTION

American Century
800-345-2021
www.americancentury.com

Ask about the American Century Strategic Asset Allocation Funds. There are three of them: conservative, moderate, and aggressive.

Dodge and Cox
800-621-3979
www.dodgeandcox.com

TOP ASSET-ALLOCATION AND BALANCED FUNDS
RANKED BY 15-YEAR ANNUALIZED RETURN

Fund Name	Ticker Symbol	Net Assets ($M)*	15-Year Annualized Return (%)	Contact Info.
Dodge & Cox Balanced	DODBX	16,500	12.60	www.dodgeandcox.com 1-800-621-3979
T. Rowe Price Capital Appreciation	PRWCX	3,711	12.25	www.troweprice.com 1-410-345-2000
Van Kampen Equity and Income A	ACEIX	10,491	12.02	www.vankampen.com 1-800-847-2424
Dreyfus Premier Balanced Opportunity J	THPBX	500	11.10	www.dreyfus.com 1-888-271-4994
American Funds American Balanced A	ABALX	37,053	11.03	www.americanfunds.com 1-800-421-0180
Vanguard Asset Allocation	VAAPX	9,479	10.88	www.vanguard.com 1-877-662-7447
Vanguard Wellington	VWELX	29,630	10.78	www.vanguard.com 1-877-662-7447
Value Line Income	VALIX	215	10.74	www.vlfunds.com 1-800-223-0818
State Farm Balanced	STFBX	1,013	10.68	www.statefarm.com 1-800-447-4930
American Funds Inc Fund of Amer A	AMECX	44,646	10.62	www.americanfunds.com 1-800-421-0180
MainStay Balanced I	MBAIX	272	10.49	www.mainstayfunds.com 1-800-624-6782
Fidelity Puritan	FPURX	22,345	10.39	www.fidelity.com 1-800-544-6666
Fidelity Balanced	FBALX	11,045	10.33	www.fidelity.com 1-800-544-6666
SB Capital & Income SmB B	SOPTX	2,270	10.30	www.smithbarney.com 1-800-221-3636
MFS Total Return A	MSFRX	10,765	10.21	www.mfs.com 1-800-637-2929
Vanguard STAR	VGSTX	9,622	10.17	www.vanguard.com 1-877-662-7447
Pax World Balanced	PAXWX	1,303	10.07	www.paxworld.com 1-800-767-1729

*Assets as of May 31, 2004. All other data updated through July 9, 2004

Ask about the Dodge and Cox Balanced Fund. This fund is consistently ranked as one of the top no-load balanced funds, with a track record going back to 1911.

Fidelity Investments
800-FIDELITY
www.fidelity.com

Ask about the Fidelity Freedom Funds. These asset-allocation funds come with a due date (e.g., 2010, 2020, 2030, 2040). Also ask about the Fidelity Balanced Fund.

T. Rowe Price
877-804-2315
www.troweprice.com

Ask about the T. Rowe Price Retirement series. Like the Fidelity Freedom Funds, these funds also come with a due date. Also ask about the T. Rowe Price Spectrum Funds.

Charles Schwab
866-855-9102
www.schwab.com

Ask about the Schwab Market Track series of funds. Also ask about Schwab's Balanced MarketMasters funds.

Scudder
800-621-1048
www.scudder.com

Ask about the Scudder Pathway Funds. Scudder also offers three asset-allocation funds: conservative, moderate, and growth.

Vanguard
877-662-7447
www.vanguard.com

Ask about the Vanguard Life Strategy Funds. Also ask about the Vanguard STAR fund. This is a "fund of funds" asset allocation product created out of various Vanguard funds. Finally, ask about the Vanguard Balanced Fund, a very low-cost balanced fund with an excellent long-term track record.

IT REALLY IS THIS SIMPLE

Investing your retirement money in a single fund may strike some people as incredibly risky. Others may think it's too easy or too simple to be a good idea. In fact, investing your Stocks slice and your Bonds slice in one fund is neither risky nor dumb. What it is, is boring.

Here's the bottom line. If you pick one good asset-allocation fund—and automate your purchases—you'll have the best kind of financial life there is: a boring one. Your portfolio will be totally diversified, professionally balanced and managed, and you will be paying yourself first—all with absolutely no effort on your part.

That's not to say you shouldn't try to educate yourself as much as possible about the financial decisions you're making. The Internet is a great resource. Here are some sites you should check out.

SOME GREAT WEB SITES FOR RESEARCHING MUTUAL FUNDS AND GENERAL FINANCIAL PLANNING

www.morningstar.com

As the saying goes, past performance is no guarantee of future results. Still, it's nice to know a fund's track record. Morningstar is the research firm that originated the concept of ranking mutual funds, and its web site makes it easy to find out which funds are thoroughbreds and which are turkeys. It also offers general descriptions of virtually every fund there is, as well as research on individual stocks. You have to subscribe to get Morningstar's detailed assessments, but general summaries are available for free.

www.valueline.com

Value Line offers more than a dozen print and electronic products that give investors access to timely information on stocks, mutual funds, special situations, options, and convertibles. The company is best known for *The Value Line Investment Survey*, which contains information and advice on approximately 1,700 stocks, more than 90 industries, the stock market, and the economy. Many experts feel it contains some of the best nonbiased research available to the public. You need to be a subscriber in order to access Value Line's products and services. At their web site, click on "Products and Services" to select the subscription that meets your needs.

http://finance.yahoo.com

Yahoo Finance offers a wealth of free information and services for both novices and veterans, including full stock and mutual fund analysis, portfolio tracking, online bill paying, message boards, research, and much, much more.

www.mfea.com

The Mutual Fund Educational Alliance is an industry group aimed at promoting the virtues of mutual funds. Its online Mutual Fund Investor's Center offers one of the largest collections of mutual fund companies, web site links, fund listings, and exclusive planning, tracking, and monitoring tools available on the Internet.

www.aol.com (keyword: david bach)

AOL Personal Finance is the leading personal finance destination on the Internet, visited by millions monthly. If you are an America Online subscriber, go to AOL (keyword: David Bach), where you will find a Money Coach Program I've created with AOL to make finishing rich even easier.

WHO WANTS TO GO TO A COCKTAIL PARTY WITH A BORING INVESTMENT PLAN?

If investing can be as simple and straightforward as following the Perfect Pie Approach or investing in an asset-allocation fund, why doesn't everyone do it? The answer is because it's boring.

Something tells me you probably have never been to a cocktail party where someone came up to you and said, "You should see my well-balanced portfolio. It's got some real estate, some bonds, and some index funds. It's very stable and I rebalance it regularly."

On the other hand, I'll bet you have had someone grab you by the arm and tell you something like this: "You really gotta buy shares in this company I heard about, because this baby is a cinch to go up. It's hot insider information—don't tell anyone."

This always gets a big laugh out of the audiences at my seminars. That's because people know it's true. Somehow we've become programmed to think investing should be interesting—even sexy. I totally disagree. Your life should be interesting. Your investment plan should be boring. Drop-dead boring.

Set up a rock-solid, drop-dead-boring investment plan, put it on "automatic pilot" by contributing to it automatically every time you get paid—and you'll be able to live an exciting life. Doesn't that make more sense?

THERE'S ALWAYS A SKEPTIC IN THE ROOM

It never fails. Every time I publish a new book, give a lecture, appear at a book signing, or conduct a seminar, there's a skeptic in the room who knows why my plan won't work. This person is one of those "yeah-butters."

Yeah, but . . . the stock market won't always go up.

Yeah, but . . . the real estate market is a bubble that's about to pop.

Yeah, but . . . a million dollars won't be worth anything in 30 years when you account for inflation.

Yeah, but . . . I can't save any money.

One of my favorite examples of this kind of "yeah-butting" was a response I got to a speech I gave in Philadelphia. I was speaking about the importance of having a boring investment plan when I noticed a guy in his forties sitting there with his arms folded across his chest and a pretty darn serious "yeah, but" look on his face. Finally, he raised his hand and said, "David, I like how you teach—it's entertaining and all—but I really think your ideas are so outdated. We're looking at baby boomers retiring, global warming, terrorism, inflation—you name it. Facing a future like that, you can't seriously believe that your simple ideas can still work. I mean, let's be honest—life is no longer simple."

LIFE MAY NOT BE SIMPLE, BUT THAT DOESN'T MEAN YOU HAVE TO MAKE IT COMPLICATED

I took what he said seriously, and I answered him with what I know for a fact—which is that every decade people say the same thing. I pointed out to him that many of my clients had lived through World War I, the Depression, World War II, the Korean War, Vietnam, the Cold War—and that like him they saw the world as a confused and confusing place. Nonetheless, they still managed to achieve some sense of security. How? By maintaining a rock-solid financial foundation. "And the way you get that," I told him, "is by taking a boring, disciplined approach to savings."

The skeptic wasn't buying it. He shook his head and kept his arms crossed. I think I heard him mutter, "Whatever."

After I finished my speech, I went to the back of the room where a table had been set up so I could sign copies of my book. The skeptic's comments had led to many interesting conversations. The most memorable involved an elderly couple in their early eighties named Nicholas and Victoria.

They appeared at the signing table carrying half a dozen copies of my book, which they wanted me to sign for their kids. As I started scribbling my name, Nicholas leaned over and said in a low voice that was almost a whisper, "You were right with that guy. My wife and I put together a really boring portfolio that was almost *exactly* like the one you described. We own a few homes. We've got money in municipal bonds that we don't have to pay taxes on. And we've got shares in a few really big mutual funds that have been around for 50 years. I started investing years ago with just $10 a month, we always saved 10% of our income—and today we are multimillionaires."

I put down the pen and looked him in the eye. "That's an amazing story," I said.

Nicholas shook his head. "Not really. Looking back, it actually wasn't that hard. We put our kids through school, and we even recently helped our daughter and her husband with a down payment on their first home."

He paused and sighed. "You know," he said as I handed him back the books he had bought, "I always thought if we could do it, anyone could, but as we watch our kids, we see how much they struggle financially. We also see how they never go without anything. It's always got to be a new car or a new computer or a new television set. Meanwhile, they don't save anything, and our other kids still rent." He gestured at my book. "We hope this will get them on the right track, because Lord knows they didn't pick up our habits."

As Nicholas gathered up the books, Victoria smiled at me and shook my hand. "You are really doing something important, David," she said. "The young people need your 'boring' advice, as you call it. It really does work, and we are living proof."

KEY "START LATE" PRINCIPLES IN CHAPTER TEN

- Trying to "time the market" almost never works; you're much better off making long-term investments in a well-diversified portfolio.
- In a complicated and crazy world, you need a boring investment plan: According to the Perfect Pie Approach, one-third of your assets should be in stocks, one-third in bonds, and one-third in real estate.
- Rather than trying to pick individual stocks, bonds, or real estate investments, you should invest in index funds that track the stock, bond, and real estate markets as a whole.
- A simpler alternative to the Perfect Pie Approach is to invest your retirement money in an asset-allocation or balanced fund.

FINISH RICH ACTION STEPS

Reviewing the principles we discussed in Chapter Ten, here is what you should be doing right now so you can Start Late and Finish Rich. Check off each step as you accomplish it.

❑ Take the money in your retirement account and invest one-third in stock-market index funds, one-third in bond funds, and one-third in real estate. Alternatively, put it into an asset-allocation or balanced fund.

❑ Educate yourself about the financial decisions you're making by visiting financial information web sites on the Internet.

By now, you should be well on your way to overcoming your late start. You're spending less, saving more, and investing intelligently. But there's more to finishing rich than that. In the next two chapters, you're going to learn how to swing the single most important investment you'll ever make: buying your own home.

CHAPTER ELEVEN

WHY RENTERS STAY POOR AND HOMEOWNERS GET RICH

Bottom line: You can't finish rich if you don't own your own home. And if you started late, you need to own someone else's home, too!

It's not simply that real estate is one of the best investments you can make. It's also that the alternative to homeowning—renting the place where you live—is one of the most financially self-destructive things you can do. So first let's look at why you should own your own home and how you can make it happen. Later on in the book, we'll cover buying other people's homes—that is, investing in rental properties.

ISN'T IT TOO LATE TO GET IN ON THE REAL ESTATE BOOM?

Is buying a home still a good investment? Home prices have recently sky-rocketed. In many areas of the country, homes have literally doubled in value in the last three years. Some people have seen their homes go up in value tenfold in a decade.

So where does that leave you? If you are still renting, you may be wondering, "Is it too late for me? Did I once again miss the boat? Is the real estate bubble about to pop?"

While no one can answer these questions definitively, what we know from history is that there has really never been a national real estate bubble. *We also know you definitely can't get rich renting!*

WHY RENTERS STAY POOR

You cannot get rich being a renter. And you certainly can't start late and finish rich renting. How do we know this? The facts pretty much speak for themselves. Across the board in North America, renters are poorer and homeowners are wealthier. According to the U.S. Federal Reserve Survey of Consumer Finances, **the average renter in 2001 had a median net worth of $4,800—while the average homeowner had a median net worth of about $171,700.**

Given this, it's obvious that a major part of how you start late and finish rich is to buy a home. And as you'll see, once you do buy a home, you should strive to pay it off early.

IF YOU'RE RENTING, DON'T GET MAD— JUST DO SOMETHING

People who rent really hate this part of my presentation. It hurts renters to hear that as long as they keep living that way, they'll probably *never* be rich.

If that's how you're feeling right now, as I said before, please don't shoot the messenger. I'm here to be your coach. I care what happens to you, and I know that if you keep renting, your chances of starting late and finishing rich are slim. You really have to buy a home. It has to be your goal—that and paying it off as early as you can (which is something we'll get into shortly). The good news is that buying your first home may be a lot easier than you think.

THE 7 THINGS YOU NEED TO KNOW ABOUT HOMEOWNERSHIP

1. You can't afford not to buy.
2. Buying can be cheaper than renting.
3. Homes make great investments.

4. The government wants you to become a homeowner.
5. You don't need a huge down payment to buy a house.
6. You don't need perfect credit or a big income to get a mortgage.
7. *It's never too late.*

YOU CAN'T AFFORD NOT TO BUY

Why is it so important to own the place you live in? Well, to begin with, there are the intangibles—the feeling of pride and control you get from being a homeowner. When you own, you have the security that comes from knowing you are building equity and living in a place that belongs to you. This is your castle. You can paint it whatever color you like, put up shelves, knock down a wall, plant a tree, or install a Jacuzzi. You're not at the mercy of a landlord who can raise your rent, impose rules, or evict you.

From a financial point of view, the argument for homeownership is equally strong. Here's the bottom line: **You can't get rich renting.**

YOU CAN EASILY WASTE HALF A MILLION ON RENT IN YOUR LIFETIME

Think about it. As a renter, you can easily spend half a million dollars or more on rent over the years ($1,500 a month for 30 years comes to $540,000) and in the end wind up just where you started—owning nothing. Or you can buy a house and spend the same amount paying down a mortgage, and in the end wind up owning your own home free and clear!

IN FACT, BUYING CAN COST YOU LESS THAN RENTING

What puts off most people about buying a home is that they get hung up on the big six-figure price tags that most houses carry these days. (According to the National Association of Realtors, the median sales price of existing single-family homes in the United States reached $170,800 in the first quarter of 2004.) Without even thinking about it, they assume they could never afford the monthly payments. What they don't realize is that if they can afford to pay their rent, they probably can afford to carry a reasonable-sized mortgage.

As of this writing (in mid-2004), interest rates are around 6.5% for a 30-

year fixed-rate mortgage. They may be higher by the time you read this, but let's use the math we have at the moment. To put it simply, for every $1,000 you pay in monthly rent, you could support roughly $160,000 worth of mortgage. In other words, if your rent is currently $2,000 a month, you could afford to make payments on a $320,000 mortgage. In most parts of the country, that would buy you a lot of home!

And that's only half the story. With all the tax advantages you get as a result of homeownership—not to mention the built-in stability of fixed mortgage payments—it can actually be cheaper to buy than to rent.

To make this point, I once ran the numbers for a client named Dorothy, a single mom in her early forties who was resisting my advice that she buy the pleasant little house she was renting for herself and her daughter. Dorothy's rent was $1,600 a month, and her landlord had offered to sell her the place for $350,000, which given comparable values in her neighborhood wasn't a bad deal. The good news was that because Dorothy believed in paying herself first, she had a little money in the bank and so was able to come up with a $50,000 down payment. The bad news was that Dorothy was scared off by the huge amount she would wind up owing the bank—that and the fact that mortgage rates were at 7% at the time, meaning that the monthly payments on a $300,000 mortgage would come to about $2,000.

"Buying that house is going to cost me $400 a month more than renting," Dorothy said to me. "That's $4,800 more a year. Now, you know me, David. I've figured out my Latte Factor, and I don't waste money. The only way I'll be able to pay that extra $400 a month is to reduce my contributions to my retirement account, and I'm sorry, but I just don't want to do that."

"I do know you, Dorothy," I replied, "and if the difference really was $400 a month you might have a point. But it's not. Don't forget—as a home-owner you'll be eligible for all sorts of tax breaks, like being able to deduct mortgage interest. When you figure them in, that $2,000-a-month mortgage actually will cost you only about $1,700 a month—meaning the real difference will only be about $100 a month, or $1,200 a year. And there's another thing. Your mortgage payment is fixed. It's going to be $2,000 a month for the next 30 years—unless, of course, you decide to pay off your mortgage sooner. Your rent, on the other hand, goes up every year."

In fact, Dorothy's rent was rising at an average rate of 5% a year. And when we worked out all the arithmetic, here's how Dorothy's cost of renting compared with the cost of buying over the next seven years.

				Monthly		Yearly
		Fixed-Rate		Difference		Difference
	Monthly	Mortgage	Monthly	After Tax	Yearly	After Tax
Yr	Rent	Payment	Difference	Savings	Difference	Savings
1	1,600	2,000	−400	−100	−4,800	−1,200
2	1,680	2,000	−320	−20	−3,840	−240
3	1,764	2,000	−236	+64	−2,832	+762
4	1,852	2,000	−148	+152	−1,776	+1,824
5	1,944	2,000	−56	+244	−672	+2,928
6	2,042	2,000	+42	+342	+504	+4,104
7	2,144	2,000	+144	+444	+1,728	+5,328

RENTING VS. BUYING: OFTEN A NO-BRAINER

What's amazing about these numbers is that based solely on the fact that Dorothy's rent would go up while her mortgage payments would remain stable, owning becomes cheaper for her than renting within just six years. And when you figure in the tax savings that come with owning your own home, the monthly cost of owning becomes cheaper than renting *in less than three years!*

By the end of Year Seven, Dorothy would be paying out $5,328 a year less in mortgage payments than she would in rent. Overall, as a homeowner, Dorothy would be more than $13,500 ahead of the game by then—and that's not counting any increases in the value of her house. And every year after that, the cost advantage of owning would only become greater and greater.

Now, to be fair, I pointed out to Dorothy that these figures did not include some of the extra costs she would incur as a homeowner, such as property taxes, insurance, and upkeep. But given the quickly widening spread between the after-tax cost of paying a mortgage versus paying rent, she is still bound to come out comfortably ahead. (It also helps that property taxes are themselves deductible.)

Talk about your no-brainers. This is why it's fair to say that you aren't really in the game of building wealth until you own some real estate. **The first landlord you should become is your own!**

So, believe me—if you want to finish rich and you are currently renting, buying a home (whether it's a house or a condo) needs to be a priority.

BUT WHAT ABOUT THE DOWN PAYMENT?

The number-one reason people put off buying a home is that they think they can't afford it. More often than not, they are wrong.

In particular, would-be homebuyers are scared off by the down payment. People often think they need to come up with thousands if not tens of thousands of dollars in cash in order to get a mortgage. This is simply not true. Remember the story I told you about my friend Christopher, who moved to Manhattan with $15,000 in credit card debt? He bought a home with a 5% down payment. How? There are all sorts of programs sponsored by developers, lenders, and even the government that can enable first-time homebuyers to finance as much as 95%, 97%, or even 100% of the purchase price. (I'll tell you about a bunch of them shortly.) While borrowing so much can be risky (if you can't afford the monthly payments), this is another fact of homeownership that may seem too good to be true, but in fact is the real deal.

YOU CAN BUY A HOUSE
EVEN IF YOUR CREDIT IS BAD

I was talking one day with my friends Brigitte and Travis about how easy it is to buy a home. In the middle of the conversation, they exchanged a glance and started asking me questions.

"Umm, David, do you think it's possible to buy a home if your credit is screwed up?"

"How bad is your credit?"

"Umm, it's not us. It's these friends of ours. They've been late on some bills, and their credit scores are really bad."

"Well, I'd tell these friends that they should go into at least five local banks and discuss their situation. Do they have jobs?"

"Oh, yes, they both work."

"That's good. If they are both working and they bring in proof of their income—like pay stubs, bank statements, and tax returns—my guess is they could get a loan even with bad credit. They'll probably get charged a higher interest rate, but they should be able to get a loan. In fact, if they are first-time homebuyers, they might even be able to get a special loan to buy a home with little or no money down."

Needless to say, Brigitte and Travis turned out to be the "friends" they were describing. And after shopping around for a while and getting turned down by several banks, they did ultimately get a no-money-down mortgage. Because their credit scores were bad, the interest rate was high—around 9%—but they got 100% financed. The mortgage even covered their closing costs.

As a result, they were able to buy a home for $525,000. That was in 2000. Three years later, they sold the house for $850,000. After commissions, they pocketed more than $250,000 tax-free. How's that for a deal!

THE GOVERNMENT WANTS YOU
TO BE A HOMEOWNER

Every state and virtually every city in the country sponsors programs aimed at making it easier for renters to become homeowners. In all, there are literally thousands of them around the country. A comprehensive list, organized by state and complete with contact information, is available on the web site of the U.S. Department of Housing and Urban Development at **www.hud.gov**.

The fact is that the government—local, state, and federal—wants you to own your own home. If it didn't, home mortgage interest wouldn't be tax-deductible. Indeed, back in 2002, the White House announced a goal of increasing the number of U.S. homeowners by 5.5 million over the next eight years. In order to make this happen, the government has earmarked billions of dollars to help first-time homebuyers handle their down payments. In addition, the government is also creating products to lower the overall cost of mortgages for first-time homebuyers.

AGENCIES AND INSTITUTIONS
THAT CAN HELP YOU BUY A HOME

U.S. DEPARTMENT OF HOUSING AND
URBAN DEVELOPMENT
www.hud.gov

HUD's mission is to create opportunities for homeownership. To this end, it offers all kinds of assistance to would-be homebuyers, including grants to help people buy a first home. If you are a first-time homebuyer, visit the HUD web site! It offers a wealth of resources on how to buy, what kind of help HUD offers, and how to qualify for assistance, as well as links to hundreds of state and local programs aimed at making homeownership easier and more affordable. Especially useful are the "100 Questions & Answers About Buying a New Home." You can even chat online with an agency representative and be referred to a housing counselor in your area.

NATIONAL COUNCIL OF STATE HOUSING FINANCE AGENCIES

www.ncsha.org

Virtually every state in the union offers special loan programs specifically created to help first-time homebuyers. The NCSHA web site is a great way to find out all about them. It contains links to housing finance agencies in every state, many of which have programs that allow you to buy a home with a down payment of less than 5%.

FANNIE MAE

800-832-2345
www.fanniemae.com

The Federal National Mortgage Association, otherwise known as Fannie Mae, doesn't lend money itself. What it does is provide the financing that makes it possible for banks to lend money to consumers. It also offers lots of good information for consumers, including an entire library of FREE reports with titles like *Opening the Door to a Home of Your Own, Choosing a Mortgage, Knowing Your Credit,* and *Borrowing Basics.* In addition, check out **www.homepath.com**, a related Fannie Mae web site that contains a consumer-friendly "For Home Buyers & Homeowners" section with helpful information on "Becoming a Home Owner," "Finding a Lender," and "Resources."

FREDDIE MAC

800-373-3343
www.freddiemac.com

Fannie Mae's younger cousin, Freddie Mac (aka the Federal Home Loan Mortgage Corporation), provides the financing that allows lenders to offer home loans that are affordable. The Freddie Mac web site has a terrific section for would-be homebuyers (at **www.freddiemac.com/homebuyers**), where you'll find a wonderful tool called "The Road To Home Ownership." It also has a related web site at **www.homesteps.com** that helps first-time homebuyers find bargain homes and get one-step loan approvals by listing foreclosure auctions and providing information about loan programs that allow would-be homeowners to buy foreclosed properties with as little as 5% down.

LOAN PROGRAMS TO CONSIDER

FHA Loans. Since 1934, the Federal Housing Administration has helped more than 30 million people become homeowners—not by lending them money but by guaranteeing their loans, thus reassuring lenders who are generally reluctant to lend to first-time buyers. FHA-guaranteed loans often cover up to 97% of the purchase price, and though they are usually meant for first homes, they can be used to buy second or third homes. For more information about how to get an FHA-guaranteed loan and referrals to FHA-approved lenders in your area, visit the HUD web site at **www.hud.gov**. Another useful site is **www.fhaloan.com**. It's not run by the FHA, but it offers reliable information.

VA Loans. If you served in the armed forces, you can get a mortgage guaranteed by the U.S. Department of Veterans Affairs—which usually means a lower interest rate than you'd otherwise get. Details are available at the VA's own web site at **www.va.gov**, as well as at **www.valoans.com**, which is privately run but is useful nonetheless.

State Bond Loans. Most states offer individual bond programs designed to help first-time homebuyers. Ask the manager or the mortgage specialist at your local bank for details. Also, as discussed earlier, visit the National Council of State Housing Finance Agencies web site (**www.ncsha.org**) for more information on these programs.

FIRST-TIME HOMEBUYER PROGRAMS— FOUND AT YOUR BANK

One of the fastest and simplest ways to find a low- or no-money-down mortgage is to check with your bank or local mortgage broker. Open the newspaper this weekend and look at the real estate section. You'll find pages of ads from mortgage brokers promoting their ability to get home-buyers the financing they need. Call a bunch of them—and several neighborhood banks as well—and ask if they offer special mortgage programs for "first-time homebuyers." If you call 10 banks and mortgage brokers, you're bound to find at least one offering this type of program.

In addition, you can look for mortgages online. Here are three of the top home mortgage web sites:

www.eloan.com
www.lendingtree.com
www.quickenloans.com

As I write this, E-Loan is running a national advertising campaign specifically promoting a "nothing down" mortgage.

HOW MUCH HOME CAN YOU AFFORD?

This is the big question. The answer is probably more than you think. How much exactly? There are a number of ways to figure out how much you can afford to spend on a home. One is to use the free calculators you'll find on Interest.com, a really useful financial information web site.

WHAT PRICE RANGE IS RIGHT FOR YOU?			
Annual Gross Income	Monthly Gross	29% of Gross	41% of Gross
$20,000	$1,667	$483	$683
$30,000	$2,500	$725	$1,025
$40,000	$3,333	$967	$1,367
$50,000	$4,176	$1,208	$1,712
$60,000	$5,000	$1,450	$2,050
$70,000	$5,833	$1,692	$2,391
$80,000	$6,667	$1,933	$2,733
$90,000	$7,500	$2,175	$3,075
$100,000	$8,333	$2,417	$3,417

Another way is to apply the FHA's rule of thumb, which is that most people can afford to spend 29% of their gross income on housing expenses—as much as 41%, if they have no debt. The table on page 147 should give you a good idea of the kind of price range your income would justify.

As the table indicates, if you earn $50,000 a year, you should be able to afford to spend at least $1,208 a month on housing—whether in the form of rent or mortgage payments. Keeping in mind that homeownership (buying) is better than home loanership (renting), check out the next table. It shows what the monthly payments would be for different amounts of 30-year mortgages at different interest rates. (It doesn't include taxes or insurance; to figure them in, you'll need to check on what they run in your area.)

TYPICAL MORTGAGE PAYMENTS

Monthly payments (principal and interest) for a 30-year, fixed-rate mortgage. Taxes, insurance not included.

Mortgage Amount	5.0%	5.5%	6.0%	6.5%	7.0%	7.5%	8%
$100,000	$537	$568	$600	$632	$668	$699	$734
$150,000	$805	$852	$899	$948	$998	$1,048	$1,100
$200,000	$1,074	$1,136	$1,199	$1,264	$1,331	$1,398	$1,468
$250,000	$1,342	$1,419	$1,499	$1,580	$1,663	$1,748	$1,834
$300,000	$1,610	$1,703	$1,799	$1,896	$1,996	$2,098	$2,201
$350,000	$1,879	$1,987	$2,098	$2,212	$2,329	$2,447	$2,568
$400,000	$2,147	$2,271	$2,398	$2,528	$2,661	$2,797	$2,935
$450,000	$2,415	$2,555	$2,698	$2,844	$2,994	$3,146	$3,302
$500,000	$2,684	$2,839	$2,998	$3,160	$3,327	$3,496	$3,665

IT'S ONLY TOO LATE IF YOU NEVER START

By now you should not only know why you need to be a homeowner, you should also know that owning your own home will probably cost you less in the long run than continuing to rent, and that you won't need to make a huge down payment. This leaves us with only the final (and perhaps most important) part of the process to consider: What kind of mortgage should you get and how can you pay it off automatically?

Before we turn to this key question, however, I want to put to rest any remaining doubts you may have about the practicality of what we're talking about here—the fact that becoming a homeowner isn't simply something you should do, it's also something you *can* do. Let me tell you about John, one of my oldest friends, who went from renting to owning a home in a few short years—and is now nearly half a million dollars richer as a result.

FROM NO DOWN PAYMENT TO A HALF-MILLION DOLLARS IN EQUITY IN FIVE YEARS

Talking to John at dinner was like experiencing déjà vu. I was explaining to him why he had to get out of the rent trap—and he was telling me for the tenth time why he couldn't afford to buy. "David, it's easy for you to say 'buy' because you're doing so well. I mean, I know Susan and I need to stop renting and buy something. But it's just too hard. We don't have any savings, Susan's pregnant and wants to stop working, and we've got credit card debt. We're never going to get out of this hole. It's too late for us."

Finally, one night, I'd heard enough. "John, we've been close friends for a long time, so you know I love you. But I gotta tell you—you got a bad case of the 'woe is me' blues. You're always saying why you can't do something. Why not change the question? What if instead of focusing on why you can't get a down payment, you focused on how you *could* get a down payment saved. Instead of asking, 'Why me?,' why not try a better question?"

"Like what?" John asked, a bit defensively.

"Well, for instance, what if you asked yourself, 'How would I buy a home in the next 18 months if my life depended on it?'"

John thought that sounded a bit extreme. I agreed it did, but then again it was meant to get him thinking differently. "Just play along," I said. "Really think about it. If your life depended on your buying a home in 18 months, how would you do it?"

John gave me that "are you done yet?" look.

I wasn't. "I'm serious," I continued. "If you had to buy a house, what would you do?"

John was silent for a moment, thinking. "Well," he finally said, "I guess Susan and I could move in with her dad, so we could stop paying rent and really focus on saving money. But can you imagine us doing that? We'd have a baby and be living with her father. It would be brutal. I'd feel like a complete loser."

He paused for a moment, then brightened. "Of course, if we *did* do it, I could probably have us out of debt in six months, and then we really could start saving some money and maybe in a year actually buy a place of our own. And the truth is that her dad's a great guy and he's more or less offered to help us numerous times."

Suddenly, there was a gleam in his eye that I hadn't seen before when he talked about his finances.

Fast-forward four years. John and Susan had a baby boy named Nathan. They lived with Susan's dad for almost two years, paid off their credit card debt, saved every penny they could, and pulled together a small down payment for a starter home in Long Beach, California.

It wasn't their "dream home" and the neighborhood wasn't exactly "hot," but the place was cute, with three bedrooms and two baths, and it cost only $220,000. Sure, it needed work—but they were more than willing to put in their share of sweat equity.

Today, John and Susan's home is worth more than $650,000. As a result of the appreciation, John has been able to refinance his mortgage, pulling out $150,000 in cash, which he's using to finance his lifelong dream of starting his own business. (He's just bought a master franchise—a concept we will cover in Part Four.) On paper, he's halfway to being a millionaire, and I'd be willing to bet he's a multimillionaire by the time he reaches 50. Most important, he loves his home, his neighborhood (which now is "hot"), and his newfound net worth.

Now, John was only in his mid-thirties when he and I had the talk that wound up changing his life. To some of you, that may not sound like a late start at all. But John felt like it was already too late for him, and that's all that counts.

Over the years, I've had as many people in their thirties come to me complaining it's too late for them as I've had people in their forties and fifties. The point is, if you are convinced it's too late for you, it doesn't matter how old you are. Whether you're 30 or 60, you're correct.

On the other hand, if you start asking the right kind of questions and get going on the road mapped out in this book, you will be able to finish rich—even if your thirties are only a distant memory. As I like to say—and this is true of finishing rich in general and becoming a homeowner in particular—it's only too late if you never start.

With this in mind, let's turn to the question of picking the right mortgage and setting up a system to pay it off automatically.

KEY "START LATE" PRINCIPLES IN CHAPTER ELEVEN

- You can't finish rich unless you own your own home.
- Buying a home can be easier and cheaper than you think—and over the long term, it usually costs you less than continuing to rent.
- It's not only that real estate is a good investment; it's also that renting drains your resources without giving you anything to show for it.
- The government wants you to be a homeowner.
- Because of this, you don't need a huge down payment, perfect credit, or a big income to get a mortgage.

FINISH RICH ACTION STEPS

Reviewing the principles we discussed in Chapter Eleven, here is what you should be doing right now so you can Start Late and Finish Rich. Check off each step as you accomplish it.

❑ Use the table on page 147 to figure out how much you can afford to spend on a home.

❑ Use the table on page 148 to figure out what the monthly mortgage payment on such a home would be. Compare this to what you're currently paying in rent.

❑ Commit to buying your own home and paying off your mortgage as quickly as you can.

CHAPTER TWELVE

HOW TO
BUY A HOME,
PAY IT OFF EARLY—
AND SAVE $71,000

We've now come to the most important part of the home-buying process: how to pay off your home and become debt-free automatically. There are an endless array of choices to make once you decide to become a home-owner: what kind of house you want, where you want it to be, how much you can afford—the list goes on and on. But while all these issues are important and must be decided carefully, from a financial point of view nothing is more important than getting the right kind of mortgage.

There are many types of mortgages: 30-year fixed-rates, 15-year fixed-rates, short-term adjustable rates, intermediate adjustable rates, and on and on. **Each type has its advantages and disadvantages.**

As a rule, I generally recommend 30-year, fixed-rate mortgages. For one thing, they are easy to understand and manage. For another, when interest rates are low—that is, when they are below 8%, as they've been since the late 1990s—they're a great deal, since they lock in that low rate for the next 30 years.

WHO WANTS TO BE MAKING MORTGAGE PAYMENTS FOR 30 YEARS?

That said, there is one obvious drawback to a 30-year mortgage. For someone who is starting late, the idea of committing yourself to a loan that will take you 30 years to pay off can sound pretty scary. And it should. I mean, who wants to be paying off a debt for 30 years? The fact is that you don't actually want to pay for your home over 30 years. Why? Because if you do, you'll be wasting hundreds of thousands of dollars.

Do you have any idea how much a $200,000 house would actually wind up costing you if you took 30 years to pay it off? Assuming a typical mortgage interest of 7%, the total payments over 30 years would amount to roughly $479,000. That's $200,000 for the house—and more than $279,000 in interest payments to the bank. Under the best of circumstances, that's a terrible deal. For someone who is starting late, it's a recipe for disaster.

TURNING A GOOD DEAL FOR THE BANK INTO A GOOD DEAL FOR YOU

In the early years of a 30-year mortgage, you're not building equity. You're just making the bank rich. That's because under most amortization schedules, less than 10% of the money you send in during the first decade is applied to paying down your principal. What happens to the other 90%? It disappears into the bank's pockets in the form of interest. That's great for the bank, but worse than useless for you.

So why do I recommend that you take out a 30-year mortgage? It's simple. Thirty-year mortgages are great for the bank only if you follow the bank's payment schedule. But if you follow a different schedule—namely, the one I'm about to share with you—a 30-year mortgage can be great for you.

MY SECRET SYSTEM FOR DEBT-FREE HOMEOWNERSHIP

In *The Automatic Millionaire*, I laid out a simple system that any homeowner can use to pay off a 30-year mortgage as much as 8 years early . . .

automatically. I called it my secret biweekly mortgage payment plan, and while it's really not a secret, it's truly automatic and it truly works.

Here's how. All you do is take the normal 30-year mortgage you have and instead of making the monthly payment the way you normally do, you split it down the middle and pay half every two weeks.

Say your mortgage payment is $2,000 a month. Under my biweekly plan, instead of sending a $2,000 check to your mortgage lender once every month, you would send him $1,000 every two weeks. At the beginning, paying $1,000 every two weeks probably won't feel any different than paying $2,000 once a month. But as anyone who's ever looked at a calendar could tell you, it's hardly the same thing. A month, after all, is a little longer than four weeks. And so what happens as a result of switching to a biweekly payment plan is that over the course of a year you gradually get further and further ahead in your payments, until by the end of the year you have paid the equivalent of not 12 but 13 monthly payments.

The math is actually quite simple. A monthly mortgage payment of $2,000 amounts to $24,000 a year. But when you make a half payment every two weeks instead of a full one once a month, you end up making 26 half payments over the course of a year. That's 26 payments of $1,000—for a total of $26,000, or one extra month's worth of payments.

WHAT COULD YOU DO
WITH AN EXTRA $71,000?

The impact of that extra month's payment is awesome. Depending on your interest rate, you will end up paying off your mortgage somewhere between five and seven years early! And that can save you tens of thousands of dollars in interest payments over the life of your mortgage.

I'm not just making these figures up. Check out the amortization schedule on page 155. It shows the difference between a monthly and a biweekly payment plan for a $200,000 30-year mortgage with an interest rate of 7%. The monthly payoff schedule winds up incurring a total of $279,017.80 in interest charges over the life of the loan. The biweekly schedule, on the other hand, runs up just $207,917.46 in interest. In other words, switching to the biweekly plan will save you more than $71,000.

If you'd like to figure out how much you could save on your own mortgage, go online and visit my web site at **www.finishrich.com**. First, click on

MONTHLY PAYMENTS VS. BIWEEKLY PAYMENTS

Principal = **$200,000**   Interest Rate = **7.00%**   Term = **30** years

Monthly Payment: **$1,330.60**   Biweekly Payment: **$665.30**

Average Interest each Month: **$775.05**   Average Interest each Biweekly Period: **$265.88**

Total Interest: **$279,017.80**   Total Interest: **$207,917.46**

Year	Principal Balance (Monthly Payments)	Principal Balance (Biweekly Payments)
1	$197968.38	$196539.56
2	$195789.89	$192829.45
3	$193453.93	$188851.65
4	$190949.09	$184586.85
5	$188263.18	$180014.34
6	$185383.10	$175111.91
7	$182294.83	$169855.78
8	$178983.30	$164220.40
9	$175432.38	$158178.43
10	$171624.77	$151700.52
11	$167541.90	$144755.22
12	$163163.88	$137308.81
13	$158469.38	$129325.13
14	$153435.50	$120765.43
15	$148037.73	$111588.13
16	$142249.76	$101748.67
17	$136043.37	$91199.30
18	$129388.32	$79888.77
19	$122252.17	$67762.17
20	$114600.16	$54760.63
21	$106394.98	$40821.01
22	$97596.64	$25875.63
23	$88162.27	$9851.93
24	$78045.90	$0
25	$67198.20	$0
26	$55566.33	$0
27	$43093.59	$0
28	$29719.19	$0
29	$15377.96	$0
30	$0	$0
Result	**Paid off in 30 years**	**Paid off in 23 years**

SOURCE: Bankrate.com "Biweekly mortgage payment calculator"

"Calculators," then look under "Mortgages" and click "Get a biweekly mortgage plan." This will take you to the best free calculator I've found on the Internet. You can then plug in your own numbers and quickly see how much you could save by switching to a biweekly payment plan.

HOW TO SET UP YOUR OWN
BIWEEKLY PAYMENT PLAN

The great thing about switching to a biweekly payment plan is that it allows you to save money over the long run without refinancing or otherwise changing your mortgage. You're simply accelerating your payment schedule.

BIWEEKLY MORTGAGE SUCCESS STORY

Dear David:

The first time we saw you on television talking about biweekly mortgage payments, we thought, "Gosh, we should do what he recommends." Well, we didn't! Then the show was repeated, so Debbie called our mortgage company to change our payments from once a month to every two weeks. Well, we didn't have the correct information they needed to set this up at that time. Now here it is a few months down the road and finally TODAY we did it!!! WOW! We were told we would save $34,000 and shave 6 years off our 30-year loan. David Bach, THANK YOU!

It's amazing how pain-LESS this is.

Much appreciation,

Mike & Debbie Riebe
Everett, WA

These days, most mortgage lenders offer programs designed to totally automate the process I've just described. (At Wells Fargo, for example, it's called the Equity Enhancement Program; CitiBank calls it The BiWeekly Advantage Plan.) To enroll, all you need to do is phone your lender or go online to its web site.

If your mortgage is with one of the larger banks, they will probably refer you to an outside company that runs the program for them. These companies generally charge a setup fee of somewhere between $200 and $400. In addition, there's a transfer charge that's assessed every time your money is moved from your checking account to your mortgage account; it ranges from $2.50 to $6.95.

A lot of companies now provide these services. To be sure you're dealing with a reputable firm, ideally consider using one that is referred to you by your bank. Chances are your bank will refer you to a company called Paymap. Paymap currently provides a biweekly mortgage payment service, called Equity Accelerator, for more than 30 financial institutions, including six of the nation's largest banks. You can contact Paymap directly at **www.paymap.com** or by calling 800-549-6445.

BIWEEKLY MORTGAGE SUCCESS STORY

Dear David,

I saw you on television a few weeks ago and immediately bought your book. I bought a second home 3 years ago and because of your book, I switched to a biweekly mortgage automatic payment system this week that will shave off 7 years of payments and save me over $100,000. Thank you for your wonderful advice.

Bruce Miller
Austin, TX

Regardless of what company you wind up using, make a point of finding out when your payment is transferred to your mortgage lender. Some companies hang on to the extra money you're putting toward your mortgage and send it to your lender in a lump sum just once a year. I'd avoid a company that does this. What they're doing is earning interest on your money for a year rather than paying off your debt right away.

WHY NOT DO IT YOURSELF?

Why spend hundreds of dollars on an outside firm when you could just as easily use your bank's online automatic bill-paying service to schedule biweekly mortgage payments for yourself? Well, it's not really that simple.

The problem is that if you split your monthly mortgage payment in half and send it in to your mortgage lender every two weeks yourself, the lender will simply send it back to you because they won't know what to do with it. Or worse, they'll stick the money in an escrow account and just let it sit there. Believe it or not, standard operating procedure at many banks is to take extra payments and hold them in a non-interest-bearing account—not use them to pay down your mortgage.

WHAT YOU COULD DO FOR FREE

You could add 10% to your regular mortgage check each month and have the money applied toward the principal. Or you could make one extra payment at the end of the year and again have it go toward your principal. But note that word "could." Let's face it—some things are much easier said than done. Just like most people won't save if they don't make it automatic—in the real world, most people won't make extra mortgage payments unless they make it automatic.

NO GOLDEN YEARS IF YOU HAVE DEBT

In the old days, it was every homeowner's goal to pay off his or her mortgage. What was nice about this simple goal was that when you reached it, you could stop working and enjoy your golden years without debt. I have no idea why this commonsense approach has lately been thrown to the winds. What I do know is that many seniors are finding themselves at retirement age with bigger mortgages and bigger payments.

In 1989, the average homeowner over age 65 had a median mortgage of $12,000. By 2001, the average nearly quadrupled to $44,000. All told, the average debt burden of borrowers between the ages of 65 and 74 doubled between 1992 and 2001. My choice for you is to become debt-free—sooner versus later.

In my experience, people who have no mortgage have less stress. Just remember this: Money may not make you happy, but debt can make you miserable . . . especially when you get older. On the other hand, think how relaxed and pleasant your golden years will be when you're living in a house that you own free and clear.

IMPORTANT NOTE: If you are starting really late (say, you are over the age of 50 and still renting), YOU SHOULD STILL BUY A HOME. The home may appreciate so much by the time you reach 70 that you could sell it and retire on the appreciation. My grandmother bought a place when she was in her eighties—and guess what? It went up in value. And even if your place doesn't appreciate dramatically, would you rather still be renting when you're in your seventies? Remember, you have to live somewhere—so regardless of your age, it makes sense to own.

KEY "START LATE" PRINCIPLES IN CHAPTER TWELVE

- By making your mortgage payments biweekly instead of once a month, you can get out of debt years earlier and save tens of thousands of dollars in interest costs.
- Most mortgage lenders offer programs designed to enable you to do this automatically.

FINISH RICH ACTION STEPS

Reviewing the principles we discussed in Chapter Twelve, here is what you should be doing right now so you can Start Late and Finish Rich. Check off each step as you accomplish it.

❑ Follow the instructions on pages 154 and 156 to find an online calculator that will show you how much you can save by making your mortgage payments biweekly.

❑ Contact your mortgage lender and arrange to set up an automatic biweekly mortgage payment plan.

Congratulations! You're now past the halfway mark on the road to finishing rich. Now that you've learned how to turbocharge your savings, let's look at how you can do the same thing to your income.

PART FOUR

MAKE MORE

CHAPTER THIRTEEN

WHO SAYS YOU CAN'T MAKE MORE?

You've just completed the most important lesson this book has to offer—how to save more. In the process, you've learned the crucial secret that rich people know and poor people don't. Simply put, it's this: "If you pay yourself first automatically and buy a home, you've got a real solid chance of being rich."

This may be the most important secret to becoming rich, but it's not the only one.

Here's another secret that rich people know.

If you can turbocharge your earning power at the same time you're turbocharging your savings ability, your chances of being able to Start Late and Finish Rich will go up exponentially.

A ROAD MAP TO JUMP-STARTING YOUR INCOME

Nothing helps people who are starting late catch up faster than increasing their earnings at the same time they are paying themselves first. So now that we've jump-started your savings by channeling a significant chunk of your income directly to you, it's time to focus on *jump-starting your income*. Doing these two things together—growing both your savings and your earnings—will give you the one-two punch you need to revolutionize your financial life.

IN THIS SECTION OF THE BOOK,
YOU WILL FIND A ROAD MAP THAT EXPLAINS:

- How extra income can turbocharge your financial freedom plan.
- How unlimited wealth can be yours—and why one good idea can be worth more than a lifetime of work.
- How to create more income by getting a raise.
- How to become a millionaire by investing in real estate on the weekends.
- How to grow your income by starting a business—without having to quit your current job.

THE MATHEMATICS OF CATCHING UP

Most people never succeed in creating additional income because they think of it as a really big thing to do. It's just too hard. It's just too much trouble.

In fact, it can be amazingly simple. To begin with, let's just focus on the math of catching up.

If you can increase your income by a few hundred dollars a month—and save all of it for your future—what do you think would happen?

As you can see on the next page, increasing your income by just a few hundred dollars a month and then saving it all can yield major-league results. So here's the question. Would it really be that hard for you to grow your income by somewhere between $100 and $1,000 a month?

Your answer should be a resounding no . . . *if* you DECIDE TODAY to focus on it.

Now, there's nothing that says you can't try to increase your income by more than $1,000 a month. But let's stick to that range. Let's say over the next 12 months you were able to grow your income by $500 a month and you saved 100% of it. Do you have any idea how much extra wealth you'd have in just 20 years?

Assuming you averaged an annual return of 10% on your money, the answer is $379,685!

EARN AND SAVE A LITTLE MORE, END UP WITH A LOT MORE

(Assumes 10% Annual Rate of Return)

Monthly Increase In Earnings	Your Extra Wealth in 10 Years	In 15 Years	In 20 Years	In 25 Years	In 30 Years
$100	$20,484	$41,447	$75,937	$132,683	$226,049
$200	$40,969	$82,894	$151,874	$265,367	$452,098
$300	$61,453	$124,341	$227,811	$398,049	$678,147
$400	$81,938	$165,788	$303,748	$530,734	$904,196
$500	$102,420	$207,235	$379,685	$663,415	$1,139,245
$600	$122,907	$248,682	$455,622	$796,101	$1,356,294
$700	$143,388	$290,129	$531,559	$928,781	$1,582,343
$800	$163,876	$331,576	$607,496	$1,061,468	$1,808,392
$900	$187,632	$373,023	$683,433	$1,194,147	$2,034,441
$1,000	$202,840	$414,470	$759,370	$1,326,830	$2,260,490

UNLIMITED WEALTH IS OUT THERE FOR THE TAKING

You may not believe this, but it's true—the amount of opportunity out there for you to make money is positively mind-boggling. We live in a world of literally unlimited wealth. And for those of us lucky enough to live in a free, prosperous country like the United States, there is no ceiling to what we can and should achieve.

THERE IS ALWAYS MONEY AVAILABLE FOR GOOD IDEAS

The secret to America's prosperity is that if you have a good idea, you can almost always find someone to help you fund it and make it happen. It's not easy, but it's doable—and people do it all the time. As I write this in mid-2004, so far this year there have been more than 15 Initial Public Offerings (in which a new company raises money by selling stock to the public) in the field of Private Equity Placements. In essence, these companies have raised money simply to invest in other people's ideas and businesses.

The incredible thing about this is that many of these new IPOs have been in the $200 million to $500 million range. One company that raised $200 million to invest in other businesses currently has a total of two employees and no business to speak of itself. Yet it will earn 2% of the $200 million it raised in annual management fees as well as 20% of any profits that it creates through its investments in other people's ideas.

This sort of thing is going on all around the world. As I write this, a friend of mine is in Asia executing a private version of this concept. He's in the midst of raising $1 billion to fund a clever little idea he got regarding the buying and selling of a group of companies. I'll spare you the intricate details. Suffice it to say that in less than 90 days, he's already gotten commitments for $400 million, and he expects to raise the remaining $600 million over the next 60 days.

Once my friend has the billion dollars he needs, he expects to be able to buy enough companies and assets to make himself another billion dollars in just a few years. To put this in perspective, keep in mind that according to the most recent Census Bureau statistics, the median household income in the United States is around $43,000 a year. From this one deal my friend is putting together, he hopes to make more than *23,000 times* what a typical American family makes in a year.

Now, my friend is a hard worker. But is he working 23,000 times harder on this deal than the average American? I don't think so. The point is that he's not working harder; he's working smarter.

And that's how you make the real money. Not by straining your muscles, but by using your brain. You get rich by exploiting your ideas.

REAL MONEY ISN'T EARNED BY THE HOUR, IT'S MADE WITH IDEAS

Getting rich with other people's money is the name of the game, if you can learn to pull it off. One of the easiest places to do this is in real estate (which we'll cover later). Just two weeks before I started writing this chapter, I spent some time with an old friend who came to New York to visit me. Actually, he didn't come to New York to visit me, although we did get together for dinner. He came to raise $100 million for a major real estate deal he was putting together in Las Vegas.

What he was selling wasn't bricks and mortar but an idea that he dreamed up in his head and then translated onto paper. During two days of "road shows," he presented his vision to the bankers, who were soon falling all over themselves to lend him the money it will take to turn his idea into reality.

By the time you read this, my friend's deal will probably have been funded, and construction will more than likely be under way. As a result, he hopes to see his net worth increase over the next few years by somewhere around $20 million—maybe more.

Not a bad return for nothing more than an idea, a little dog-and-pony show for the bankers, and some flawless execution.

AND THEN THERE'S DONALD TRUMP

If ever there was an example of someone who knows how to make a fortune with ideas, it's Donald Trump. Most people think Trump is rich because of real estate. Not so. He is rich because of the ideas he has. Real estate is simply the vehicle he uses to execute his ideas. It's the tool he uses to make his ideas real—and himself rich.

Take 40 Wall Street, a 72-story building in downtown Manhattan that was built in 1929. When Trump bought it in 1995, the building was empty and in need of renovation. As a result, Trump was able to acquire it for a down payment of only $1 million. What Trump saw that others didn't was that the run-down building could be transformed into a showplace.

Today 40 Wall Street is filled with class-A tenants and, as of this writing, is reportedly worth more than $400 million. Says Trump, who may now sell the building for 400 times what he originally put into it: "It was the best deal I ever made in real estate."

WHY NOT YOU?

I admit it. These examples of people who have made fortunes with their ideas are VERY extreme. But I'm sharing them with you for a reason.

When most people hear stories like these—or when they read about famous people like Donald Trump—they ask themselves, "Why not me?" And then their brain goes to a place that says, "Well, they got lucky" or "I could never do what they do." What's sad is that they don't let their brain go to a place that asks, "I wonder how I could do what they do?"

YOU HAVE TO ASK THE QUESTION
TO GET THE ANSWER

Look, you may never raise $100 million or buy a building with a million-dollar down payment and then watch its value skyrocket to $400 million. But if "they can do that," why can't you get a raise of 5%? Or maybe buy your first home? Or figure out how to retire comfortably with enough income to enjoy your life?

And really—how hard would it be to maybe earn an extra $500 to $1,000 a month with your own business?

If people can create multimillion-dollar fortunes out of thin air, who says you aren't special enough to do at least some of what I just suggested? So let me put the question to you: Why not you? Who says you can't earn more? Who says you can't make a fortune?

I know what you're thinking. You're saying to yourself, "There's no way I can make more money right now." You know what? You're wrong. Later on in Part Four, I'm going to share with you a bunch of ideas that range from how to raise your salary by at least 10% in just four weeks to how to start your own business and earn a few thousand extra dollars a month to how you can buy a few homes over the next five or ten years and multiply your net worth. Now, if you have no experience in achieving success, it is normal to simply shut down mentally when you hear this sort of thing— to say, "Forget it. It can't be done. That just won't work for me."

YOU HAVE NO IDEA—RIGHT NOW— WHAT YOU CAN DO

Well, think again. Allow me to suggest that as long as you base your expectations on your experience, you actually have no idea what will work for you in the future. Your experience has taken you to where you are today. All you know is just enough to be who you are and where you are at this moment.

To get to the next level, you need to acquire new knowledge and to take new action.

Unless you really believe you can get rich scrimping and coupon-clipping and taking advantage of the early-bird special, I seriously suggest you give yourself a break and just try to see what would happen if you really absorbed what's in this chapter and followed through on what it recommends.

READ THIS SECTION EVERY MONTH FOR A YEAR

Here's a challenge. I want you to reread this section on turbocharging your income once a month for a year. As your money coach, I truly believe that if you do this and act on the advice, by the end of the year you'll be earning at least 10% more income. Even better, if you act on the ideas I'm going to give you, your income will grow by as much as 25%. And if you go hard-core—pedal to the metal, as they say—you could double your income.

This may seem far-fetched, but the honest-to-goodness truth is you'll never know unless you try it.

YOU CAN THINK POOR OR THINK RICH— THE CHOICE IS YOURS

For most people, money is very tangible. A job pays a set number of dollars an hour. It's a straightforward amount that people can see and understand. You may be living this kind of life.

According to the federal government's Bureau of Labor Statistics, the average wage earner in America makes around $36,000 a year, or roughly $17.60 an hour. For these people, life is not easy. Perhaps you're one of them, which is why you bought this book. You want a better life. You want to earn more.

LET'S START WITH YOUR CURRENT INCOME— DO YOU WANT MORE?

So let's get started. Let's begin by looking at your current income and see-ing if we can get you a raise. This may not seem very dramatic, but if the only thing you did was to get yourself a 10% raise in the next 30 days—and you saved all that newfound money—your entire financial future would MASSIVELY improve.

You think I'm exaggerating? Let's take the average working person I just mentioned, the one who makes $36,000 a year. That's $3,000 a month, so a 10% raise would amount to $300 more a month. Put the entire amount into a tax-deferred retirement account and what does that get you? Well, according to the table on page 165, if you're 35 and you start banking an extra $300 a month, by the time you're 65, you'll have an extra $678,147 to live on.

Is that massive enough for you?

With that in mind, let's start with what you have. After that, we can look at what to do next.

WOULD YOU HIRE YOU?

Before I get into the specifics of my system for getting a raise, let me ask you something: "If you were running a company, would you hire you? And if you would, would you pay you what you're currently being paid?"

I ask these questions in my seminars, and they almost always get a big laugh. Why? Because people always laugh at truths—particularly uncomfortable ones. And people seem to think the idea of hiring themselves is REALLY FUNNY.

And, in truth, it often is.

HAVE YOU SEEN THE
SMOKING-BREAK CREW?

Traveling around the world as I do to speak and coach, I get to see all kinds of workers. The ones who really amaze me are what I call "the smoking-break crew."

You know whom I'm talking about. Every few hours, they gather at the loading dock or on the sidewalk just next to the building entrance for a cigarette. Now, I know smoking is an addiction. But that's beside the point. I mean, drinking can be an addiction, too, but you don't see people having a cocktail hour at work two or three times a day. So why is it okay to go outside for a smoking break every few hours?

Nonetheless, that's just what millions of people do every day. They stop working every two or three hours, get up from their desks, and go outside to grab a cigarette and enjoy a little wind-down time, chitchatting with their friends at the smokers' pit.

If you are you one of them, be honest and calculate how much of your time—which your employer is paying you for—is wasted smoking. Such calculations are actually done all the time, and I can tell you that not counting the medical and health insurance costs associated with smoking, the working time it wastes is enormous.

Let's say you waste just 30 minutes a day smoking. That's probably a conservative estimate, if you include the time you prepare for your smoking break—finding a friend to go with you—and then actually smoking, then getting back to your desk or workstation. That's ten hours a month wasted. More than 120 hours—or 15 full workdays—a year, all paid for and wasted. And your employer knows that you and your fellow smokers actually waste more than 30 minutes a day.

So if you are that smoker, be honest. Would you really want to have someone like you as an employee?

By the way, I'm not trying to pick on smokers. I just want you to see the math and understand the cost associated with it, so you can ask yourself, "Is this helping me make more money?" The chances are the answer is "no"—not to mention how much the cost of a pack of cigarettes a day can add up to.

DRIVING THE BOSS CRAZY

The first thing you need to consider before you ask for a raise is what your boss thinks of you. Obviously, if he regards you as a mediocre employee, he or she probably won't react well to your request. Unfortunately, many employees are surprisingly in the dark about what their bosses think of them. They don't even know what bothers bosses in general.

Well, as it happens, I have some unique insight here. That's because I run my own company and employ a number of people—all of whom are great (I swear I'm not picking on anyone at my company). It's also because I'm around entrepreneurs every day. Most of my friends own their own businesses, and I get to hear from them just how difficult their employee issues are.

So based on my experience and what I've heard from others, here's a list of the kind of things that people do at work that keep their bosses up at night, worried on the weekends, and generally drive them crazy.

WHY BOSSES OFTEN HATE THEIR EMPLOYEES

- They don't do their job.
- They don't do what they say they will do.
- They come to work late.
- They come to work with personal problems.
- They wait to be told what to do.
- They punch the clock.
- They are content with mediocrity.
- They complain.

- They gossip.
- They never say thank you.
- They have bad attitudes.
- They smoke—and take smoking breaks.
- They surf the Internet, check personal e-mails, and spend time Instant Messaging their friends.
- They lie.
- They steal.
- They do good work, not great work.

WHY GOOD EMPLOYEES DOING GOOD WORK *DOESN'T WORK*

I saved the "good work, not great work" issue for last because it's the single biggest problem that all bosses face. When you talk to truly successful business owners, they will tell you that it's not the bad employees who concern them, because those people ultimately will quit or get fired. No, what really bugs them are the good employees, the ones who do what it takes to be okay, but never enough to be great. Bosses don't hate these good employees, but they don't love them either.

Why should you care? It's simple. I'm sharing these gripes with you not to make you feel sorry for your boss, but because they are so common across all industries that if you were to use them as a checklist of all the things NOT to do at work, you'd become one of those great employees that bosses treasure. And that would put you in the driver's seat when it comes to asking for a raise.

The number-one challenge facing virtually every employer and boss in America is finding great employees. Employers will pay twice as much for a great employee as they pay for a good employee. Why? Because a great employee is worth more than twice as much as a good employee—and maybe four to five times as much as a bad employee. An entire team of great employees can transform a business . . . and possibly change the world.

FROM GOOD TO GREAT

There's a classic book on this subject called *Good to Great* by Jim Collins. It's become a kind of business bible for both smart business owners and smart employees. Collins spent years identifying a set of elite companies that had made the leap from good to great and then continued to perform at the same high level for at least 15 years. What he found was that these great companies produced cumulative stock returns that outperformed the overall market by a factor of seven!

Having studied these companies in detail, Collins was able in his book to explain in layman's terms how to take a company from good to great. Every single business owner I know has a copy of this book, which is probably why it's sold over a million copies.

The interesting thing about Collins's findings is that virtually everyone I know who's read the book says the same thing when I ask them what they think is its most valuable lesson. They all point to what he has to say about the importance of hiring great employees.

TO BE A GREAT COMPANY, YOU NEED GREAT PEOPLE

As Collins sees it, it's not the direction of the company that matters most. Nor is it corporate strategy or the vision thing. What you need to do, he says, is to think of a company as a bus. And before you worry about where the bus is going, you need to focus on who's on the bus. Don't worry about which seats they are sitting in (that is, job titles or job duties). Just get the right people on the bus. Once you have the right people, you can figure out everything else.

Think about it. Millions of business owners are reading this book and focusing on trying to "get the right people on the bus." This should tell you something breathtaking about the way business works in America today. Basically, companies are figuring out that achieving greatness is not so much about visionary, charismatic leaders as it is about assembling a group of GREAT EMPLOYEES.

As an employee—and possibly a future business owner yourself—you should regard this as truly priceless knowledge.

Now, armed with this newfound knowledge, let's look at how you can use it to increase your income.

KEY "START LATE" PRINCIPLES IN CHAPTER THIRTEEN

- Turbocharging your earning power at the same time you're paying yourself first gives you the one-two punch you really need to start late and finish rich.

- It's easier than you think to grow your income—the amount of opportunity out there for you to make money is positively mind-boggling.
- You don't get rich by working hard; you get rich by working smart.
- Nothing will increase your income faster than getting a raise. If this were the only thing you did—and you saved all your additional income—your entire financial future would MASSIVELY improve.
- Because it takes great employees to make great companies, most bosses will pay great employees great wages.

FINISH RICH ACTION STEPS

Reviewing the principles we discussed in Chapter Thirteen, here is what you should be doing right now so you can Start Late and Finish Rich. Check off each step as you accomplish it.

❑ Use the table on page 165 to see how big a difference a small increase in your income can make.

❑ Commit to becoming not just a good employee but a great employee.

❑ Commit to asking for a raise.

CHAPTER FOURTEEN

A FOUR-WEEK ACTION PLAN TO GET A RAISE

Nothing will increase your income faster than getting a raise. Nothing.

You walk into your employer's office and you say, "I want a raise."

Your employer says, "Okay."

You walk out of the office and you are now richer.

If you earn $50,000 a year and you get a 10% raise, you've immediately increased your annual income by $5,000. Now, it's true that getting a raise isn't the only way you could come up with an additional $5,000 a year. You could also try to cut your expenses by that much. But how hard would that be? If you're already on top of your Latte Factor (and I know you are), the answer probably is "pretty darn hard."

Alternatively, you could try to generate an additional $5,000 a year from interest on your savings. Of course, with money market rates running around 1%, you'd need to save roughly half a million dollars to generate $5,000 a year in interest income. That's a little worrisome, right? That could take a while. Then again, in a matter of minutes you could go get a raise and be earning more money on your next paycheck.

WHY GETTING A RAISE
IS NOT IMPOSSIBLE

Does this sound impossible? It shouldn't. People get raises every single day. Right now, as you read this, someone somewhere is asking for and getting a raise. Why isn't this person you?

Are you self-employed? Well, that's fine—but it's not an excuse for not being able to get a raise. If you run your own business, the way you get a raise is by increasing your prices. "No way," you say. "My customers wouldn't stand for it." Really? Why wouldn't they? Right now, someone somewhere is raising the price he charges for some combination of goods and services. Why not you?

Consider, if you will, what I've done with my own business. The fee I charge to give a speech has increased tenfold in less than five years. Why did my fee go up so much? Because I kept stretching my comfort level and raising it.

Now, it's true that I'm better known than I used to be because I've published best-selling books. And I draw bigger crowds now and have become a better speaker than I was five years ago. But the bottom-line real reason I'm able to charge *10 times* more today for virtually the exact same speech I gave five years ago is simply that I decided to charge more.

To be honest, in the beginning I was very uncomfortable raising my fees. Then I realized that no one was going to offer me more money out of the blue. If I wanted to be paid more (and I did), I'd have to ask for it. And, yes, it's true that sometimes when you ask for more, the answer is "No." Not everyone agrees to pay me 10 times my old fee, but enough groups do so that I now earn more speaking only 30 days a year than I used to earn speaking 150 days a year.

I work less and earn more. That's the idea, right? So why not you? As I write this, my agent says (and has proven to me) that I'm not raising my fees fast enough. I recently spoke at an event with Dr. Phil in front of 5,000 people, after which I found out that many of the other speakers were getting two to three times what I was charging! Meanwhile, my reviews at this huge event were off the charts. My agent says it's time to double my fee—again. That would amount to a twentyfold increase in five years.

THE MARKET DOESN'T PAY YOU WHAT YOU'RE WORTH—IT PAYS YOU WHAT IT HAS TO . . . AND WHAT YOU'RE WILLING TO ACCEPT!

The reason I'm sharing my situation with you is not to brag but to coach. Whether you are an employee or an entrepreneur, the bottom line in life is that you only get what you go for.

I've often illustrated this point with the story of my dry cleaner. He increases his prices by 5% every six months. So one day you go into his store, and the shirt that used to cost $1.50 to clean now costs $1.57.

Guess what? Virtually no customers storm out and take their business elsewhere. Why not? Because my dry cleaner does great work, and a seven-cent increase doesn't seem like a big deal.

Then, six months later, the cost of cleaning that same shirt goes up to $1.65. Again, no one leaves his establishment. And every year my dry cleaner's income increases by more than 20% because of compounded growth and new customers. As a result, he's a millionaire many times over.

WHAT KIND OF BRAND ARE YOU?

What you need to understand is that nothing determines your value in the marketplace more than how you position yourself. To get people to think of you in a certain way—say, as a valuable asset who deserves to be compensated handsomely—you've got to present yourself in a certain way. The current buzzword for this is branding. But whatever you call it—whether it's branding or presentation or self-promotion—the fact is that it doesn't just happen. You've got to make it happen.

So what's your brand at work?

What follows is a list of questions that should help you figure out what kind of brand you're projecting to your boss. Keep in mind that there's no point in not answering these questions honestly. If you fudge, you're only fooling yourself. And don't say, "I don't know the answer." Instead, say, "If I did know the answer, what might it be?"

THE PERSONAL BRAND QUESTIONS
YOU NEED TO ASK YOURSELF

- As an employee, do you stand out or blend in?
- If you left your company, would it be hurt or helped?
- Do you come to work on time, early, or late?
- Do you have a written plan for your career that describes how you add value at work, or do you wing it?
- Do you have a relationship with the person who determines whether you should get a raise? Do you know anything about his or her family? Does he or she know anything about yours?
- Do you really care about the company you work for or is it just a job?
- Do you spend any time, money, and/or effort learning new job skills so you can add greater value to your company?
- Do you have a vision of where you want to be with your employer in three to five years?
- Does your employer *know* you have a vision?

HMM . . . SOMETHING TO THINK ABOUT?

These questions are meant to get you thinking. And don't worry if you don't like your answers. The fact is that you can totally turn around your career in 90 days. How do I know this? Because I've seen people do it.

I've seen people go from being on the verge of being fired to doubling their income in six months by getting their act together.

All it takes is turning around the impression people have of you.

Notice that I said "impression." It's not enough just to do great work. Your bosses have to be aware of what you're doing. If no one notices, it's really not going to do you much good, is it?

A FOUR-WEEK ACTION PLAN
TO GET A RAISE

Let's cut to the chase. Decide today you want a raise. Decide today you deserve a raise. Decide today you will go and get a raise.

WEEK ONE
DECIDE WHAT YOU WANT

The reason most people are "stuck" in life is that they don't know what they want. This sounds simple because it *is* simple. You have to decide what you want, put it in writing, and then move forward toward it. Doing this doesn't mean you are guaranteed to achieve your goal, but it will give you direction. And direction is crucial. You will never get anywhere in life without it.

Direction starts with specific action. So now move toward your specific action.

As a first step, write down EXACTLY what you want to achieve, how you're going to do it, and when.

Since you're going for a raise, list the following on a sheet of paper: your name, how much you're currently earning, how much of a raise you're looking for, what percentage it represents, what your new annual salary will total, when you're going to start trying to make it happen, and what your deadline is for making it happen.

In addition, you should include the name of the supervisor you need to ask and when you intend to meet with him or her.

The sheet should look something like this:

SALARY INCREASE ACTION PLAN

My name is _____ .

My current salary is $_____ a year.

I want (and deserve) a $_____ raise, which amounts to an increase of ____%.

I am going to start trying to make it happen no later than _____ [insert date], and I intend to get it by _____ [insert date].

The supervisor whose approval I will need to get is _____, and I will meet with him or her to make my request no later than _____ [insert date].

Signed: _____

Don't worry right now about whether this is doable. Simply write it out and get specific.

WHY THIS IS NECESSARY

Some people are skeptical about the need to write down their intentions. But believe me—it works. Just talking and thinking about your goals isn't enough. If you are serious about wanting to achieve them, you've got to be specific and concrete, complete with details and deadlines. And there is no better way I know of to do that than to write them down.

BUT MY COMPANY DOESN'T GIVE MERIT RAISES

Many people work for employers who award pay increases based solely on length of service. Others are at companies with a strict policy of doing performance reviews only once a year. If this describes your situation, you may be tempted to give up hope.

Don't. Over the years, I've seen government workers, people with tightly regulated union jobs, and employees of huge bureaucratic corporations swear up and down that there's no way they could get a raise on their own schedule—only to try this approach and receive one.

Consider this story.

FROM $15 AN HOUR TO $80,000 A YEAR

After waiting patiently for nearly an hour, a woman came up to me at a book signing I was doing in Ottawa, Canada. Her name was Katrina, and by the time she reached me she was almost in tears.

"David," she said, "I know you hear this every day, but I have to thank you from the bottom of my heart."

"Well, you're welcome," I replied. "But what for?"

"For telling me to go for it. I was earning around $15 an hour at a clothing store when I first read your book *Smart Women Finish Rich*. I hadn't completed my education, and I didn't really believe I had much of a future. Then I decided to try your step-by-step plan to get a raise.

"At first, my boss said no—no one was getting raises that year. But I was relentless. I knew that if I added more value at work, they'd have to give me a raise. So I went out of my way to help the customers. Whatever they needed, I was there with a smile and a helping hand. I came to work early and I always stayed late, looking for ways to improve what we did.

"Then one day a new customer saw me interacting with one of our regulars. She saw that I knew the customer's name and that I had a real rapport with her. When I finished with that customer, she approached me and asked if I was happy at my job. I told her I was, but I added that I was also looking to do and be more—and that I wanted to make more. She told me she owned a clothing store downtown and asked if I'd be interested in visiting her store to discuss a job. I said, 'Sure.'

"I met with her later that day and got a job offer for $20 an hour plus commission! Within 90 days, I was the highest-paid person in the store. By the end of the year, I was the store manager—earning more than $35 an hour. Today I manage three stores, I earn more than $80,000 a year plus bonuses, I've got more than $20,000 in savings, and last year I bought a home!

"And that's not even the best part. Just this week, another woman approached me and asked if I had any interest in owning my own business. I told her I'd always dreamed of having my own store, and she said she was planning to open one and was looking for a partner. All this happened in less than three years—simply because I went for it!"

So just because your employer's rules or policy don't allow for merit raises, don't throw in the towel. Once you start the ball rolling, you never can tell where it—and you—will end up.

THE FIRST PERSON YOU NEED TO QUESTION IS YOURSELF

When I say you need to go for it, I don't mean you should just go charging into your boss's office without first thinking long and hard about how you're going to present your request for a raise. While it's true that you only get what you ask for, just asking doesn't by itself do the job. You've got to give your boss a reason to say yes. So now that you're definitely committed to asking for your raise, let's start the process of figuring out why you deserve it.

The first person you need to question is yourself. If you work for an employer who does give performance-based raises or bonuses, think about the last time you got one (assuming you ever have). Did you proactively do something to get this raise or did you simply wait passively to be rewarded? Did you do or say something to make sure your job performance was noticed by a supervisor or did you simply wait for your regularly scheduled annual review? Did you draft a written explanation of why you deserved a raise or did you simply go through your company's normal performance-review process "reactively"?

Be honest. Your answers to these questions should tell you a lot about why you are earning what you earn right now.

If you are self-employed or run your own business, ask yourself the following: When was the last time you raised your rates? Did you do so because your costs went up or because you felt you were adding more value in the marketplace and knew your customers would be willing to pay for it? Do you have a consistent system for raising your rates or do you do it more or less randomly?

Your answers will tell you a lot about how you are running your business right now.

At this point, whether you work for yourself or for someone else, you should be beginning to have an idea of the strengths and weaknesses of your case for a raise.

WEEK TWO
ASK YOURSELF THE SEVEN MAGIC QUESTIONS

What exactly do you do at work that makes you so valuable that people are actually willing to pay you for your time and effort? I've talked about this for years with my clients. You can go to work and be busy all day long "doing things." But are these "things" really connected to the kind of productive, result-oriented work that makes you money?

Too many people spend their lifetimes essentially pushing paper and forwarding e-mails. Either that or they devote themselves to what I call "rearranging the deck chairs on the *Titanic*." Are you one of these people? Here's what it comes down to: Are you productive or do you spend most of your time doing what basically amounts to busywork?

A good way to find out is to put yourself in your boss's shoes (or, if you're self-employed, one of your customers' shoes) and try to imagine how he or she would answer what I call the Seven Magic Questions.

THE SEVEN MAGIC QUESTIONS

1. What is the most important thing I do for my boss?
2. What does my boss think I'm uniquely talented at?
3. What would my boss be afraid to tell me about my job or how I do it?
4. What would my boss say I could do to add more value to my job?
5. What could I do to be my boss's "dream team" employee?

6. Knowing what he or she has learned about me in all the time I've worked here, would my boss hire me today?
7. What would my boss say it would take for me to get a raise in the next six months?

Why do I think it's a better idea to try to imagine your boss's answers than to ask him the questions directly? Because they are incredibly searching questions that could open a Pandora's box. Look at question No. 6 again: Knowing what you know about me, would you hire me today? This question says it all. And the answer will be immediately obvious in your boss's body language. If he or she squirms, can't look you in the eye, doesn't quickly and strongly answer "Yes"—you've got a problem.

Do you really want to find this out? Actually, you do. The alternative is to wait to be fired—or worse, continue to work at a job, maybe for years, with no real potential for growth. But it's better to acquire this knowledge on your own—so you can do something about it BEFORE you bring it to your boss's (or customer's) attention.

THE BRUTAL TRUTH

If you are not prepared to be completely, painfully honest with yourself, you shouldn't bother going through this exercise. Because chances are that if you did ask your boss these questions, a lot of his or her answers wouldn't be entirely pleasant. In fact, some of them are likely to be downright awful. But don't shy away from recognizing this. The sad, brutal truth is that we are all guilty of wasting valuable time putting energy into relationships and jobs that offer us no real potential for gain. And as unpleasant as it may be to hear the truth, the sooner you face up to it, the better off you will be.

Once you've answered all the questions, start thinking about what changes you'd have to make in your work habits to transform all the negative answers into positive ones. In other words, what specifically would you have to do to become not just a good but a great employee? On this basis, begin working up an action plan designed to maximize your value as an employee.

WEEK THREE
LEARN THE 20/60/20 PRINCIPLE™

If you are an employee, you can come to work and just do your job and get what you get. Alternatively, you can come to work with an action plan and create your future for yourself. It's pretty much one or the other.

Over the years, I've noticed the same thing at just about every workplace I've seen. Employees always seem to break down into three basic groups: about 20% fall into the bottom group, about 60% fall into the middle group, and about 20% are in the top group. I call this my 20/60/20 Rule™.

Here's how I define these groups.

BOTTOM 20%
HAVE NO CLUE

The people in this group barely manage to get to work on time. They are really employed or in business in spite of themselves. You run into these people every day. You work next to them. They are literally everywhere. You see them in restaurants and stores and at the airport. They are teaching your children, working for the phone company, sorting the mail. Office buildings are filled with them.

MIDDLE 60%
WANT A CLUE

Most workers are basically good people. They want to do well. They may be frustrated at times, but for the most part they are honest, hardworking folks doing what they think they are supposed to do. They went to school, got a job—and now they are working. They also work as teachers, letter carriers, waitresses, salesclerks—and in the cubicle next to you or the office down the hall. Although they try hard, for them life never seems easy.

TOP 20%
HAVE A CLUE

The top 20% get it. They know that you get only what you go for. They come to work with specific career and income goals. They manage their direction in life. They know how to make friends and influence people, as the saying goes. They are winners. You can see it in how they dress, talk, act, and live. Their lives have purpose and meaning. They are what are called "specifically intentioned" individuals.

THE CHOSEN FEW: OWN THE CLUE (THE CLUE CREATORS)

Within that top 20% is a very small group of people who go one step further. They go beyond simply having a clue to *owning* the clue. In addition to deciding for themselves how their day is going to go, these people also stay focused on moving forward toward the outcome of their desires. As a result, they tend to run things. They fire the bottom 20%; they manage, hire, and give raises to the middle 60%; and they lead the top 20%. They are what I call "Clue Creators."

YOU KNOW WHERE YOU FIT IN

Now let me suggest something that may get you mad at me. **You already know exactly which of these categories you belong to.** Your friends and family also know. So do your co-workers, as well as your boss or customers. And if this makes you furious, it's probably because you don't like the person you happen to be right now.

Please don't shoot the messenger. If you don't like the image of yourself that you see, then change. In this context, feeling uncomfortable is good. *Your life starts to change the moment you feel uncomfortable.*

I've personally lived in all three categories. I can tell you for a fact that the air is better in the top 20%—and it's MUCH, MUCH better in the "Chosen Few" category, where the "clue is created." The people in this category live more, do more, and are more. It's a fun place to be. It's not always easy, but neither is life in the bottom 20% or the middle 60%.

NOW WRITE YOUR ACTION PLAN

It should be clear by now that you don't move into that top 20%—and certainly not into the "Chosen Few" category—simply by wishing and hoping. You've got to make a plan and then act on it. The same goes for getting a raise.

So where do you start? It's simple, really. Back in Week Two, we raised the question of how much of what you do is productive and how much is busywork. What you need to do now is maximize the productive effort and minimize the rest.

THE PARETO PRINCIPLE

I've written before about something called the *Pareto Principle*. Back in 1906, an Italian economist named Vilfredo Pareto noticed that 20% of the Italian people owned 80% of Italy's total wealth. In the century since then, Pareto's observation has come to be known as the 80-20 Rule, which basically says that a small number of causes is responsible for a large percentage of the effect—or, to put it crudely, 20% of what you do accounts for 80% of your results. In other words, 80% of your effort really doesn't matter all that much.

What does this have to do with asking for a raise? Well, if you're going to make yourself more valuable to your employer, you need to figure out which of your efforts account for most of the value you add on the job. That is, you need to identify the 20% of what you do that produces the 80% of your results. Once you've done that, you can write an action plan designed to maximize your most productive activities—and minimize the useless busywork that takes up the bulk of your time without producing anything worthwhile.

LISTEN AND YOU WILL LEARN

To be perfectly honest, after having thought deeply about what your boss or your customer would likely have to say about where and how you add value (and where and how you don't), it shouldn't be hard to figure out where your effort belongs and where you're wasting your time. The plain truth is that it should already be clear to you. So take note of it. And then take action.

WEEK FOUR
ASK FOR THE RAISE

By now, you should be feeling pretty confident. Why? Because you know exactly why you are entitled to be paid more for your time and effort. And as they say, knowledge is power.

You've already asked yourself the **Seven Magic Questions**—an exercise that showed you where you stand. You've also figured out how to maximize your value to the people who pay you by identifying your most productive activities and focusing on them, and you've written down your conclusions in a succinct action plan.

So now it's time to approach your boss and ask for the raise. Or if you're self-employed, it's time to raise your prices.

People being what they are, some friends or family members may try to dissuade you from taking such a bold step. Ignore them. Believe me, there is no downside to what you are about to do. The worst thing that could happen is that your request is turned down—in which case you've learned something important (namely, that it may be time to start looking for a new job or perhaps a new career, or maybe that you need to focus harder on how to add more value).

If you have a boss, make an appointment with him or her. Know exactly how much you want to ask for, and consider putting it in percentage terms. A humble request for a 5% raise starting in the next 90 days may be easier for your boss to handle than a demand for a $2,500 raise—even if both amount to the same thing.

Similarly, ask for a raise in monthly or biweekly amounts. For instance, instead of saying, "I want an increase of $2,500 a year," you might say, "I'm looking for you to increase my compensation by $50 a week" [or "$10 a day"].

WHAT WOULD IT TAKE FOR ME TO GET A RAISE IN THE NEXT SIX MONTHS?

Another approach is simply to ask, "What would it take for me to get a raise in the next six months?" Pose the question and then be quiet—let your boss lay out what you'll need to do to get that raise. Write down what he says, do it, and then follow up with your boss once you've done what he asked of you. You may even want to ask for a 90-day review meeting to see if you are progressing toward your six-month goal of getting a raise.

What if you're self-employed? Again, if you are self-employed, you simply need to raise your rates. Though some businesses send out an explanatory letter or announcement when they raise prices, there is no law that says you have to say anything to anyone.

Not saying anything is exactly what the new owners did at my favorite neighborhood burrito place, which was recently bought out by a major company that plans to expand it. One day my "Border Burrito" (with jalapeños and sour cream) was $5.95—and a day later it was $6.95. No sign, no explanation—and they raised the price a buck! Guess what? I flinched . . . and paid the new price. What I am going to do? Find a new favorite burrito place? I'm telling you—this is "real-world advice" that people are using around you and on you all the time!

BECOME A CLUE CREATOR!
WIN A FREE FINISHRICH EDUCATIONAL PROGRAM

When you take charge of your career, I want to hear about it. Visit my web site at **www.finishrich.com** and click on Start Late, Finish Rich. There you'll find our online form to share your success story. Each month I'll hold a competition for the best story—and the winner will receive our updated complete FinishRich Educational Package (worth $399) as our gift to you! So get going and let us know how you do—your success may inspire someone else to take action.

KEY "START LATE" PRINCIPLES IN CHAPTER FOURTEEN

- You only get what you go for; to get a raise, you have to ask for it.
- By changing the impression people have of you, you can totally turn around your career.
- According to the 80-20 Rule, 20% of what you do accounts for 80% of your results. In order to transform yourself into a great worker who adds so much value that your bosses or customers will be happy to pay you more, you need to figure out which of your efforts account for most of the value you add.

Congratulations! You're ready to shift your earning power into high gear by maximizing your value to your current employer (or customers). But this is only the first part of turbocharging your income. Now it's time to really put the pedal to the metal—and learn how to develop an entirely new income stream . . . without having to leave your current job.

FINISH RICH ACTION STEPS

Reviewing the principles we discussed in Chapter Fourteen, here is what you should be doing right now so you can Start Late and Finish Rich. Check off each step as you accomplish it.

❑ Identify your personal brand by asking yourself the questions on page 178.

❑ Write down exactly how much of a raise you will ask for, whom you will need to ask, and when you will ask them.

❑ Figure out what your boss thinks of you by asking yourself the Seven Magic Questions on pages 182–83.

❑ Based on your answers, draw up an action plan designed to maximize your most productive activities while minimizing the useless busywork.

❑ Bring your action plan to your boss and ask for the raise.

BECOMING YOUR OWN BOSS— WITHOUT QUITTING YOUR DAY JOB

If I'm going to bet on a business—let me be the one who owns it.

—David Bach

Let's get straight to the point—creating a second stream of income can change your life. As I said before, if all you did was spend less and save more, you could probably start late and finish rich. But if you spend less, save more, and MAKE more, nothing will stop you from achieving your goal of financial freedom. And if you ALSO develop a second income stream, you can finish even richer than you might have if you'd started early.

WEALTH IS ALL AROUND YOU

Part of finishing rich is understanding that wealth is all around us. Everywhere! Every day, people who are not as smart as you are making money in every kind of business you can think of. Look around. Just about everything you can see right now is the result of a business that someone owns.

Just about everything you use, consume, or enjoy—someone's business created it, manufactured it, sold it, shipped it, or serviced it. And these days, what with the Internet and corporate downsizing and jobs being shipped overseas, it is both crucial and smart to consider starting your own business . . . while you still have a job that provides you with a paycheck.

THE NEXT WAVE OF MILLIONAIRES IS BEING CREATED AT HOME

The American Dream of owning your own business is coming true. According to the Bureau of Labor Statistics, there are currently more than 18 million home-based businesses in the United States, generating an estimated $427 billion a year in revenues. One out of every six working adults in the United States is connected with one, more than half of them on a part-time basis. By 2005, says *Newsweek* magazine, fully half of all households will be involved in some sort of home-based business.

As a result, most experts expect the next wave of millionaires to be dominated by small-business entrepreneurs, especially those with home-based businesses. Indeed, a survey by *Money* magazine found that one out of every five home-based businesses produces an annual gross income of $100,000 to $500,000. And the Small Business Administration reports that nearly 20,000 entrepreneurs have already grossed more than $1 million a year operating from home.

NOW IT'S YOUR TURN TO JOIN THEM

I'm not suggesting here that you quit your day job (not yet, anyway). After all, while it might not make you rich in the long run, your day job BRINGS YOU INCOME. What I want to do in this chapter is introduce you to a number of different approaches to creating a business you can run on the side while you keep your day job. As you will see, becoming your own boss is not easy. But it's not impossible.

Depending on your interests and abilities, there are all sorts of things you can do to develop an additional source of income. You can perform a service (like painting houses or editing résumés) or you can make something and market it (like cookies or jewelry) or you can buy something and re-sell it. You can take a skill you use at your regular job (like word processing or graphic design) and offer it on a freelance basis—on your own time, of course! Or you can turn a hobby into a side business (like cooking into catering or sewing into tailoring). Finally, instead of you working for extra money, you can put your money to work for you by investing in real estate.

In this chapter, and the five that follow, we will look at:
- The six myths about starting your own business
- Why the government wants you to start a business
- Free resources that can help you, from SBA to SCORE and more
- How to start a home-based business
- How to make money in real estate
- How to start a business on eBay
- How to make money in direct selling
- How to make money in franchising

In this section of the book, I'm not just going to be your coach. I'm also going to be a tour guide, exposing you to a variety of different ways to build a second stream of income. You may decide to do more than one, only one—or none. But whatever the outcome, it's worth at least taking a look at what some of the possibilities are.

Ready?

THE MYTH ABOUT BEING IN BUSINESS FOR YOURSELF

To begin with, let's consider some of the many myths that discourage people from even considering going into business for themselves. Separating the facts from the fictions can totally transform your attitude—and make the difference between never getting started and finishing rich.

MYTH NO. I
YOU NEED A LOT OF MONEY TO START

The reality of most small businesses is that starting them takes less money than you think. The average start-up cost of the companies on *Inc.* magazine's 2004 list of America's 500 fastest-growing small businesses was $25,000—and many of them were started with $5,000 or less. In fact, many businesses today are started with less than $1,000. (Later, I'll share a great example of this: **A business started by a woman with an initial investment of $3,000 that she eventually sold for nearly $1 billion!**)

MYTH NO. 2
YOU NEED TO HAVE EXPERIENCE

Friends and relatives may warn that you need to have experience in business in order to be able to start one. Don't let these people steal your dreams. While experience certainly helps, action beats inaction any day of the week. Besides, you don't have to go for it alone. These days, it's easy to be in business for yourself but not by yourself. As you'll discover in this chapter, there are so many resources out there to help you build a home-based business and second stream of income that you may wonder why you waited so long to do this. There are countless companies in the business of helping you get your business off the ground with training and mentoring systems designed to help you succeed. In addition, the government now offers training, and there are many volunteer organizations staffed by veteran entrepreneurs whose experience you can tap.

MYTH NO. 3
YOU NEED A LOT OF TIME

The naysayers—who, I promise you, will come out of the woodwork the minute they find out you're planning to start a business on the side—will insist you don't have the time to start a business. "You're too busy!" they'll argue. You have a job, kids, household chores—whatever. The bottom line is this: In most cases, you need no more than one to two hours a day to get a business going on the side—which is why I say you not only should but also *can* do it without quitting your day job. If you commit two hours a day to a new venture, that's 60 hours a month, or roughly 720 hours a year. If you put that kind of effort into starting a business on the side over the next five years, I promise you—you'll succeed. What would you have to give up? Television and maybe a little sleep. Wake up an hour a day early and skip the TV at night, and you'll have the time. If you can't commit to an hour or two a day to start a business, you're not ready to do this.

MYTH NO. 4
NINE OUT OF TEN NEW BUSINESSES FAIL

The biggest myth about starting your own business is that you have a 90% chance of failing within one year. This much-heralded statistic doesn't match up with what we see in the real world. According to the Small Business Administration, two-thirds of all new businesses survive at least two years, and about half survive at least four.

MYTH NO. 5
YOU NEED A LOT OF STUFF TO GET STARTED

The idea that you need a business plan and business cards and stationery and a phone line and an office and so on and so forth to start your business simply is not true. The only things you absolutely need to start a business are passion, commitment, desire, and a willingness to take action. I know this from experience. I started and ran FinishRich, Inc., to the point where it was bringing in $1 million in annual revenue, *without* having an office, a business plan, business cards, or stationery. What I did have was passion and commitment.

MYTH NO. 6
YOU HAVE TO BE PASSIONATE ABOUT THE PARTICULAR BUSINESS YOU CHOOSE

I'm a big believer in the idea that if you do what you love, the money will follow. But I also recognize that this cliché has held many people back from starting their own businesses. Why? Because they don't know "what they love"—or because they believe that "what they love" can't make money. If your goal is to earn an extra $500 a month, that in and of itself can be enough of a reason to start your own business! People become successful in business all the time even though they aren't really turned on by the actual product or service they happen to produce or sell. What they're passionate about is being an entrepreneur and being their own boss. If you really want to be your own boss and are dedicated and willing to work hard, then you have what it takes to start your own business.

WHY THE GOVERNMENT WANTS YOU TO START YOUR OWN BUSINESS

The government wants you to start your own business because small businesses are the fuel that drives our economy. According to the Small Business Administration, there were 23.7 million small businesses in the United

States in 2003, providing employment for more than 57 million workers—which is to say roughly half the jobs in the country.

Even more important, small businesses are responsible for creating the lion's share of new jobs in the United States. Throughout the 1990s, they generated between 60% and 80% of new jobs, and in 2000 and 2001 (the most recent years for which data is available) they accounted for *all* of the net new jobs in the United States. The government knows that a business being started today in your garage, kitchen, or even dorm room could be a future Fortune 500 company that someday will employ thousands of people.

HOW THE GOVERNMENT HELPS YOU BECOME RICH

In order to encourage people to start their own business, the government has created a wide variety of tax breaks for business owners.

The most obvious and immediately useful of these are the benefits you get from a self-employed retirement account. When you own your own business, you are allowed to put more money in a pretax retirement account than an employee. As we discussed in Chapter Nine, a self-employed person can save up to $41,000 pretax in a SEP IRA or a One-Person 401(k)/Profit-Sharing plan. By contrast, as of this writing (in 2004), the most an employee under 50 could contribute to a 401(k) plan is just $14,000. In other words, if you're self-employed, you can save at least $27,000 more a year tax-free than an employee can. This is a huge difference. (If you're already contributing to a 401(k) or other qualified retirement plan at work, your ability to contribute to a SEP IRA or a One-Person 401(k)/Profit-Sharing plan may be limited. Check with your accountant.)

THANKS TO THE GOVERNMENT, WE GET $54,000 A YEAR MORE FOR OUR FUTURE!

In 2003, my wife and I both maxed out our retirement accounts as self-employed business owners (we used One-Person 401(k)/Profit-Sharing Plans, which I discussed on page 112). Using this new type of retirement account, we were able to save a total of $80,000 ($40,000 each) in completely tax-deductible contributions to pretax retirement accounts. Had we been employees, we would have been able to put away a total of only $26,000 tax-free ($13,000 each). So because we had our own business, we were able to save an *extra* $54,000 pretax!

In all, we've been able to save nearly $200,000 in our retirement accounts in less than three years by fully funding them. As employees, it would have taken us nearly 15 years to do the same thing!

Consider this. Michelle and I are in our late thirties. If we continue to fund our retirement accounts at the rate of $80,000 a year for ten years and we earn a 10% return on that money, by the time we're in our late fifties, we will have more than $5 million in retirement funds. By the time we're in our late sixties, we'll have more than $15 million!

HITTING THE TAX-FREE JACKPOT AS A BUSINESS-OWNING COUPLE				
(Assumes 10% Annual Rate of Return)				
Tax-Free Maximum Investment (Monthly)	10 Years	20 Years	30 Years	40 Years
$6,667	$1,365,701	$5,062,712	$15,070,672	$42,162,638

Now, what about you?

You don't think you could afford to save nearly that much? OK, let's be negative and say you won't really go for it big-time. What would happen if you went for it just small-time?

Let's say you start a home-based business that earns you only $1,000 a month (or $12,000 a year). And let's say you set up a One-Person 401(k)/Profit-Sharing plan and decided to fund it with only $4,000 a year (or $333 a month). Here's what would happen to you: In 20 years, you'd have an extra $252,010. In 30 years, you'd have more than $750,000!

EVEN GOING FOR IT SMALL-TIME PAYS OFF				
(Assumes 10% Annual Rate of Return)				
Monthly Investment	10 Years	20 Years	30 Years	40 Years
$333	$68,281	$253,120	$753,488	$2,108,005

The point is that on the basis of retirement benefits alone, the case for starting your own business is overwhelming.

FREE RESOURCES THAT CAN
HELP YOU GET STARTED

Whatever kind of home-based business you're interested in, the Small Business Administration is a great place to get started. Over its 50-year history, the SBA has backed nearly $200 billion in loans to small businesses—more than half that amount in the last decade. In 2003 alone, the agency helped nearly 75,000 small businesses get financing, whether in the form of loans or venture capital.

The SBA is an agency of the federal government—which is to say it's funded with your tax dollars. Since you're paying for it, you might as well check it out—especially since it doesn't charge anything for its many services.

To begin with, I recommend you spend a few hours browsing through the SBA's web site at **www.sba.gov**. The site is packed with an unbelievable amount of free advice and information for anyone considering starting his or her own business, including:

- **Start-up Basics.** A very solid tutorial covering just about everything you need to know about starting a business. (Look under the SBA Development Program.)
- **Planning.** An entire section filled with valuable tips on every aspect of business planning.
- **Marketing.** Individualized prep programs that show how to develop effective low-cost or no-cost marketing plans for a new small business.
- **Financing.** Nearly everything you need to know about financing your business, including what it will take, how much you might need, and how to get a small-business loan.
- **Workshops.** A complete list of the many workshops and expos the SBA holds around the country throughout the year.

The SBA site also includes a section designed for women (the agency has an Office of Women Business Ownership, the goal of which is to promote the growth of women-owned businesses) as well as a section for business-oriented teenagers interested in becoming the next Bill Gates.

SBA LOANS—WHAT YOU NEED TO KNOW

While the SBA offers numerous loan programs designed to help small businesses, the agency itself does no lending. Rather, like the FHA, it guarantees loans made by approved banks and other lenders. SBA-guaranteed loans range from a few thousand dollars to an upper limit of around $1.5 million.

SBA's business loan program exists to help ensure financing for small businesses that need money to buy inventory or equipment, acquire property, or pay for essential services but might normally have a difficult time with traditional lenders. By guaranteeing loans, the SBA shifts the risk from the lender to the government—making lenders much more willing to back new small businesses.

The agency has essentially three basic loan programs. (Since they are constantly changing, you should visit the SBA web site for details.)

BASIC 7(A) LOAN GUARANTY

This is the SBA's primary loan program (as well as its most flexible), designed to help qualified small businesses get loans of up to $1.5 million that might not otherwise be funded. The financing comes from commercial lending institutions (like banks), and terms range up to 10 years for working capital to 25 years for fixed assets.

CERTIFIED DEVELOPMENT COMPANY (CDC) 504 LOAN PROGRAM

This program guarantees long-term, fixed-rate financing of up to $1.3 million for businesses looking to acquire real estate or machinery and equipment for expansion or modernization. The loans themselves are actually made by certified development companies, which are private nonprofit corporations established to promote regional or community economic development. As of this writing, there are 270 of them nationwide.

MICROLOAN 7(M) LOAN PROGRAM

This program provides short-term loans (maximum: six years) of up to $35,000 for small business start-ups. The money must be used to purchase inventory, supplies, or fixtures; it cannot be used to buy real estate. The average loan amount is just over $11,000, and in 2003 the agency helped nearly 2,300 entrepreneurs in this way.

In addition to guaranteeing loans, the SBA offers a Surety Bonding Program that helps small and minority companies win government contracts by providing guarantee bonds for jobs worth up to $2 million. The SBA also oversees an extensive investment program, licensing what are called

Small Business Investment Companies (SBICs), which are privately run firms that specialize in providing venture capital to small business start-ups. In 2003, some 448 SBICs invested nearly $2.5 billion in more than 2,600 small businesses.

SOUNDS LIKE A LOT OF LOANS—
HOW DO I GET ONE?

SBA loans are not easy to get. The agency expects you to have a well-defined business—and a written plan explaining how you intend to pay back the loan. In short, you must have your act together.

For details, go to the SBA web site, click on "Starting Your Business," then, under Financing, click on "Applying for a Loan." It will tell you exactly what you need to do.

KNOWING THE SCORE—
ANOTHER GREAT RESOURCE

As good as it is, the SBA is hardly the only great resource for people who want to start their own business. Since 1964, the Special Corps of Retired Executives, or SCORE, has helped more than 6.5 million aspiring entrepreneurs get started—most of them with home-based businesses.

SCORE has a nucleus of 10,500 volunteer business counselors who make themselves available 24/7 to help you get your small business up and running—from concept to start-up to fully financed entity. You can get advice and information by visiting SCORE's web site at **www.score.org** or by stopping in at one of the organization's 389 chapter offices throughout the country. Either way, SCORE provides hands-on counseling from experienced businesspeople—everything from how to write a business plan to how to get financing to how to figure out how much to charge your customers. And it's all free!

Among other things, SCORE will help you formulate your business concept, outline your plan of action, and either teach you how to write a business plan or get you in touch with somebody who can do it for you. SCORE also has dozens of business alliances with institutional partners who can help you get everything else you need to make your business dream real—from setting up your corporation to actually funding it. These include:

- **Circle Lending.** A lending institution and money source that has developed a free how-to workbook (that you can download) to help small-business owners understand finance and loan issues.
- **The Companies Corporation.** A Delaware incorporation specialist that provides free informational workbooks, including *How to Incorporate Your Business* and *How to Really Start Your Business.*
- **Creativeworks.** A marketing and advertising agency based in St. Louis that donates tools to help new businesses learn how to create marketing programs.
- **Easi Media.** A developer of software that helps small businesses learn how to use media to build their businesses.
- **Ford Motor Company.** The giant automaker sponsors a national business-plan writing contest, judged by SCORE counselors. The grand prize is $50,000, and two runners-up get $25,000 each.
- **National Business Association.** A 40,000-member advocacy organization that helps members of the small-business community achieve both personal and professional goals.

RESOURCES FOR WOMEN ENTREPRENEURS

Anybody who thinks of business as a man's world is living in the wrong century. The fact is, by a wide margin, most entrepreneurs these days are women. Indeed, when it comes to starting new businesses in the United States, women currently outnumber men by 2 to 1.

Reflecting this, there is no end of resources aimed at smoothing the path for women entrepreneurs. One of the best is a government outfit called Women Entrepreneurship in the 21st Century, or Women-21 for short. A partnership of the SBA and the U.S. Department of Labor, Women-21 has an excellent web site, **www.women-21.gov,** that accurately describes itself as "a premier one-stop federal resource for targeted information, registration for online programs, and networking opportunities to help women entrepreneurs navigate the ever-changing business world."

Women-21 boasts a long list of partners, many of them nonprofit, offering help for women interested in starting new businesses. I've listed a few of them below. But if you want to get a real sense of the array of resources available to women entrepreneurs, visit the Women-21 web site.

- **The Association of Women's Business Centers** (www.womensbusinesscenters.org). A national nonprofit organization representing women business owners, the AWBC provides educational, training, technical assistance, mentoring, development, and financing opportunities.

- **Black Women Enterprises.** Dedicated to advancing the interests of Black women business owners (though everyone is welcome to join), BWE provides educational, networking, and technical resources for its members.

- **eWomenNetwork.com**. An invaluable networking resource, eWomenNetwork has a searchable online directory that boasts the world's largest photographic profile database of female business own- ers and corporate professionals. With more than 10,000 members and 80 U.S. and Canadian chapters, eWomenNetwork provides women entrepreneurs with a steady stream of new contacts and business- development opportunities as well as a cost-effective way to promote themselves and their businesses.

- **MANA, A National Latina Organization** (www.hermana.org). MANA is a nonprofit advocacy organization that promotes Latin women in business and community service.

- **National Association of Women Business Owners** (www.nawbo.org). With more than 8,000 members in more than 80 chapters around the country, NAWBO calls itself "the voice of America's women-owned businesses." In addition to providing unparalleled networking possibilities, NAWBO lobbies vigorously on economic and public policy issues affecting women business owners.

- **National Women Business Owners Corporation** (www.nwboc.org). The NWBOC, a sister organization of the National Association of Women Business Owners and the Center for Women's Business Research, runs a national certification program for women-owned and -controlled businesses that can help them compete for corporate and government contracts. More than 100 private and public agen- cies now accept NWBOC certification.

SO LET'S GET STARTED

Most home-based businesses never get off the ground because most peo- ple get mired in minutiae. They don't realize there are really only three rules to follow to start a home-based business:

1. Ready
2. Aim
3. Fire

Okay, I'm kidding. There are actually four rules you need to follow.

RULE NO. 1
MAKE A DECISION

Nothing happens in your life until you make a decision.

So make one. Decide you are ready to start a business at home. Find a spot in your house. Pick a day on your calendar and get started.

Your first day in business can be spent reading books on how to start a business. In fact, you probably should spend a lot more than just your first day doing research. At the very least, you should check out all the web sites listed in this chapter. Since you are not going to quit your day job to do this, we're realistically talking about a few weeks of Internet browsing at night or in the morning before you leave for work.

But get started. A cause set in motion creates action that begets results.

RULE NO. 2
PICK A FIELD

I have no idea what kind of business you should start—and maybe right now neither do you. That's okay. Just don't spend a decade deciding.

One of my best friends has spent 15 years trying to find the "right business" for himself. That's 15 years of waiting. Meanwhile, he hasn't started a single business. Don't worry if you don't get it right the first go-around. You're not signing up for life. Just pick something that gets you excited and get going.

It's all about making a decision. I had one friend, Gary, who paid his way through college painting dorm rooms. When he lost his corporate job, I suggested that he start a painting business. He reacted as if I'd insulted him. "I didn't go to college to start a painting business!" he huffed.

"So what did you go to college for?" I asked him.

He said to make money, to which I replied, "Well, how much are you making right now?"

Two weeks later, he had posted flyers all over town announcing, "I paint houses cheap!" He's been working steadily ever since, and within 12 months was earning four times what he made in his corporate cubicle job. Today, he employs a crew of ten—and more important, he's happy!

RULE NO. 3
GET HELP

Considering how many resources there are out there to help you, it's silly to try to go it alone. So make a point of exploring all the web sites and resources I list in this chapter. You're not even close to being the first person to start a new business at home in your spare time. More than 20 million other Americans have gone before you—so take advantage of their experience.

RULE NO. 4
MAKE IT LEGAL

Even though I said earlier that you don't need a lot of "stuff" to start a business, you do need to be legal. After all, you don't want the IRS showing up at your doorstep. To keep them off your back—and your enterprise on the right side of the law—you will need to set up a legal structure for your business. For the kind of thing we're talking about, there are basically three structures to choose from: sole proprietorship, partnership, and corporation. For more information on this subject, go to the IRS web site at **www.irs.gov** and request Publication #334, "Tax Guide for Small Business." Also, if you are selling retail products, you will more than likely need a State Tax Resale Number. (To find out how and where to get one, go to a good search engine like www.google.com and insert your state name and the phrase "sales tax department" in the search line, or call your local Chamber of Commerce.) In its "Starting Your Business" section, the SBA web site has a terrific primer on everything you need to know about the legal aspects of starting a business.

Now that we've got the general principles behind us, let's look at some specific businesses tailor-made for people looking to create a second, potentially life-changing stream of income for themselves: buying and selling on eBay, direct selling, and investing in real estate on the weekends. In addition, we'll look at a new full-time line of work you might want to consider if you're currently unemployed, retired, or ready to leave your current job: franchising.

KEY "START LATE" PRINCIPLES IN
CHAPTER FIFTEEN

- If—in addition to spending less, saving more, and increasing your current salary—you ALSO develop a second income stream, nothing will stop you from starting late and finishing rich.
- The next wave of millionaires is likely to be dominated by small-business entrepreneurs, especially those with home-based businesses.
- You don't need a lot of money, time, experience, or "stuff" to start your own business.
- The government wants you to start your own business—and it offers numerous programs and tax breaks to make doing so easier and more attractive.
- All you really need to do to get started is to make up your mind and pick a field. Then take advantage of all the free resources available to you, and create a legal structure.

FINISH RICH ACTION STEPS

Reviewing the principles we discussed in Chapter Fifteen, here is what you should be doing right now so you can Start Late and Finish Rich. Check off each step as you accomplish it.

❑ Visit the Small Business Administration web site (at **www.sba.gov**) to sample the huge amount of free services, information, and advice available to people who are thinking of starting their own businesses.

❑ Visit the SCORE web site (at **www.score.org**) to see the kind of help you can get from retired executives.

❑ Commit to starting your own business.

❑ Follow the four rules on pages 202–203.

CHAPTER SIXTEEN

MAKE MORE ...
ON EBAY

The hugely popular online auction site eBay may well provide the simplest way there is to start a business at home without quitting your day job. That's because it's become not just a place where millions of people buy stuff, but also a serious place to sell stuff—which means you can use it to create a home-based business (and a second income source) on the side.

Three things made me decide I had to include eBay in this section on starting a business.

The first involved my father. Just a few years ago, he didn't know how to click a mouse. So you can imagine how shocked I was when I went over to his house one day not too long ago and discovered him bidding on cars on eBay. Little did I know that my conservative dad had a longing to own a red Cadillac convertible! Since then, he has bought two Cadillacs on eBay— one of which he turned around and sold (again, using eBay) for a nice little profit. If my dad can make money on eBay, anyone can.

Then I found out that one of my friends, Mary, had made $2,500 in less than a month selling clothes on eBay. "I can't believe how easy it is," she told me. "The truth is, I could make a business out of this if I wanted to." With her second child on the way, and a desire to work from home, who knows—maybe she will.

Finally, I read about Kim from Kansas in *BusinessWeek*. Kim started selling antiques for fun on eBay in 1998. Today, her eBay-based antiques business grosses more than $100,000 a month (that's a million dollars–plus a year)—and she still runs it from her home, where she's taking care of her two kids, ages four and ten.

Kim's story pushed me over the edge. It was time for me to check out eBay for myself and find out what the fuss was all about. Could eBay really be as great as everyone says it is? And, more important, could it be a reliable and effective tool that you can use to make more money?

Having done the research, I've come to the conclusion that the answers are "Yes!" and "Yes!"

THE AMERICAN DREAM FINDS A HOME ON THE INTERNET

eBay pretty much epitomizes today's home-based businesses. Certainly, it's the ultimate example of what can happen when you combine the old-fashioned desire to run a business at home with twenty-first-century Internet technology.

Started as an online auction site in 1995 by Pierre M. Omidyar, eBay has truly become "the World's Online Marketplace" (which is how it describes itself) for all sorts of goods and services. eBay claims that people spend more time on eBay than on any other web site, and I can believe it. As of April 2004, eBay boasted more than 100 million registered users—nearly half of whom had bid for, bought, or listed something in the previous 12 months.

This vast crowd of buyers and sellers comprises an unbelievable marketplace for anyone who dreams of starting their own business. In fact, like Kim from Kansas, many eBay users have taken advantage of eBay's amazing breadth and scope to do just that. Some started out with no other goal than simply to see if they could get some money for all that junk cluttering up their garage. Others were more strategic, recognizing eBay as perhaps the most potent sales tool the world has ever seen, and deciding to use it to grow their own empires.

THE GOLD MINE AT EBAY

In 2003, nearly $24 billion worth of merchandise changed hands on eBay. That amounts to more than $65 million in sales every day. With the business growing at a phenomenal rate (between 2001 and 2003, gross revenues nearly tripled), eBay's sales volume these days is probably somewhere around $100 million a day—and, believe me, not all of it is generated by people who are simply cleaning out their garages or attics. In fact, according to published reports, eBay provides a marketing platform for an estimated 430,000 Internet entrepreneurs who individually gross anywhere from $100 to $1 million a month.

How do they do it? It's simple, really. Although there are thousands of variations, you can make money on eBay in basically two ways.

You can use eBay as a low-cost (i.e., virtually free) way to offer some product or service you already have to millions of potential buyers.

Or you can use it to find some undervalued commodity that you can resell for a higher price—either because you know how to add value (say, by refurbishing it) or because you have some sort of special expertise (like a knowledge of antiques or cars or rare coins) that enables you to spot a bargain where others might not see it.

CHECK OUT THESE EBAY
SUCCESS STORIES

LAURIE THE BOX LADY

Laurie is a stylish, semiretired real estate agent who uses eBay to sell boxes from Tiffany & Co., Neiman Marcus, and other fancy retailers to status-conscious gift-givers who like the idea of wrapping their presents in upscale packaging. Like most eBay entrepreneurs, she developed her business by accident. In an effort to get rid of a bunch of boxes she'd accumulated as a result of her own purchases at posh stores, she posted a listing on eBay and was stunned by the response. Now something of a "box wrangler," Laurie sells around 60 image-boosting boxes a month on eBay at an average price of $5 each. Her out-of-pocket? A little sweat equity and a few dollars' worth of gas. Her profit? Virtually 100%.

GETTING OFF THE ROAD—
AND ON THE INTERNET

Michael is a southern California entrepreneur who has made a fortune trolling on eBay for battered, often virtually unrecognizable antiques—everything from rusty old butchers' scales to semidestroyed chaise longues—which he then restores and resells for very hefty profits. Before eBay, Michael used to have to travel around the country constantly, both to find disintegrated treasures and to attend collectors' fairs where he could sell his restored masterpieces. Now he is able find all the "junk" he can use without ever leaving home, courtesy of eBay, which he also uses as a no-cost sales force. "Now, if I miss one of these collectors' conventions, it's not the end of the world," he says happily. In effect, he's transformed what had been a very time-intensive road show into a low-overhead, home-based operation—in the process, doubling his profit margin.

A HOBBY BECOMES A THRIVING BUSINESS

When Jenny lost her job as an assistant at an insurance company, it occurred to her that she might be able to make a little money selling some of the fanciful "junk jewelry" she made as a hobby. She didn't know much about the Internet, but when a friend suggested she try eBay, she decided to give it a try. The decision changed her life. A few quick sales followed by even more requests for her low-cost designer jewelry turned Jenny into an overnight entrepreneur. Suddenly, she was making, marketing, and selling far greater quantities of her pieces than she had ever imagined possible. Before long, she was earning more than $6,000 a month and literally couldn't produce enough jewelry to keep up with demand. Now, two years later, she has a thriving business with a staff of four who do nothing but put together jewelry pieces based on her designs. Her monthly net has nearly tripled, and now she's discussing an exclusive contract with a major retail chain.

HOW EBAY HELPS YOU
GROW YOUR BUSINESS

One of the things that makes the world of online auctions such a sensible alternative for people who are looking to develop a new income stream is that eBay makes it easy for newbies to get started. The eBay web site (at **www.ebay.com**) is chock-full of chat rooms, services, tutorials, and tools—many of them free—designed to get you up and running as quickly as possible.

Probably the best route for beginners is to click on the "Services" link on the eBay home page, then click on the button at the top of the Services page that says, "New to eBay? Start here." This takes you to the eBay Learning Center, where you will find free tutorials that cover the basics of buying and selling on eBay. **The Learning Center** also contains links to an impressive array of tools and services, including eBay University, where for $20 you can take an excellent online course that covers all the basics of setting up an eBay-related business. The "university" also offers more advanced one-day classroom seminars in various locations around the country for $39 each.

One of the greatest resources eBay has to offer is the **eBay Community,** a vast collection of message boards, chat rooms, answer centers, and community groups that attract everyone from first-time fun shoppers to senior managers of Fortune 500 companies. What all these people have in common is a desire to learn more about how to do business on eBay. As a result, the Community sponsors countless workshops and events on a variety of practical topics (ranging from "How to Buy a Vehicle on eBay" to "Selling to Canadians"). A complete schedule can be accessed on the eBay web site's "Community" page.

For many people, the best thing about eBay is that it enables you to do business all over the world and interact with countless other people without ever leaving home. Such is the magic of the Internet.

Then again, there are many people who like to leave home and who like to interact with others face-to-face. If you're one of these, eBay may not be for you. Instead, you might want to consider the subject of the next chapter—direct selling.

KEY "START LATE" PRINCIPLES IN CHAPTER SIXTEEN

- eBay may be the ultimate example of what happens when you combine the old-fashioned desire to start a home-based business with twenty-first-century Internet technology.

- You can use eBay to offer some product or service you already have to millions of potential customers.
- Or you can use it to find some undervalued commodity that you can resell for a higher price.
- One of eBay's great advantages is that it offers countless services, tutorials, and tools designed to make it easy for novices to get started.

FINISH RICH ACTION STEP

Reviewing the principles we discussed in Chapter Sixteen, here is what you should be doing right now so you can Start Late and Finish Rich. Check off this step when you've accomplished it.

❑ Visit the eBay web site (at **www.ebay.com**) to see what it's like— and whether or not it's for you.

CHAPTER SEVENTEEN

MAKE MORE ...
IN DIRECT SELLING

Chances are, the concept of direct selling (or, as it's also called, network marketing, multilevel marketing, party plan marketing, and one-to-one marketing) rings a bell. You may be familiar with it from the likes of a local Avon lady or Mary Kay specialist who may have once rung your doorbell, or from a neighborhood Tupperware party you attended a few years ago. Perhaps you've purchased something from a friend who at some point went into direct selling as a side career.

It's also possible that at some point this kind of business turned you off. If you're like me, maybe someone you know—probably a relative, friend, or coworker—once came up to you and asked, "Can you do me a favor and come to this meeting with me? I'm looking at a new business opportunity, and I want to share it with you and see what you think."

Because you're a good guy or gal, you said okay—only to find that your friend had suckered you into an "opportunity meeting" for a new multi-level marketing business.

DOES THIS SOUND FAMILIAR?

After being harangued for an hour or so about how you can make a fortune—with overly enthusiastic people delivering emotional testimonials about how much money they were supposedly making and a bunch of group cheers where everyone had to get up and yell, "Whoopee!"—the meeting broke up into smaller groups, where your friend and a bunch of other people tried to sign you up.

Maybe you did sign—and, as a result, ended up with $4,000 worth of water filters sitting in your garage. Or several hundred boxes of some superdeluxe nutritional products that supposedly allow you to eat cheeseburgers and watch TV and still lose weight. Or a special water ball that goes in your washing machine and does your laundry for a hundred years. Or amazing knives that cut through telephone books.

It's not surprising that your memories of the experience aren't fond ones.

This practice of pressuring people into buying a "distributorship" and, along with it, a ton of stuff they don't need and will never be able to sell is known as "front-loading"—and it's illegal, as is most of what the authorities call "pyramid schemes." The good news is that pyramid schemes are NOT what this section is about. So please keep reading.

THE DIRECT-SELLING INDUSTRY— AN OBJECTIVE LOOK

I've started this section talking about the negative side of direct selling because if you've been exposed to it before (as I've been), then like me you may think this entire industry is a sham. Truth be told, I felt this way for nearly two decades (ever since the first bad meeting I was roped into attending). Whenever someone would try to talk to me about the industry, I would turn and head the other way.

All the same, I don't think you (or I) should dismiss direct selling out of hand. The fact is, the industry has changed enough in recent years to be worth a second look. What used to be a fly-by-night business of scammers now boasts a fair share of publicly traded multinational giants and well-established privately held companies with revenues in the billions. As a result, I've come to believe that direct selling now deserves serious consideration as a possible way to create a second, home-based income stream for yourself.

WHEN WARREN BUFFETT TAKES NOTICE, IT'S NOTICEABLE

To be honest, what got me to reconsider my negative attitude about direct selling was Warren Buffett. When I read in *Fortune* magazine that Warren Buffett, the billionaire investor and one of the world's richest men, was investing in a direct-selling company, I decided maybe I was missing something.

For those of you who are not familiar with Warren Buffett, he's a widely admired, Nebraska-based financial guru (known popularly as "The Oracle of Omaha") who's built a fortune estimated at more than $40 billion. He's done this mainly by making long-term investments in boring, cash-cow industries like insurance and consumer products and soft drinks. So for him to invest in a direct-selling company meant something in that industry must have changed.

DIRECT SELLING—OVER $80 BILLION A YEAR AND GROWING

What may have attracted Mr. Buffett's attention to direct selling is the fact that the industry is really booming. According to the *Direct Selling Association (DSA)*, more than 13.3 million Americans were involved in direct selling in 2003, generating total revenues of just under $30 billion. Worldwide, some 47 million participants racked up sales of $88 billion.

Even more impressive (or surprising), studies show that more than one in two American adults have purchased goods or services from a direct-selling representative.

WHAT EXACTLY IS DIRECT SELLING?

Direct selling, network marketing, multilevel marketing, party-plan marketing, and one-to-one marketing are all variations on the same theme. As the DSA defines it, "Direct selling is the sale of a consumer product or service, person to person, away from a fixed retail location." Generally speaking, the person doing the selling is an independent contractor—usually called a distributor or a consultant—who basically contracts with the manufacturer to sell products ranging from nutritional supplements to makeup to rubber stamps. The sales typically take place through in-home product demonstrations, parties (think Tupperware), meetings, or one-on-one interactions ("Avon calling!").

In addition to selling your product, you also recruit others to sell products for you. These so-called "downstream" distributors pay you a percentage of their sales—just as you pay a percentage of your sales "upstream" to the person who recruited you. The idea is to recruit so many people that an increasing amount of your income comes from their efforts, not your own. Indeed, in network and multilevel marketing, recruiting others is often a primary point of the business.

The reason you recruit others is so you can earn passive income from their sales and obtain new customers for your products or services. In truth, the best passive income in direct selling or network marketing comes from satisfied customers reordering products or services you previously sold to them. If the entire business is focused on the recruitment of more sales representatives—and not on the selling or consumption of services or products—something is amiss.

WHAT DIRECT SELLING IS NOT!

- It's not about getting you to buy a ton of products up front—which, as I noted above, is considered pyramiding and is illegal.
- It's not a get-rich-quick business. Any company that presents it as such should be avoided.
- It's not expensive to get into. In most cases, you can get started with an investment of less than $300, and often under $100—but you may need to invest a few thousand to really get it off the ground.
- It's not for the lazy. This business will not make you money while you're sleeping or sitting on the sofa watching TV.
- It's not necessarily about roping in your family and friends. If your supplier seems to focus more on getting you to recruit buddies and relatives rather than on selling and introducing the quality products or services it is providing, you're with the wrong company.

WHY CONSIDER DIRECT SELLING AS A HOME-BASED BUSINESS OPPORTUNITY?

I know I'm going out on a limb here by recommending direct selling as a business to consider. I'm doing this because it really can be an excellent source of additional income. To me, what many people see as a downside to direct selling is actually an upside. The fact that most people don't get rich in this industry, but instead "only" make an extra $500 to a $1,000 a month, is exactly what excites me.

As I noted earlier, the average wage earner in America makes around $36,000 a year. If you're in that range, earning an extra $500 to $1,000 a month amounts to an increase in your income of anywhere from 16% to 33%! Saving just a quarter of that could represent the difference between being able to retire and having to work until you drop. And if you're lucky enough to be earning more than the average, the extra income could be what winds up buying you your financial freedom.

13 REASONS TO CONSIDER DIRECT SELLING

REASON NO. 1
THE MOMENT YOU JOIN A DIRECT-SELLING COMPANY, YOU ARE IN BUSINESS

Generally, when you start a new business, the first weeks and months (sometimes years) are spent developing relationships, finding reliable suppliers, testing marketing plans, and the like. Not so in direct selling. Once you find a company that's right for you, it's all there, ready to go—suppliers, marketing plans, training, you name it. You can start going after customers from day one.

REASON NO. 2
YOU DON'T HAVE TO REINVENT THE WHEEL

The hardest part of becoming your own boss is figuring out what business you're in. What are you selling? Who are your customers? What's the best sales approach? Will it even be profitable? A direct-selling company that's been in business for a while and has a proven track record (which is the only kind to join) has long since figured all this out.

REASON NO. 3
YOU DON'T HAVE TO DO IT ALL YOURSELF

Trust me, as an entrepreneur who's created a business from scratch and is now creating a new industry (financial lifestyle education that works)—it's hard! I spend tons of time and lots of money going to coaching programs, attending entrepreneur clinics, and taking marketing courses. I've had to go out and find all of this support on my own. When you join a top-notch direct-selling company, they provide you with an entire training system that usually includes "learning in a box" (e.g., at-home study courses as well as extensive audio, video, and book resources) along with regular training and motivational seminars.

My only warning about this aspect of direct selling is to be careful that you don't become a professional "training junkie." Unfortunately, some people get so hooked on the courses and the workshops that they forget why they signed up in the first place. All the training and motivation in the world is useless if you don't actually go out and sell some product.

REASON NO. 4
YOU WILL BE FORCED TO STRETCH YOURSELF

Let's be totally honest here—you're not going to start a business (any business) at home in your extra hours without massive effort. And you're not going to succeed at direct selling without really working hard.

There are occasionally a few exceptions—and, believe me, if you join this industry, you will hear about people who supposedly made tons of money without lifting a finger. But they are the exceptions! Anyone who gets involved in direct selling is going to have some really bad days. Remember, you are going to be presenting a product or service to people, and some of them (maybe a lot of them) are going to REJECT YOU! At that point, you will either quit or stretch yourself. All personal growth—and, along with it, income growth—comes after that stretch, not before.

REASON NO. 5
YOU WILL FIND MENTORS AND EXPERTS

While groups like SCORE can help, the fact is that when you start a business, it's often hard to find experienced mentors with the time and inclination to help guide you to success. This problem does not exist in direct selling. Since the person who introduces you to the business gets paid only if you succeed, he or she has a vested interest in seeing that you succeed. This means you should be very careful about the person you allow to sign you up, since he or she will become your mentor.

REASON NO. 6
YOU CAN CREATE PASSIVE INCOME

The hardest dollar you will ever earn is the one you are paid in exchange for your time. Whether you earn $5.15 an hour minimum wage or $500 an hour like my trademark attorney, people who get paid by the hour are trading time for money—and there are only so many hours in a day. The key to being rich, therefore, is getting money to come to you 24 hours a day without your having to be working all the time. In direct selling, as you build a customer base, you not only earn money from your own efforts but, as you get other people to start their own businesses, you begin earning money from their efforts as well. This idea of earning money from others people's efforts—or what is known as passive income—is not unethical, by the way. It's called being a "business owner."

REASON NO. 7
YOU MAY MAKE A NEW CIRCLE OF FRIENDS

Here's something you may not realize: A lot of the people you hang out with today are really about your past. You may have a ton of friends you made 5, 10, maybe 20 years ago who have no desire to do or be more than they are right now. And the moment you tell them what you are doing, whether it's going into direct selling, buying a house, paying yourself first, or simply learning about all of this, they are going to put you down and tell you you're being stupid.

This will hurt and upset you, and you will find yourself tempted to "throw in the towel" in an effort not to alienate your old friends. After all, the only alternative is to make new friends. And when you are older, making new friends is not easy.

The beauty of direct selling is that you join a team of people who have similar interests and dreams to do and be more. As a result, you may find yourself building a whole new world of new friends.

REASON NO. 8
YOU DON'T HAVE TO RETIRE

In Chapter Twenty-two, you'll learn why I think retirement is a myth. The beauty of a direct-selling business is that if you are successful and enjoy it, no one can force you to retire from it. You won't get downsized or outsourced into retirement. Many retirees find that direct selling is a nice way to supplement their Social Security checks or fixed income while staying active and socially involved.

REASON NO. 9
YOU GET TO HELP OTHER PEOPLE

Direct selling may be the ultimate "people" business. It's all about helping and being helped by the people you work with—not only your customers but your colleagues, whom you mentor and who mentor you. Not every line of work gives you the opportunity to do this and to make a good living at the same time.

This aspect of direct selling is one of its great strengths. Whether you get involved in direct selling or some other business, what will make you successful is your desire to help other people. If you work from that place with integrity and honest intentions, you will lead a life of significance—and you will be a better person at the end of the day. You will also earn more money.

REASON NO. 10
YOU MAKE YOUR OWN HOURS

Direct selling tends to attract women, couples, and families looking for a way to balance their lives with their need for additional income. Because you decide how hard you want to work and how much you want to earn, you can create the life you desire in this business. No one is out there insisting, "You have to do this full-time!" While some direct-selling people do work 60 or more hours a week, the choice is theirs—and yours. (Indeed, according to the DSA, more than 85% of direct salespeople work fewer than 30 hours a week.)

The best advice I can give you along these lines is "don't quit your day job"—or even think about it—until your direct-selling income outstrips your regular income. (This applies to any new business you may start.)

REASON NO. 11
TAX INCENTIVES!

As I noted earlier, the tax advantages to owning your own business are huge. It's not just the great retirement accounts business owners qualify for. There's also the fact that many daily activities—such as travel, telephone conversations, entertainment, and the like—can turn out to be legitimate business expenses that are at least partly tax-deductible. One of the great things about direct selling is that the business is so intertwined in your life that many normal activities become business-related—and, hence, deductible. (For details on what constitutes a legal tax write-off, consult your tax advisor or visit **www.irs.gov** and request Publication #535, "Deducting Business Expenses.")

REASON NO. 12
DIRECT SELLING IS LESS EXPENSIVE TO GET INTO THAN MANY OTHER BUSINESSES

As I noted earlier, some direct-selling companies sell start-up kits for as low as $200; some are even $10—or free! There are not many other businesses where you can get started on such a small initial investment—especially when you consider that you'll be associating yourself with an established company that will more than likely provide you with a completely automated accounting and billing system, as well as introductory training, access to professional marketing materials, and business and personal development resources.

REASON NO. 13
IT'S A FAMILY BUSINESS

While working with your spouse and children might not be tops on your list, a direct-selling business is an excellent way for you and your family to spend time together. Meeting new friends together, sharing products you love with others, and taking the incentive trips many companies reward distributors are just some of the opportunities. And that doesn't include the extra time you can spend with your family once your business has been established. There is no boss to tell you when you have to work.

Often, children can help you in certain aspects of your business, giving you an excellent environment to teach them self-reliance and responsibility. Lastly, many direct-selling companies allow children to either inherit the business you have built or start a business under you, giving them multiple options as they plan their own lives and careers.

FIVE MAJOR DOWNSIDES OF DIRECT SELLING

Okay, we've looked at the major reasons why you should consider direct selling as a possible home-based business you could run. But that doesn't mean you should run blindly to the first direct-selling company you can find and sign up. There are some risks involved in this industry, and it's important that you weigh them before you make any commitments.

First, despite the presence of a growing number of respectable players and various federal and state laws designed to protect home-based business owners, the nature of direct selling creates a fertile environment for con artists—and many direct-selling companies that appear legitimate or seem to be growing fast are really making only their owners rich. In my view, the single biggest problem in the industry is the high percentage of businesses that pop up and then disappear in just a year or two.

The "business explosion" rate in this industry is shocking. One minute a company is bragging about doing $30 million in its second year (you're reasonably impressed). Then, six months later, it's out of business (and you've wasted six months—not to mention all the money you put into it). This happens a lot. I've seen hardworking people spend a decade in this industry going from one company to the next because of this "explosion rate," all the while getting nowhere fast.

Second, the business is overly prone to what I call the "old razzle-dazzle." It's easy for unsavory operators to prey on people's desire to get rich quick. They show off their cars and jewelry and brag about their vacations. They tease you with images of the "good life"—and tell you that you can have it, too!

Well, that's not entirely untrue. You *can* have the good life, if you're willing to work for it. But anyone who uses this approach to sell you on the business is, in my opinion, trying to "razzle-dazzle" you, and they and their business should be avoided.

Third, for all its progress, the industry still suffers from a taint. The fact that direct-selling revenues now approach $100 billion a year, that Warren Buffett has invested in it (through his Berkshire Hathaway holding company), that companies with household names such as Avon, Citicorp, Sara Lee, and Time Warner all have very large direct-selling operations, and that the government has ruled it's completely legal hasn't yet been able to counter the "Are you kidding me? You're doing what!?" reaction that being involved in direct selling tends to elicit.

It is what it is. You will have to decide how much you care about what other people think. Of course, the funny thing about caring what other people think is that if we all really knew how little time other people spent thinking about us, we'd never worry about it. Trust me, as you read this right now, the chances are that nobody is thinking about you. Sort of brings a smile to your face, doesn't it? That's because you know I speak the truth.

Fourth, it's not easy to find the right company to sign up with. It requires a lot of research, and that takes time. If you're not willing to spend that time, you could wind up making a huge mistake.

Finally, most people who enter this business wind up dropping out. It's repeatedly reported that 90% of people who join a direct-selling company quit within 90 days. You may find this depressing—even intimidating—but it's important that you be aware of it. At the same time, you should keep in mind that while a 90% attrition rate may seem extraordinarily high, it is not uncommon in other industries. When I was training to become a financial advisor, the instructor at my firm told everyone in my training class to look to our left and to our right—both people would be out of the business within three years. It turned out the instructor was being optimistic. He should have said, "Look to your left, your right, in front of you, behind you, and diagonally." The attrition rate was that high.

PUTTING THE ODDS IN YOUR FAVOR
IN DIRECT SELLING

The best way to maximize your chances of succeeding at direct selling is to choose the right company the first time you try. This is not easy. Here are five tips for how to do this.

TIP NO. 1
ONLY GET INTO A BUSINESS
YOU ARE PASSIONATE ABOUT

If I were getting involved in direct selling (I'm not because I need to stay neutral, so don't e-mail or call me about this), I would go straight into financial services, since it's what my educational background and professional training has been in. Right now, there is a company (whose name I won't mention because I'm not making specific recommendations here) that is in the business of helping people save money, buy insurance, and pay their home down early. This company is owned by one of the largest publicly traded financial-services firms in the world. Because this company is in an industry that is directly aligned with my own core values and interests and training, I could start with them tomorrow and easily devote 40 hours a week to it.

Remember, direct selling is a "people business," in which you have to share with others your passion for the product or service you're offering, whether it be health, wellness, travel, legal protection, clothing, collectibles, home furnishing, or something else. So you need to find a business that you want to talk about all day and dream about all night.

TIP NO. 2
ONLY SIGN UP WITH AN ESTABLISHED COMPANY

The best way to avoid heartache is never to be "first" in this business. There's too much risk in being first—and while I know all the stories about how it's the pioneers who get very rich, it's too much of a risk for people who want to start late and finish rich. Find me a company that's publicly traded, that's already doing a billion dollars a year in sales (and there are already six), that has an established track record of earnings and growth—

and the odds are in your favor they won't be going out of business anytime soon. Of course, anything is possible (look at Enron). But you do have a better chance of not losing your shirt. At a minimum, I'd want to see revenues of $50 million a year and at least five years of solid earnings and growth before I signed up with anyone.

TIP NO. 3
VISIT THE COMPANY HEADQUARTERS AND MEET THE MANAGEMENT

Nothing beats a face-to-face meeting at company headquarters. It's by far the best way to get a good sense of what kind of people are running the company, how it's doing, and where it's going. You'll get a sense of their integrity, and whether or not they are people you can trust. Go with your gut on this one. Even if it costs you $1,000 to make the trip, you should do it. And if the company doesn't roll out the red carpet to meet you, then cross them off your list. If you can't afford the expense or the time, then study the materials you get from the company extensively and completely. Really read (don't just flip through) the entire distributor agreement and ask questions about items you do not understand. In addition, meet the company's leaders who are in your local area and attend some company events prior to signing up.

TIP NO. 4
READ THE FINANCIALS

Seriously. No joke. You are making a HUGE MISTAKE if you sign up with any kind of company, direct selling or otherwise, without first taking a close look at its financial records. Whether you are buying real estate, investing in a franchise, or getting into direct selling, you have to look at the numbers. This is why I recommend that you consider only direct-selling companies whose financials you can obtain. This is easiest if the company is public, since by law the financial results of publicly traded companies must be made public—meaning you can either get them from the company itself or by going online. You should also check the company's history with your local Better Business Bureau, your state's Attorney General, and the Federal Trade Commission. Specifically, you want to look for some simple things: Does the company make money? Does the company have debt—and if so, how much and why? What's the attrition rate of people who join the business? This kind of information should be readily available from a publicly traded company. If the company you're considering is not publicly traded, they still should be willing to show you their financials. If they're not, don't get involved—PERIOD!

TIP NO. 5
CONSIDER ONLY DSA MEMBERS

The Direct Selling Association has essentially become the Better Business Bureau of this industry. As of this writing, there are more than 1,000 well-established direct-selling companies in business. Of these, fewer than 200 have applied and been approved for DSA membership. As this statistic indicates, the DSA sets a very high standard. Visit its web site at **www.dsa.org** and check out its membership requirements and Code of Ethics. Among other things, it subjects companies to a yearlong review process before it lets them join—and to discourage "front-loading," it requires members to repurchase unsold materials from distributors for at least 90% of the original cost within 12 months of the original purchase.

AND NOW BACK TO WARREN BUFFETT

One of the first direct-selling companies Warren Buffett invested in was an outfit called Kirby Company (vacuum cleaners). He then purchased World Book (educational products) and, most recently, The Pampered Chef. The story of the founder of The Pampered Chef, Doris Christopher, is a great example of direct selling at its best—and what can happen if you have the courage to start your own home-based business.

FROM A $3,000 START-UP TO
A BILLION-DOLLAR GIANT

Back in 1980, Doris Christopher was looking for a business she could start that would allow her to stay home with her two young children. An educator and home economist, she was convinced that women not only wanted but also needed professional-quality kitchen tools for everyday use. So in

1980, with only $3,000 in cash and boundless faith in her sense of the marketplace, she launched **The Pampered Chef.**

Capitalizing on her natural abilities as both a teacher and a cook, she pulled together a small but top-quality line of professional cooking utensils and began not so much selling them as teaching other women how to use them.

Her products were so well suited to direct selling and demonstrations that Doris soon realized that the best sales technique for them was essentially to throw a party. People loved to eat, they loved to cook, and they loved to get together to socialize. Of course, a lot of pots and pans were sold at these parties, and soon friends of hers began asking if they could organize sales parties of their own.

Realizing she could have a much bigger business if she recruited a team of people to sell for her, Doris decided to set up a direct-selling company—a woman-to-woman network in the tradition of other powerful direct-selling giants such as Avon, Mary Kay, and Tupperware.

Doris knew that if she built a company based on integrity, service, and above all else quality products, she could really grow her business. She was right. Over the years, The Pampered Chef has mushroomed into a $750-million-a-year company with 70,000 active independent kitchen consultants in four countries.

Eventually, Warren Buffett would notice not just the value in Doris's business but the integrity of its founder and CEO. In December 2002, he bought The Pampered Chef.

DON'T QUIT YOUR DAY JOB—
AT LEAST NOT YET

The purpose of the last two chapters was to expose you to two different ways of growing your income. I'm not here to suggest that you must take up buying and selling on eBay or joining a direct-selling company. Whether or not starting a second business makes sense for you—and what that business should be—is ultimately something only you can decide.

Hopefully, you've gotten excited about one or more of the ideas I've presented. But no matter how excited you may be, I implore you, DON'T QUIT YOUR DAY JOB.

If you wind up following through on one of these approaches—and you wind up succeeding at it so well that your new stream of income outstrips what you are currently earning—THEN you can consider leaving your day job. But only then, and only if you're confident the new income stream will continue to grow. Remember, the idea is to supplement your basic income, not replace it. You quit your day job only if you think you can make even more money by doing so.

This is exactly what happened to me. I started FinishRich, Inc., on the side (working on it in the early morning and at night) while I kept my day job as a senior vice president at Morgan Stanley and a partner of The Bach Group.

In all, I spent four years developing FinishRich, Inc., before I quit my day job. In that time, I not only built up our savings but I also was able to prove to myself (and my wife, Michelle) that my new business was sound. I didn't leave my day job until I felt extraordinarily confident that FinishRich, Inc., was working.

KEY "START LATE" PRINCIPLES IN CHAPTER SEVENTEEN

- Although the direct-selling industry has attracted more than its share of shady operators, it also boasts some extremely respectable multi-national giants—and, as a result, deserves serious consideration as a possible business.
- Legitimate direct selling is not a get-rich-quick business, but if you are willing to work hard, it can be quite lucrative.
- Among its many advantages is that you are buying into an existing enterprise that's designed to help you get started.
- You should consider signing up only with established companies that are members of the Direct Selling Association—and then only after checking out their financials and meeting their management.

FINISH RICH ACTION STEPS

Reviewing the principles we discussed in Chapter Seventeen, here is what you should be doing right now so you can Start Late and Finish Rich. Check off each step as you accomplish it.

❑ Visit the Direct Selling Association web site (at **www.dsa.org**) to learn how legitimate direct-selling companies operate.

❑ If you have any friends or relatives who've been involved with direct selling, ask them about their experiences.

CHAPTER EIGHTEEN

MAKE MORE ...
IN FRANCHISING

In turning to the subject of franchising, I feel like I've come full circle. Why? Because back in 1993, with two years of real estate under my belt and some money in the bank, I decided I wanted to get into franchising.

With that as my aim, I spent six months researching the industry, attending conferences and expos, narrowing my search down to specific businesses, and interviewing actual franchisees about their success and satisfaction. In the end, I didn't pull the trigger and actually buy a franchise. Instead, I entered the investment business. But my interest in franchises never really died (and researching the subject for this book brought back a lot of memories).

What always appealed to me about franchising—and may appeal to you—is the opportunity to buy into a proven business system. As I noted earlier, franchising is not really something you can do on the side while you keep your regular job. But if you are looking for a new career path, a second start in life, or a different approach to starting late and finishing rich, franchising is definitely something you should consider.

WHAT IS FRANCHISING?

Franchising is all about systems. When you buy a franchise, what you are buying is an existing system for branding and marketing a particular service or a product. Think about McDonald's for a second. McDonald's has a system for selling burgers and fries that is now recognized all over the world. Obviously, the McDonald's brand is about more than just burgers and fries—it's about a restaurant that serves food quickly and with a smile (and sometimes it's even healthy food). The moment you see the McDonald's Golden Arches, whether you're in Tennessee or Timbuktu, you instantly know what to expect.

When a milk-shake-mixer salesman named Ray Kroc first came across the original McDonald's restaurant, it was nothing more than a popular burger joint run by two brothers. Kroc was struck by the fact that the McDonald brothers were so successful yet owned only one restaurant. Since they were averse to expanding, he took it upon himself to make it happen. What Kroc did was figure out what made the original McDonald's so popular and then translate that into a detailed system that specified everything from how a McDonald's restaurant should look to how the food should be prepared to how the counter people should interact with customers. Kroc's real brilliance, however, wasn't in designing a popular restaurant. Rather, it was in realizing that instead of running around the country trying to open and manage branches himself, he could do much better licensing his system to independent entrepreneurs, who by following it (and Kroc made sure they did) would wind up with a McDonald's restaurant that looked, smelled, and felt exactly like every other one.

By 2003, there were more than 30,000 McDonald's restaurants in 119 countries around the world, generating more than $17 billion a year in revenues.

HOW'S THAT FOR A SYSTEM?

So when you buy a franchise, you are buying a license to use a system that was created by someone else—a "franchisor." As the "franchisee," you do not own the system. You are merely paying for the right to use it. Most franchisees pay an up-front fee for this right (known as the franchise fee) and then a royalty on all the sales their business generates (the licensing fee or royalty).

But becoming a franchisee is not only a matter of paying fees and royalties to the franchisor. You also have to commit to following the franchisor's system religiously. This means using their building plans, their price schedules, their menus and recipes, their suppliers, and on and on.

There is a good reason for this. The main reason franchises work so well is that most consumers like to know in advance what they are going to get. If you drive into a strange town looking for somewhere to have lunch and you see two hamburger places—one, a local café called "Dave's Burgers," the other a McDonald's—chances are you'll head to the McDonald's. That's because even though you've never been in this town before, you know exactly what you're going to find there—what's on the menu, how much it will cost, how it will taste. This wouldn't be the case if McDonald's allowed its franchisees any leeway in how they operated their individual restaurants.

So if you're looking for a business in which you can create new concepts on a whim, franchising probably isn't for you. On the other hand, if you're looking for something in which hard work can pay off big-time, keep reading.

YOU NAME IT, THERE'S A FRANCHISE FOR IT

If you live anywhere in the developed world, the odds are almost certain that sometime this week—and quite possibly today—you did business with a franchise.

In the old days, people heard the word *franchise* and thought hamburgers. Today, the franchising industry is EVERYTHING. It's the real estate firm you used to buy your home, the accounting firm you used to do your tax returns, the salon where you got your hair cut, the store you ducked into to pick up some groceries, the gourmet coffee shop where you had that latte, the private post office you visited to send a package and pick up your mail, the tutoring academy your kid attends to boost his math grades.

According to the International Franchise Association, the franchise industry is now a $1-trillion-a-year business. That's *trillion* with a "t."

In all, according to the IFA, franchise outlets account for 40% of all retail sales in the United States—and employ more than 8 million people, or one out of every nine working Americans. In 2004, reports *Entrepreneur* magazine, there were more than 1,500 different kinds of franchised businesses operating more than 320,000 franchise units. That works out to about one out of every 12 retail establishments in the country.

To put it mildly, the growth of franchising has been truly mind-boggling. Yet how surprising is that? When you consider that a big part of the American dream is to own and run your own business, it's not very surprising at all.

Each year, *Entrepreneur* magazine produces what it calls its Franchise 500 list, a rating of the best franchise companies based on size, financial strength, stability, growth-rate track record, start-up costs, litigation, percentage of terminations, and whether the company provides financing. Below is the list of *Entrepreneur*'s top 10 franchises for 2004. (The complete list of all 500 is available at **www.entrepreneur.com.**)

ENTREPRENEUR'S TOP 10 FRANCHISES

Top Ten Franchises	Top Ten Low-Cost Franchises	Top Ten Home-Based Franchises
1. Subway	1. Curves	1. Jani-King
2. Curves	2. 7-Eleven Inc.	2. Chem-Dry
3. Quizno's	3. Jackson Hewitt Tax Service	3. Service Master Clean
4. 7-Eleven Inc.	4. Jani-King	4. Snap-on Tools
5. Jackson Hewitt Tax Service	5. Kuman Math and Reading Center	5. Jan-Pro Franchising
6. The UPS Store	6. Chem-Dry	6. Jazzercize Inc.
7. McDonald's	7. Service Master Clean	7. Matco Tools
8. Jani-King	8. REMAX International	8. Servpro
9. Dunkin' Donuts	9. Jan-Pro Franchising	9. CleanNet USA Inc.
10. Baskin-Robbins USA Co.	10. Merle Norman	10. Coverall Cleaning Concepts

WHAT FRANCHISING IS NOT!

Before we look at why you may want to consider buying into a franchise, let's dispel a few myths about the franchising industry.

MYTH NO. 1
FRANCHISING IS EASY

The fact that you're buying an already existing, proven system is no guarantee that you will be a success. You will have to market and run the business (or find and hire competent managers to do it for you). Most successful franchisees will tell you that the secret to making it in franchising is being committed to doing whatever it takes to be successful. It is not unusual for new franchisees to work upward of 50 hours a week to get their business off the ground. Many will tell you they work more than 70 hours a week. What's more, most franchises take at least a year to start generating profits—which means if you don't have savings to live on, you may need to work a day or part-time job on the side to keep the income coming in while you get your new business off the ground.

MYTH NO. 2
FRANCHISING IS BORING

Some entrepreneurs look down on the franchise business because they think it's boring. "You have to follow their rules and use their systems," they complain. "You can't be creative." In fact, opening a franchise and then growing it can be extremely exciting, not to mention profitable. Many successful franchisees go on to own franchises in multiple locations—a process that can lead to becoming what's called an "area developer" (in which you control the franchise rights to a specific area) or, even better, a "master franchisee" (where you control an entire region, state, or country). In effect, you can develop your own mini-empire inside the larger franchise empire. Does that sound boring to you?

MYTH NO. 3
FRANCHISING IS EXPENSIVE

The most common misconception people have about franchising is that you need to have a million dollars to get a franchise. While it's true that some franchises do carry seven-figure price tags, others can be had for as little as $10,000. Indeed, 90% of all franchises charge an initial fee of less than $100,000. So, yes, if you want to buy a franchise for a Courtyard by Marriott hotel, you should be prepared to spend upward of $5 million. Then again, the estimated initial investment for a Lawn Doctor franchise is just $83,300, with a liquid capital requirement of only $50,000.

What's more, many franchisors now offer either in-house or third-party financing to help you make the transition from someone else's employee to business owner as smoothly as possible. And some will help you finance the purchase of additional franchises once you have proven yourself successful.

12 REASONS TO CONSIDER
BUYING A FRANCHISE

REASON NO. 1
YOU WANT TO RUN A BUSINESS, NOT CREATE ONE

This is not a small thing. In fact, it is one of the most important issues about franchising that you need to understand and come to terms with. As I said before, many entrepreneurs are NOT cut out for franchising. Why? Because as often as not, an entrepreneur is the kind of guy or gal who likes to create, to improvise, to act quickly, to break the rules, to challenge or change the system. If any of these phrases describe you, you probably should consider something other than franchising. On the other hand, if you enjoy working with systems, can follow directions, and have both money and time to invest, franchising can truly be your dream second career.

REASON NO. 2
YOU ARE LOOKING TO MAKE A CAREER CHANGE

Franchising can be a great solution for someone in their forties, fifties, and even sixties who is ready to leave the corporate world. You may have something put away in savings—you certainly have years of experience under your belt—and you are ready to make a little money for yourself instead of for someone else. If this describes you, it's definitely time to consider getting into a franchise. Many victims of "corporate downsizing" are now successful franchisees—growing a business and building their own net worth, instead of their bosses'—and loving it.

REASON NO. 3
YOU HAVE SOME MONEY TO INVEST

While it doesn't necessarily take millions, you can't get into franchising as inexpensively as you can get into direct-selling or home-based businesses, in which start-up costs can run as low as $500 or less. If someone offers to sell you a franchise for $500, run. It's a scam. Realistically, the start-up costs for most decent franchises will run you upward of $50,000.

IMPORTANT TIP

Callers to my radio show have asked me whether they should use money from their 401(k) plans or other retirement accounts to buy a franchise. My answer is usually no—but it depends. I once got a call from a 57-year-old man who had $400,000 in his IRA and wanted to use $50,000 of it to buy the rights to an existing franchise that was already up and running. In his case, he could afford to take the risk—and he was able to do what is called a 72(t) withdrawal from his IRA that allowed him to avoid the normal early-distribution penalties.

REASON NO. 4
YOU HAVE MANAGEMENT EXPERIENCE

These days, many midlevel managers in corporate America are scrambling to keep their jobs. Guess what? The management skills you've developed and used at your company over the last 10 or 20 years may be the exact management skills required to run a franchise and manage employees.

REASON NO. 5
YOU HAVE SALES EXPERIENCE

As with management experience, sales experience can also apply directly to franchising. Many franchises are totally sales-driven. One great example is the business of producing those coupon packets we all seem to get in the mail every few weeks. This is a franchise business, in which the franchisees go out and sell local merchants on the idea of offering discount coupons to attract new customers. (The franchisee then prints up the coupons and mails them out, in return for which the merchant pays him or her.) If you're good at selling, there's a franchise that can match your ability.

REASON NO. 6
YOU CAN FOLLOW RULES AND SYSTEMS

If you are good at following rules and systems, you are perfect for franchising. Franchisors want people who can follow a program. Personally, I'm terrible at following someone else's system. I can't even get myself to read an instruction manual, much less do what it tells me to do. But if you can, you're in the right place.

REASON NO. 7
YOU WANT A SECOND BUSINESS

While I don't necessarily recommend this, many franchisees start and run their franchises as second businesses. As I write this, my close friend John (the one whom I convinced to buy a house) just became an "area developer" in southern California for a franchise. In order to maintain his income while he gets the new business up and running, he's starting the business on the side while he keeps his corporate job. As a result, he is currently working upward of 80 hours a week. It's not easy, but it is leading him to realize his dream of owning his own business.

REASON NO. 8
YOU'VE JUST DECIDED TO RETIRE OR YOU WANT TO RETIRE

Franchising can be a terrific second career for retirees who are bored with golf or worried about running out of money—or both. The key is to pick a franchise that matches your personality, your job skills, and your physical capabilities. If you're 60, you may not want to run a sandwich shop because that may require you to employ a team of teenagers to make the sandwiches and man the cash register. On the other hand, maybe you love golf and want to own a driving range (yep, there's a franchise for that, too).

REASON NO. 9
YOU ENJOY PEOPLE

This is such a cliché, but I have to include it. If you love working with people, you've got a future in franchising. If you don't like people, you may not. While there are exceptions to this rule, as a franchisee you'll be taking on a whole new world of responsibilities—all of which involve dealing with people, whether they are employees, customers, vendors, or your franchisors. Most people in the business will tell you that the most successful franchisees tend to be those who are really good with people.

REASON NO. 10
YOU ARE INTERNALLY MOTIVATED

Franchising is tailor-made for motivated individuals, the kind of people who are known as "get it done" guys or gals. Running a franchise takes constant "get up and go." Particularly at the beginning, you need to be a self-starter. When franchisors are asked what makes a successful franchisee, the answers invariably involve having a huge capacity for hard work and a willingness to do whatever it takes to succeed.

REASON NO. 11
YOU WANT TO BE RICH

One of the great things about franchising is that the opportunities it offers are virtually endless. Franchisors want their franchisees to make money. That's because they make money when you make money. Every time you open another location, they make more money. So you've got a team on your side, wanting to see you become rich. That's not to say they are going to make you rich. You have to do that yourself, using the systems they provide, along with your own sweat and tears.

REASON NO. 12
YOU'VE GOT A FAMILY THAT SUPPORTS YOU

Franchising is a business that can be very rewarding for the family—if everyone pitches in or at least supports the business owner, whether it's Mom, Dad, or both. I went to school with a kid named Barry whose dad owned five McDonald's franchises. We all thought he was the coolest kid around because he could eat at McDonald's for free. But then, as a teenager, he and his brother had to work at one of his dad's McDonald's. That wasn't so cool—until his senior year in high school, when he showed up driving a BMW. Suddenly, he was cool again. Five years after college, Barry was running the family business, and last I heard, they were up to 25 franchises generating $30 million a year, and he owned a 7,000-square-foot home on a golf course in a nice gated community. Pretty darn cool—a family fortune made through franchising.

The catch is that your family must be willing to support you. Running a franchise can be extremely demanding. If your spouse and kids don't have an "all hands on deck" mentality, your business—or your family—will suffer.

FIVE MAJOR DOWNSIDES
TO FRANCHISING

First, you need real money to get started. You may not need a million dollars, but you will need something, more than likely at least $10,000. Many franchise businesses can't get off the ground for less than $100,000. In addition, you will also need money to tide you over while the business gets up and running. This is something many franchisees don't adequately take into account. To be on the safe side, you may want to have as much as a year's worth of expenses in the bank on top of what you'll need to get the business running.

Second, you have to follow the rules. I know I already discussed this, but it's worth repeating. If you are a rebel, stay away from franchising. You will rebel yourself right out of business. If you don't follow the rules scrupulously, the franchisor will fire you and take back your franchise without hesitation—and you could lose a fortune.

Third, as I said, it's not easy. Owning a franchise (especially in the food sector) can be brutally hard work, involving long hours and often physical labor.

Fourth, you may have to relocate in order to get the franchise rights you want because the territory where you happen to live is already taken.

Finally, you may fail. It's difficult to know just what the failure rate is in franchising. The industry has promoted the idea that in sharp contrast to the overall business failure rate of 90%, 85% of franchisees are successful. As I noted in Chapter Fifteen, however, that often-cited 90% failure rate is a bogus number—and my guess is that so is franchising's supposed 85% success rate. Still, my research does show that if you find a successful franchisor with a solid management team and you do the right things, you've got a solid chance of succeeding. But it's not guaranteed. And guess what? Nothing in this book is! You don't get dreams with guarantees. Life doesn't work that way.

PUTTING THE ODDS IN YOUR FAVOR
IN FRANCHISING

As I mentioned, I did months of research when I was thinking of getting into franchising. One thing I learned is that you can easily lose a fortune—and waste years of your life—if you don't do your homework.

The secret to franchising is the same as that in any business. You want to find an "unfair" advantage—something that will cut the time it takes you to achieve success. You can spend 20 years and become a success in franchising, or you can spend five years. The fastest way to go from learning to acting is to learn from the best. When you learn from someone who has been there, you get faster, smarter, more successful results.

With this in mind, here are six tips to maximize your chances of making it in franchising based on multiple interviews and research I did on franchising.

TIP NO. 1
READ THE UFOC!

UFOC stands for Uniform Franchise Offering Circular. As a regulated industry, franchising is governed by a strict series of federal and state laws and regulations—one of which requires franchisors to provide potential franchisees with a document that details their financials, management, legal history, fee structure, and much, much more. The UFOC is supposed to be written in "plain English" so you can understand it, but having read my fair share, I must tell you that most are filled with legalese that seems deliberately designed to put you to sleep. Still, you MUST READ THIS—and you must have it reviewed by an attorney who specializes in franchises, not your local attorney. (And don't use an attorney recommended by the franchisor. Find your own.)

Specifically, what you want to get out of the UFOC are four categories of numbers: what it costs to start a typical franchise, what it costs to run one, how much a typical franchise grosses, and how much profit it makes. You should be able to find all the answers in the UFOC, but in some cases you'll have to dig for them.

WHAT DOES IT *REALLY* COST
TO START A FRANCHISE?

Every franchise is different. But there are some pretty standard costs. First, you have your franchise fee. But this is usually just the starting point. You can read in a glossy brochure (under "Initial Franchise Fee") that your franchise fee will be $25,000. But if you read more closely (under "Initial Investment"), you will find that you will also need to come up with another

$75,000 to open the store. And by the way, you will need to spend another $50,000 on top of that for leasehold improvements (also found under "Initial Investment")—and, oh yes, there's also the required participation in the company's marketing co-op program, transfer fees, audit costs, and so on (all listed under "Other Fees").

WHAT DOES THE BUSINESS *REALLY* MAKE?

After you are clear on the costs and investment requirements, the next critical question is: Does the business make money? This is often hard to figure out from the UFOC. Something like three-quarters of all franchise companies do *not* include profit estimates in their UFOCs. And those that do make them difficult to figure out. If you look under "Earnings Claims" in the UFOC, you'll probably find a range of gross revenues, earnings, and profit figures. Keep in mind that ranges are not averages. You can't look at a UFOC that says most businesses gross between $200,000 and $250,000 per location and net between $50,000 and $75,000—and then split the figures down the middle and figure, "Well, I guess I can expect to do around $225,000 gross and around $60,000 in profit." That's a classic rookie mistake.

Obviously, you need to find out this information before you buy into a franchise. Why don't franchisors provide it? I could provide you with pages of excuses, like these: *We don't want our competitors to see our numbers.* Or: *Our business is spread over such a large region that you can't compare earnings on an apple-to-apple basis.* Or: *The numbers our franchisees provide aren't audited, so we can't vouch for them.*

None of this cuts much ice with me. If you're going to invest your time and money, you need more than a "take my word for it" on the numbers. Which leads us to Tip No. 2.

TIP NO. 2
TALK TO PEOPLE WHO ALREADY OWN A FRANCHISE

One thing you will find in most UFOCs is a list of names of current franchisees along with their contact information. Contact them. For his part, the franchisor will give you the names of some happy franchisers as references. Go meet with them, by all means. But make sure you talk to some franchisees the company didn't suggest. The stories they tell you may well turn out to be very different from what you hear from the company guys.

This is exactly what I found when I was looking at buying a fast-food franchise back in the early 1990s. When I asked the franchisor for the names of the top three franchisees in my region, he put me in touch with Nos. 2 and 3 but wouldn't give me No. 1's name. "He's too busy to speak to potential franchisees because he's so successful," the franchisor insisted.

I didn't argue. Instead, I drove out to the No. 1 location, bought a meal, and sat down to watch the store operate for an hour. Then I asked to speak to the manager. I told him what I was doing and asked if I could speak to the owner. Guess what? The manager *was* the owner. He said, "Come back at 3 P.M. when it's dead in here, and I'll tell you whatever you want to know."

He wound up sharing quite a lot with me. First, he told me that his net profit was between $35,000 and $55,000 a store—roughly 40% less than the franchisor had suggested. Second, he told me that the business was a nightmare to run because employees were young and the average turnover was about ten weeks! Third, he told me he didn't start to make any profits until he owned three stores. Fourth, he told me he would sell his stores in a heartbeat if he could get the right price.

This was a heck of a lot more than I could have learned from any UFOC. But I didn't just take his word for it. Over the next two weeks, I went on to interview five other owners—three of whom, it turned out, also were looking to sell. I interpreted this as either a huge opportunity to buy them all or a huge sign to stay away. After thinking it over, I decided to stay away.

TIP NO. 3
WORK AT THE FRANCHISE BEFORE YOU BUY

One of the best ways to get a sense of what you may be getting yourself into is to get yourself a job at the franchise so you can see what the business looks like from behind the counter. Many successful franchisees do this before they buy. If you're going to be an owner/operator (and chances are you will), you should find out if you would enjoy working in the franchise. Also, if you work in a franchise for a while (a few weeks to a few months), you will learn things you could never learn as an owner. Some people may consider this "beneath them," but this is silly. Given that you're considering investing $50,000 or more of your life savings, what's a month of your time? And you *are* getting paid, even if it's only minimum wage.

TIP NO. 4
LOOK INTO BUYING AN EXISTING FRANCHISE

Meeting those franchise owners who wanted to get out of the business made me aware of something the franchisors don't exactly like to advertise: the fact that almost every franchisor has franchisees who are looking to sell! In fact, studies indicate that about 10% of franchisees sell their franchises every year. This is the hidden little secret of the industry—and they try to keep it that way, because they don't like to encourage franchisee sales. For one thing, they don't help the growth numbers. For another, most people who sell franchises are paid commissions. If you buy a "used" franchise direct from its current owner, the franchisor's salesperson is probably not going to get paid.

So how do you find a franchisee who wants to sell? Let me share a low-tech method that is surprisingly simple. You visit the location of a franchise, as I did. You get to know the owner. You find out how his business is doing and you ask him if he has ever considered selling.

I did this 10 times and found four owners within a 50-mile radius who were interested in selling their franchises. This is useful even if you don't wind up buying from any of them, because when you find out what a franchisee is willing to sell his or her business for, you get a real feeling for the business's true value.

In recent years, some of the smarter franchisors started including listings of franchisees who want to sell on their web sites. In addition, there are franchise brokers and consultants who can help (generally for a fee).

TIP NO. 5
CATCH THE GROWTH CURVE—AND PROSPER

There are certain franchise businesses that simply explode. One minute they have 50 stores, then 100 stores, then 1,000, then 4,000. When you see a franchise mushroom like this, there's usually a reason—and the reason is usually strong profits and great word of mouth.

It wasn't so long ago that the founder of Subway, which at the time had 5,000 franchise locations, said he wanted to surpass McDonald's. Everyone laughed at him and said Subway's expansion couldn't continue. He's the one laughing now. Subway has more than 40,000 locations and continues to grow.

Often, all you have to do to catch a growth curve is pay attention.

A classic recent example of an exploding franchise is a company called Curves. Please understand up front that I'm not recommending you buy a Curves franchise. Rather, I'm using it as an example of how you can often spot a franchising trend and jump on it to make money.

CURVES CATCHES THE WAVE

Curves is a fitness center for women. Started in 1992 by Gary Heavin, Curves began selling franchises in 1995. By 2004, it boasted more than 7,000 locations and ranked second (just behind Subway) on *Entrepreneur* magazine's list of Top 500 Franchises.

I first heard of Curves when I was doing a series of *Smart Women Finish Rich* seminars in Dallas and Houston. At a book signing following one of the seminars, I noticed a group of women waiting in line all wearing buttons that said, "Ask Me About Curves." A bubbly woman named Mary Kate seemed to be their ringleader, so as I signed her book, I did. "What's the deal with Curves?" I asked her.

"Oh, it's a franchise," she said. "A gym for women where you get your entire workout done in less than 30 minutes. It's the best thing I've ever done. I read your book *Smart Women Finish Rich*, asked for a raise, my boss said no, and I quit! Six months later, I bought a Curves franchise."

Mary Kate leaned into me. "David," she said, "I'm telling you—these things are gold mines! I've got three now and they are all profitable! Best of all, they cost me only $35,000 each to buy, and the last one—I took it over from a woman who didn't enjoy running it—I got for nothing down."

My curiosity was piqued. When I got home from my trip, I suggested to my wife that maybe she should look into buying a Curves franchise. Two days later, my mom called, and when I asked her how she was doing, she said, "I'm doing great. I finally joined a gym like you suggested and I'm actually going to it. It's this great gym for women only where you can get in and out in 30 minutes."

"Let me guess, Mom," I said. "You're going to Curves."

"Yeah," she replied. "How did you know?"

"LET ME GUESS—YOU'RE GOING TO CURVES?"

A few weeks later, I was at the CNN studios in New York for an interview. Rochelle, who always does my makeup before I go on, was really looking healthy, so I casually told her, "You look like you've been working out."

"I am," she said. "I just started going to this great place for women."

"Let me guess—you're going to Curves?"

"Yeah, how'd you know?" Rochelle laughed. "You know, they're really amazing places. I told my daughter—you should open one of these."

I swear this is an entirely true story, and I share it because it's such a classic example of how you can discover a growth company right in front of your eyes. The trick, of course, is to act quickly.

TIP NO. 6
KNOW WHAT TO WATCH OUT FOR

According to Russell J. Frith, the CEO of Lawn Doctor, Inc., and former chairman of the International Franchise Association, these are the top eight things to watch out for when buying a franchise.

1. Start-up franchises or those that are undercapitalized. They may lack an executable strategic plan, have a low level of support, or, worse, they may not stay in business.

2. Franchises in overcrowded categories—for example, fast-food restaurants. It may be difficult to break through the clutter.

3. Antiquated business models. Some well-known franchises are well recognized but have failed to keep up with the changing business environment. They are unlikely to evolve, which could impede growth.

4. Franchises riddled with litigation. Avoid companies that have an abundance of lawsuits filed by their franchisees. (This would be disclosed in the UFOC.)

5. Franchisors that are growing too fast. While it's important to catch a growing trend, some franchisors have been known to expand too fast to be able to handle and service the growth.

6. Franchisors that don't invite you in to visit their corporate headquarters. Good companies promote what's known as a "discovery day"—visits to headquarters to meet the management.

7. Franchisors that push too hard to "close you." Franchisors should have a process that moves things forward, but not at the cost of making you feel uncomfortable, not answering all your questions, or making it difficult for you to do your due diligence.

8. Unhappy franchisees. While every franchisor will have operators who are not happy, the majority should be. You should be con-

cerned if you talk to several franchise owners who are not satisfied. (Contact information for franchisees is listed in the UFOC.)

Frith also recommends that you review the franchise agreement thoroughly to ensure you are comfortable with the obligations of both parties. You may want to go over the documents with an attorney to make sure you have a clear understanding. In addition, he says, be sure the franchise you are considering has a long-term expectancy and is not based on a fad.

RESOURCES FOR FINDING A FRANCHISE

Now that you know all the reasons to consider buying a franchise as well as how to go about it, here are some resources to help you find the particular company that may be right for you.

www.entrepreneur.com

The best place to start researching franchise companies is probably the web site of *Entrepreneur* magazine. For starters, it's loaded with free information. I particularly like *Entrepreneur*'s Top Ten and Franchise 500 lists. The site also contains some of the best articles and research I've seen on both franchises and home-based businesses.

www.franchise.org

Your second stop should definitely be the web site of the International Franchise Associations, founded in 1960 as a membership organization of franchisors, franchisees, and suppliers. Its web site is a one-stop shopping experience for franchise information.

www.frandata.com

If you're looking for the UFOC of a particular franchise company, this web site is the place to go. Not only can you purchase UFOCs for thousands of franchises here, you can also get detailed information and analysis of earnings claims. The reports are not cheap, but they are enormously useful and filled with information you should consider before you invest in a franchise.

As should be clear by now, franchising requires a major commitment. But then so does finishing rich if you're starting late. So as I said, if you're currently unemployed or prematurely retired or just generally looking for a new path to wealth, it's definitely worth considering.

KEY "START LATE" PRINCIPLES IN CHAPTER EIGHTEEN

- Franchising is not something you can do in your spare time. It makes most sense for someone who is looking for a new career path.
- Franchising lets you buy into a proven business system.
- Franchisees not only have to pay fees and royalties to the franchisor; they also have to follow his system religiously. So if you're the kind of person who likes to go his own way, it's probably not for you.
- Franchising means a lot more than just fast food; these days it includes everything from tax services to private post offices.
- You don't have to have a lot of money to buy into a good franchise.
- Before you sign up to buy a franchise, investigate the franchisor thoroughly.

FINISH RICH ACTION STEPS

Reviewing the principles we discussed in Chapter Eighteen, here is what you should be doing right now so you can Start Late and Finish Rich. Check off each step as you accomplish it.

❑ If franchising appeals to you, visit the *Entrepreneur* magazine and International Franchising Associations web sites to learn more.

❑ If you are seriously considering buying a franchise, read the company's Uniform Franchise Offering circular carefully.

CHAPTER NINETEEN

GET RICH INVESTING IN REAL ESTATE ... ON THE WEEKEND

In my five previous books about personal finance and investing, I didn't spend a lot of time on real estate except to implore my readers to buy their own homes. So why am I devoting two entire chapters to real estate investing now?

The answer is simple. Investing in real estate is one of the easiest ways I know to finish rich. For people who are starting late, it's practically a lifesaver.

THE "PERFECT" BUSINESS FOR PEOPLE STARTING LATE

Almost any way you look at it, real estate is virtually the "perfect" business for late starters looking to turbocharge their earning power. Here's what makes it so great.

First, with just one properly managed purchase of a property, you can instantly create $500 to $1,000 a month in extra income. The trick is to buy a house that you can rent out for enough to generate a positive cash flow—meaning the rent more than covers your mortgage payment, taxes, and maintenance. **It's not easy, but people do it every day.**

Second, you can make this extra income without the hassle or expense of having to hire employees, something that most businesses require.

Third, once you've found and rented the property, you really don't have to do much, if any, work. (Maintenance and repairs can easily be outsourced.)

Fourth, you have a business with built-in growth potential. As the property increases in value, the value of your new "business" goes up along with it.

Fifth, you have a business that you can sell without having to pay capital gains taxes. (You can avoid them by doing what's called a "1031 exchange"—something we'll discuss later on.)

For all these reasons and more, investing in real estate is a wonderful business to consider. So let's take a look at how you can do it.

THE REAL DEAL ABOUT "NO MONEY DOWN"

One of the main things that gets novices excited about investing in real estate is the idea that you can buy properties with no money down. But can you really? The infomercials say you can. The newspaper ads that invite you to a free seminar say it's easy!

But do you know anyone who has actually done it?

Not long ago, at a seminar I was doing in New York City, a woman named Monica raised her hand and said she had a very specific question about real estate. "Should I set up an LLC or a Nevada corporation to put my real estate investment company into?" she asked me. (An LLC, by the way, is a Limited Liability Corporation. Don't worry if you don't know what this is. Monica certainly didn't.)

"It depends," I replied. "What type of real estate do you own?"

"Actually, I don't own any . . . yet," Monica admitted. "I just read this book that says I should buy real estate and I should put it in an LLC or a Nevada corporation, because then my assets will be protected from lawsuits. What do you think about Nevada corporations? This book I have says they are great."

"Well, let me ask you something," I said. "Do you have a lot of assets?"

Monica started to stammer. "Not really."

"Do you owe credit card debt?"

"Umm, yes, I do."

"How much?"

Monica blushed. "I guess about $40,000."

The audience started to laugh.

"Now, wait a minute," I said. "Let's not laugh. Let's encourage her." I looked at Monica. "You're hoping you can get out of debt by investing in real estate and you want to be rich, right?"

"Yes," Monica said with a sigh. "That's exactly right." She paused and sighed again. "The problem is, I just don't know where to start. This book I read makes it sound so complicated. This Nevada corporation thing, and then this Limited Liability Company idea. And I'm not really clear: How exactly do I buy real estate with no money down, anyway? The book didn't really explain it. It just said that rich people do it all the time."

LEARNING THE TRUTH
FROM A REAL-LIFE "BETA TEST"

I knew the book Monica was talking about. It was a very popular book at the time, and it actually contained some valuable information and insights. So I didn't want to pick on it. Instead, I posed a question to the audience: "How many of you have seen one of those 'Buy Real Estate with No Money Down' infomercials?"

Nearly every hand went up.

"Great," I said. "Now let me ask you all something. How many of you have ever bought real estate with no money down?"

Out of more than 200 people in the room, only one hand went up. "I see a really huge percentage of you are buying real estate with no money down," I said with a grin. Everyone laughed. "Now, how many of you have set up an LLC or a Nevada corporation to shelter your real estate assets?"

No hands went up.

"Interesting. Now one last question. How many of you have parents or grandparents who told you the best investment they ever made was their home?"

This time, nearly EVERY hand went up.

"Isn't that interesting?" I said. "We just did a real-life 'beta test' of what seems to work in the real world. What we learned is that almost no one understands—or trusts—all the rigmarole about buying real estate with no money down. But buying a home and owning it for a while can turn out to be a great investment. Not a good investment—a GREAT investment."

I then turned back to Monica. "Rather then worrying about an LLC or Nevada Corporation, maybe you should focus first on buying your own home. What do you think?"

Monica looked at me, relieved and smiling. "That seems to make sense," she said. "I thought that other stuff seemed awfully complicated."

BUY A HOME, LIVE IN IT, RENT IT— THEN DO IT AGAIN

My approach to real estate investing is not a get-rich-quick scheme. Rather, it's a get-rich-slowly approach. I certainly have no intention of doing what a lot of those real estate books and infomercials do—which is to overwhelm or excite you with all sorts of ideas and facts, and then leave you to figure out the details on your own.

Instead, I want to share with you a specific plan for how you can become a real estate investor on the weekends. As it happens, you really *can* buy real estate with little or no money down, and you don't have to be rich to do it. Of course, no-down-payment mortgages are generally easiest to get when you're buying your own home. So if you're not already a homeowner, you must become one before you do anything else with real estate! If this sounds unrealistic or impractical, go back and reread Chapters Eleven and Twelve to remind yourself how easy it is to buy a house for yourself (even if you don't make all that much money) and how important it is to stop renting.

Once you've bought your own home, I want you to live in it for a while, then rent it out and buy a second home. You live in the second home for a while, then rent *it* out, and repeat the process with a third home, a fourth home, a fifth home—and so on.

Don't think this is impossible, because it's actually quite doable. The idea of owning four or five homes may strike you today as being way beyond your means or your abilities, but keep in mind that we're not talking about doing it all at once or even quickly. We're talking about a plan that you will execute over the next 5 or 10 or 20 years.

You'll start out doing very simple deals. As you progress from one purchase to the next, you'll learn more and more about real estate, so eventually you'll be able to advance to the bigger deals and more sophisticated strategies that rich people use. But in the beginning, we'll keep it simple.

The fact is that when it comes to money, simple usually works.

HOW I INCREASED MY NET WORTH BY A MILLION DOLLARS IN 10 YEARS WITHOUT REALLY TRYING

To be perfectly honest, I made my first million in stocks, not real estate. For me, investing in the stock market was easier than investing in real estate because stocks are what I grew up with. When you buy a stock or a bond or a mutual fund, you don't have problems with backed-up plumbing or a leaky roof. You don't need strong credit. And you don't need to work with a bank to get a loan.

That said, I've been able to create a million dollars in real estate equity for myself in 10 years—and 99% of it happened in less than 5 years.

How did I do it?

Basically by purchasing a total of three homes, each of which I bought not as an investment but as a place to live.

As I mentioned back in Chapter One, I bought my first home right out of college with a friend. I was just starting out as a commercial real estate agent, and I was earning $1,250 a month. I later became very successful in real estate, working on more than 50 corporate lease transactions totaling more than half a million square feet of office space. But at the time I wasn't earning enough to live on, so I had to borrow money from my employer each month to make ends meet.

Nonetheless, my friend and I somehow managed to scrape together about $25,000 ($12,500 each), which we put toward a down payment on a total fixer-upper in Danville, California, a suburb in the San Francisco Bay area. The house cost us $220,000, and I remember at the time I had just enough savings to pay my half of the mortgage for six months. I remember telling my father, "Well, I'll either figure out how to make money selling and leasing real estate really quickly, or I'll lose my house to foreclosure."

He said, "Nothing will motivate you like the possibility of losing your home."

After six months, I was still struggling to make ends meet. So my friend and I decided to rent out the third bedroom to another friend of ours. The rent our new roommate paid lowered what it actually cost me to live in the house to less than $500 a month. Not a bad deal. I was 24 and co-owned a three-bedroom home that cost me less than $500 a month.

UNFORTUNATELY, REAL ESTATE DOESN'T ALWAYS GO UP

After two years working in the real estate business, I was doing very well. I was also getting sick of living in the suburbs. So my friend and I moved out of the Danville house and began renting out the whole place. The rent covered our mortgage payments, and about three years later we sold the house for $225,000—just $5,000 more than we'd paid for it. After figuring in the broker's commission, we basically broke even.

As I mentioned earlier, the house is currently worth more than $700,000. **I wish we hadn't sold it.**

MY SECOND AND THIRD PURCHASES WENT MORE SMOOTHLY

I bought my second home in the late 1990s in San Francisco. It was a really gorgeous two-bedroom condo in the Marina district that cost me $640,000. My friend Jeff told me I was an idiot for spending so much on a condo.

Three years later, Michelle and I moved to New York and began renting the place to a tenant who took better care of it than we did. And the year after that we sold it for $900,000—pocketing all of the $260,000 profit tax-free. (Under current tax law, unmarried homeowners who sell a house they've lived in for at least two of the last five years don't have to pay any taxes on the first $250,000 in profits they make on the sale. For married homeowners, the first $500,000 is tax-free.)

A year later, we bought a condo in New York City for a little over $2 million. As of this writing (some two years later), our condo has appreciated by nearly 50%. Since we can again sell our house and make another $500,000 tax-free (because we've owned and lived in it for more two years), my wife and I are now thinking about selling this home and buying a smaller place in the same neighborhood.

Once again, I'm sharing this story with you not to brag but to coach. My point is that I haven't really been trying to get rich by investing in real estate.

My vehicle is stocks and bonds. Yet over the last five years, because of real estate investments, my net worth has grown by more than a million dollars.

The moral here is not to impress you with what I've done, but to show you just how easy getting rich can sometimes be when you are buying and selling homes. When I bought my $2-million condo in New York, I was very nervous about the price—and stretching to buy such an expensive place. To make matters worse, many of my friends told me I was crazy (once again the "you're crazy" gang comes out to say hello). One of those friends had lived in New York for 10 years and was still renting. I told him, "You're the one who's crazy. You're spending $4,000 a month on rent when you could buy your own place for a million dollars. That's $48,000 a year you're spending on rent—money right down the drain."

Well, here we are two years later and my friend is still renting. Only now what he could have purchased for a million dollars in New York City is going for more than $1.5 million. And by the way, his rent has gone up, so he's really spent more than $100,000 in rent over the last two years. He's now highly motivated to buy—11 years of renting later.

Remember, people have to live somewhere—so go buy a home!

YOUR HOME IS AN ASSET

"David, is my home an asset?"

I get this question a lot these days, because there are some experts who insist your home is not an asset. An asset, they say, is something that generates income. And if you're living in your home (as opposed to renting it out), it's costing you money, they say, not making you money. So, technically, it's a liability. Then again, there's technical validity and there's real-world validity.

As I see it, if you buy a home for $250,000 and its value rises to $500,000, you're looking at a tax-free $250,000 capital gain when you sell. If you sell it and pocket $250,000 tax-free, that looks like a nice asset to me.

Now, I realize that technically it may not be considered an actual asset until you sell, but in my book, if it looks like an asset and smells like an asset and walks like an asset—then, darn it, it just *might* end up being an asset.

Why do I say this? Well, take my condo in New York. The bank will lend me money in a heartbeat on the appreciated value of my home, money I can use to buy more real estate. Money I can use to buy more assets. Alternatively, I could rent out my home this minute and enjoy a positive cash flow of more than $30,000 a year. Or I could sell it and pocket a profit of more than $500,000 tax-free. What's more, if I were to move to a new community where homes don't cost millions of dollars, I could practically retire just on the appreciation of my real estate in New York over the last two years.

So the question isn't really whether a home is an asset. The question really is: Will *your* home be an asset? Again, I don't know what will happen to you, but I do know that if you ask your parents (or any other older homeowners you know), you will more than likely find out their home was their best investment ever and probably their largest asset.

IN THE REAL WORLD, PEOPLE USE THEIR HOMES AS ASSETS EVERY DAY

There's an assumption that older people who have a lot of money in their homes don't really have an asset because they're not willing to sell their home and downsize in order to use the equity. *That's just not real-world thinking.*

As I write this, close friends of my parents are selling their home in the Bay Area and moving to Arizona. They got really lucky. About four years ago, they bought a new home in a retirement community for about $500,000. In less than three years, the market exploded for this type of home in this specific development, and they just sold it for nearly $900,000— receiving a tax-free windfall of $400,000! They're now moving to Arizona, to a retirement community where houses cost 25% of what they do in California, and they are going to use much of the profit they made to retire on.

THE TRUTH ABOUT WHY REAL ESTATE MAKES PEOPLE RICH

When I was a little kid, my parents bought a new home in the San Francisco suburb of Moraga for $110,000. Ours was only the second home on our block, and I thought my parents were insane.

Move to a street with no other homes? What were they thinking?

In fact, our little suburb was booming and the schools were great. I remember my mom telling my dad we should buy some of the undeveloped lots on our street. At the time, they were going for $15,000 each. My dad shook his head and told my mom, "Bobbi, that's crazy."

Fast-forward several years. By the time our street was fully developed, those lots were valued at $75,000. Today, they would go for $500,000. My parents wound up selling the house I grew up in for $750,000. They couldn't believe their luck. Five years later, that same home changed hands again—this time for more than $1 million.

I'm sure you've heard plenty of stories like this. The question is, why does this sort of thing happen so often? The answer has to do with the nature of real estate. Real estate is a unique investment. What makes it unique are four fundamental characteristics that you'll find listed in every book, course, or videotape on the subject:

- Leverage
- Income
- Tax Advantages
- Appreciation

Let's take a close look at each of these and see why they will make it so much easier for you to start late and finish rich.

LEVERAGE

Leverage is what you get when you use what is called "OPM," which stands for "other people's money." Buying properties with OPM gives you huge financial advantages, and it is what smart dealmakers use to get rich. It's what you will use to buy real estate—the "other person" in this case being your bank or mortgage lender.

Here's how it works. If you find a home for, say, $250,000, you shouldn't have too much trouble finding a bank or other institution willing to lend you at least 80% of the purchase price—meaning you'll need to come up with only 20% of the purchase price, or $50,000, for a cash down payment.

Now let's say that home increases in value by 10%. So now it's worth $275,000, or $25,000 more than the original purchase price. What kind of return do you think you'd realize if you were to sell the house for $25,000 more than you paid for it?

If your answer is 10%, you're wrong. Remember, you put down only $50,000 in cash. The bank put up the rest of the money. But the bank has no claim on any of the profits you may realize from a sale. The only thing due the bank is repayment of the money it loaned you (plus interest, of course). Even though you invested just $50,000—or only a fifth of the purchase price—you get to keep all the profits. And a $25,000 profit on a $50,000 investment amounts to a *50% return!*

Not too shabby.

This is the power of leverage.

This is exactly what happened in Las Vegas a few years ago (and is still happening as I write this), except the leverage was even better. In 2003, people were buying homes in Las Vegas for $250,000 with down payments of just 5%, or $12,500. Happily for them, over the next year, the value of the homes shot up by more than 30%. So now they were worth $325,000. The new owners then sold the homes at a profit of $87,500 each. Given that their initial investment was only $12,500, this amounted to a return of 700%!

As much as I like stocks and bonds and mutual funds, the fact is that you simply cannot get this kind of return out of them. Why? Because you can't get this kind of leverage. No one will lend you 80% or 90% or 95% of the purchase price to buy stocks, bonds, or mutual funds. Nor will anyone lend this type of money to buy gold, artwork, antiques, stamps, limited partnerships, diamonds, or any other "hot" investment vehicles.

Real estate is the one asset that financial institutions will lend you tons of money to buy. That's because of its other three characteristics: It can produce income, it offers tax advantages, and it usually grows in value. As a result, many banks will lend you far more than 80% of the purchase price. In fact, many will happily lend you 100% of the price—and some will lend you even more (through what are called "hybrid loans" that can total 110% to 125% of the home's value).

INCOME

There's an old saying that the three secrets to successful real estate investing are location, location, location. In fact, that's not strictly true. The real key to real estate investing is **income, income, income**. Think about it. What makes location important is its connection to income. A good location is good because its desirability or convenience enables the owner to charge higher rents—that is, to produce more income. A bad location is bad because it doesn't.

The more income a property can generate, the better your chance of being able to collect more in rent than you have to spend on mortgage payments, maintenance, insurance premiums, and property taxes. This is called positive cash flow. If you can demonstrate the likelihood of a positive cash flow, you will have no trouble getting someone else to lend you the money to buy the property—and the more likely it is that the value of your property will ultimately go up.

Let's say you own a home on which the mortgage payment and other expenses total $1,500 a month. If you can rent it out for $1,800 a month, you will have $300 a month, or $3,600 a year, in positive cash flow. What's great about this isn't simply that you've earned $3,600. It's that someone else (your tenant) is paying down your mortgage for you as well as covering all the other expenses of ownership, while you get all the benefit of any increase in the total value of the house. Your tenant is literally footing the bill for you to get rich.

TAX ADVANTAGES

There are lots of ways to make money, but very few of them come with all the tax advantages that real estate can offer. I've already noted the fact that if you sell your primary home, the government lets you keep the first $250,000 in profit tax-free ($500,000 if you're married). In addition, the interest you pay on the mortgage for your primary residence (up to $1 million) is tax-deductible. And if you own rental property, you may be eligible to deduct what's called depreciation, which can offset some of your otherwise taxable positive cash flow. As a result, you can find yourself literally making tax-free money while you sleep.

APPRECIATION

While it has its ups and downs, over the long haul real estate has proven to be one of the most consistent and reliable growth investments around. On average, real estate values have appreciated at an average rate of 6.3% a year since 1968, when the National Association of Realtors started keeping track.

Some people compare this to stock market returns (which have averaged nearly twice that over the last 50 years) and turn up their noses. What they are ignoring is that a 6% annual return on an investment that is often 80% leveraged is actually worth five times more than the same return from an unleveraged investment (such as a stock or bond).

Say you own a $100,000 piece of real estate that goes up in value by 6% over the course of a year. That's an increase of $6,000. But your actual down payment was only 20% of the total cost, or just $20,000. And a $6,000 profit on a $20,000 investment amounts to a return of 30%. There aren't many stocks or bonds that can produce results like that on a regular basis.

HOW TO GET RICH BY BUYING
5 PROPERTIES IN 10 YEARS

I want you to look closely at the following chart and consider what would happen if, over the next ten years, you purchased five homes that only

BIG PROFITS FROM YOUR REAL ESTATE INVESTMENT

The table below illustrates the dramatic profit from your real estate investment after 10 years. For example, purchasing a $100,000 property with a 5% initial down payment results in a profit that is 1,482% of your original investment.

COMPARISON OF INITIAL INVESTMENT TO RESULTING PROPERTY VALUE

Value of Property	Initial Investment of 5%	Property Value After 10 Years	Profit	% Increase
$100,000	$5,000	$179,100	$74,100	1482%
$150,000	$7,500	$268,700	$111,200	1483%
$200,000	$10,000	$358,200	$148,200	1482%
$250,000	$12,500	$447,800	$185,300	1482%
$300,000	$15,000	$537,300	$222,300	1482%
$350,000	$17,500	$626,800	$259,300	1482%
$400,000	$20,000	$716,400	$296,400	1482%
$450,000	$22,500	$805,900	$333,400	1482%
$500,000	$25,000	$895,500	$370,500	1482%
$550,000	$27,500	$985,000	$407,500	1482%
$600,000	$30,000	$1,074,600	$444,600	1482%
$650,000	$32,500	$1,164,100	$481,600	1482%
$700,000	$35,000	$1,253,600	$518,600	1482%
$750,000	$37,500	$1,343,200	$555,700	1482%
$800,000	$40,000	$1,432,700	$592,700	1482%
$850,000	$42,500	$1,522,300	$629,800	1482%
$900,000	$45,000	$1,611,800	$666,800	1482%
$1,000,000	$50,000	$1,790,900	$740,900	1482%

Value of Property	Initial Investment of 10%	Property Value After 10 Years	Profit	% Increase
$100,000	$10,000	$179,100	$69,100	691%
$150,000	$15,000	$268,700	$103,700	691%
$200,000	$20,000	$358,200	$138,200	691%
$250,000	$25,000	$447,800	$172,800	691%
$300,000	$30,000	$537,300	$207,300	691%
$350,000	$35,000	$626,800	$241,800	691%
$400,000	$40,000	$716,400	$276,400	691%
$450,000	$45,000	$805,900	$310,900	691%
$500,000	$50,000	$895,500	$345,500	691%
$550,000	$55,000	$985,000	$380,000	691%
$600,000	$60,000	$1,074,600	$414,600	691%
$650,000	$65,000	$1,164,100	$449,100	691%
$700,000	$70,000	$1,253,600	$483,600	691%
$750,000	$75,000	$1,343,200	$518,200	691%
$800,000	$80,000	$1,432,700	$552,700	691%
$850,000	$85,000	$1,522,300	$587,300	691%
$900,000	$90,000	$1,611,800	$621,800	691%
$1,000,000	$100,000	$1,790,900	$690,900	691%

Assumption: Appreciation is 6% annually.

BIG PROFITS FROM YOUR REAL ESTATE INVESTMENT

(continued)

COMPARISON OF INITIAL INVESTMENT TO RESULTING PROPERTY VALUE

Value of Property	Initial Investment of 20%	Property Value After 10 Years	Profit	% Increase
$100,000	$20,000	$179,100	$59,100	296%
$150,000	$30,000	$268,700	$88,700	296%
$200,000	$40,000	$358,200	$118,200	296%
$250,000	$50,000	$447,800	$147,800	296%
$300,000	$60,000	$537,300	$177,300	296%
$350,000	$70,000	$626,800	$206,800	295%
$400,000	$80,000	$716,400	$236,400	296%
$450,000	$90,000	$805,900	$265,900	295%
$500,000	$100,000	$895,500	$295,500	296%
$550,000	$110,000	$985,000	$325,000	295%
$600,000	$120,000	$1,074,600	$354,600	296%
$650,000	$130,000	$1,164,100	$384,100	295%
$700,000	$140,000	$1,253,600	$413,600	295%
$750,000	$150,000	$1,343,200	$443,200	295%
$800,000	$160,000	$1,432,700	$472,700	295%
$850,000	$170,000	$1,522,300	$502,300	295%
$900,000	$180,000	$1,611,800	$531,800	295%
$1,000,000	$200,000	$1,790,900	$590,900	295%

Assumption: Appreciation is 6% annually.

broke even on a cash-flow basis (meaning the rent you were able to collect covered all your costs but didn't make you any profit) and simply appreciated in value over time.

The numbers speak for themselves. When it comes to catching up, nothing will make it easier to start late and finish rich than . . .

BUYING A SECOND HOUSE WHILE YOU'RE STILL PAYING OFF YOUR FIRST

Beginners at the real estate game sometimes have a problem with this concept. How, they wonder, can you get a bank to lend you money to buy a second (or third or fourth) house while you're still paying off the mortgage on your first home?

In fact, it's simple—provided you can show the bank that the rental property you want to buy will generate a positive cash flow. Of course, you'll still need to come up with a down payment. Often, an easy way to do this is by using the equity you have accumulated in your first home. Here's a great example of how this can work:

Not long ago, I was sitting at dinner with my friend Robert. Robert is normally an upbeat kind of guy. But this particular evening he seemed angry.

When I finally asked what was bugging him, he practically exploded. "I can't believe it," he said. "You know that great loft we've got downtown—the one I spent six months looking for? Well, guess what? The landlord is selling it, and we've got to move again. We'd have never leased the place if we knew he wanted to sell."

TAKE LEMONS AND MAKE LEMONADE

"Well, Robert," I said, "instead of being bummed about having to move, why don't you buy it? Make the guy an offer. Do you have any idea how much he wants for it?"

When Robert told me his landlord was thinking of listing the place for $500,000, I almost fell out of my chair.

"BUY IT!" I yelled at him. "It's a no-brainer. The place is worth at least $700,000!"

Robert shook his head. "It's not a no-brainer. For one thing, we don't have the money for a down payment. For another, we're already carrying a mortgage on the house we own in the country. And, anyway, how do you know it's worth more than $500,000?"

"Robert," I said, "I know the market in downtown Manhattan. Look, I'll make this simple for you. Here's what you do. First, call a real estate agent tomorrow. They can find comparables and tell you in minutes how much a place is worth—and they'll do it for free, if you tell them you are looking to buy or sell.

"Second, call your mortgage broker and find out if they'll let you refinance your place in the country. You bought it two years ago for $150,000, right?"

Robert nodded.

"It's worth more now, isn't it?" I asked.

Robert nodded again. "Yeah. I heard we could get upward of $250,000 for it."

"Great," I said. "That means you have more than $100,000 in equity in the country place, so your broker will be happy to refinance it for you. If your landlord agrees to sell you the loft for $500,000, I'll bet you won't need to put down more than $75,000. Your mortgage broker can probably do both loans at once for you and will be happy to get all the business.

"There's one other thing. Make your landlord a direct offer. Offer him $500,000 and remind him that if he sells to you directly, he'll save both the 6% commission and the transfer fees he'd have to pay if he listed the property with a broker. On a $500,000 sale, that's a saving of at least $35,000!

"And it probably wouldn't hurt to remind him—nicely, of course—that your lease has six more months to run, and that if he insists on showing your place to potential buyers, you can't guarantee that you'll be able to keep the place clean or be available to show it whenever he'd like—which could make it difficult for him to sell it."

Robert stared at me for a long time. And then he went out and did exactly what I suggested.

Within three months, he had refinanced his country home and purchased the loft for $500,000. At the end of the deal, his overheads had actually gone down!

His mortgage payments on the loft (including taxes and insurance) totaled $2,900 a month—$500 a month less than his rent had been! And his new mortgage on the country house cost him only $300 a month more than the old one. So he came out of the deal owning both his apartment in New York and his house in the country—and spending $200 a month less than before.

WHAT I LOVE ABOUT THIS STORY

When I first met Robert, two years earlier, he was a lifelong renter. Today, he owns two homes and is building equity in both! In two short years, he's increased his net worth by more than $300,000. In his early forties, he is on his way to starting late and finishing rich!

So don't view already owning one home as an obstacle to buying a second. In fact, it's the solution, not the problem.

Think outside of the box. Robert thought he had a problem when he heard his landlord wanted to sell. I immediately saw it as an opportunity. Same situation—except that Robert's view of it would have had him moving, while mine wound up making him rich! And that's really how life works—every minute of every day.

THE WEEKEND WARRIOR APPROACH TO REAL ESTATE INVESTING

People often make getting rich in real estate more difficult than it has to be. In fact, there is no reason why you can't do everything you need to do on the weekends. The only exception may be visiting the bank, and with more and more banks being open on Saturdays, even that may not be a problem.

My Weekend Warrior approach to real estate investing is tailor-made for late starters who can't afford to take time off from their regular occupations to develop and maintain a second income stream. Just follow these steps, and before you know it you will be building your own personal real estate empire.

STEP ONE
DECIDE WHERE YOU'RE GOING TO LOOK

You shouldn't have to get on a plane and fly to some other state to start investing in real estate. You should be able to open your Saturday or Sunday paper, look at the ads, and then get in your car and drive to an "open house."

So the first thing you should do to begin my Weekend Warrior approach to real estate is take out a map and decide how far from home you're willing to go to look for properties. My experience is that you shouldn't have to extend your weekend real estate search beyond 5 to 10 miles of where you live. If you live in a major city, you should be able to do your entire search within less than three miles. Some of you may be able to build your entire real estate empire within a 20-block radius of home.

Within ten miles of where you live, there are dozens if not hundreds of homes for sale right now. Remember, you need to buy only one in the next 12 months to start building wealth.

STEP TWO
GET YOUR CREDIT ACT TOGETHER

It's not hard to get a real estate loan. It's not easy, but it's not hard. The reason is simple. Banks are in business to lend you money. And they especially love lending money on real estate. In fact, lending you money on real estate is a "no-brainer." After all, the bank knows that if you default on the loan, it can collect what it's owed by selling off the property. It also knows that the likelihood that you will default on your loan and go into foreclosure is almost ZERO! In 2004, banks foreclosed on fewer than 1.3% of all mortgage loans. In other words, roughly 99 out of every 100 mortgages work out just fine—pretty good odds for both you and the bank.

Moreover, many banks make real estate loans with the sole intention of "packaging" the loan and immediately selling it to another lender. This way, they collect the up-front fees and then sell the risk to someone else.

So understand this going in: When it comes to real estate, banks *want* to lend you money! They are literally sitting around hoping you will come in and ask. All you have to do is qualify.

That said, one of your goals should still be to present yourself in the best possible light to lenders. Think of your meeting with a potential lender as a job interview. You want to make a good impression. The thing is, in this interview, how well you come across has nothing to do with how well you dress, what your GPA was in college, or what you want to be when you grow up.

WHAT YOUR LENDER REALLY CARES ABOUT

Along with your current income and employment status, the factor that matters most to lenders is your credit score. In effect, your credit score is your financial GPA. It's based on how much debt you currently owe, how much available credit you have, and what kind of payment record you've compiled over the years. As far as lenders are concerned, these factors provide an excellent indication of how risky it might be to lend you money now.

The higher your credit score, the less risky the bank considers you to be. The lower your score, the more likely they figure you are to pay late or default entirely. Based on your score, the bank will thus decide the following (and they'll do it immediately):

• Whether or not to lend you money at all
• How much to lend you
• What interest rate to charge you

Given all this, it makes a great deal of sense to find out your credit score before you sit down with a lender. The easiest way to do this is to go online to **www.myfico.com**. This is the web site of Fair Isaac & Co., which runs the most influential credit-rating system around. FICO is not the only credit-scoring system banks use, but it is by far the most popular, figuring in three out of every four U.S. credit applications. FICO scores range from 300 (really bad credit) to 850 (ideal borrower). Anything over 720 is considered very good.

You actually have three credit scores, one for each of the three major credit-reporting bureaus: Equifax, Experian, and TransUnion. FICO explains the difference by noting that since the credit bureaus don't share data with one another, each of them may have different data on you. According to FICO, nearly a third of credit users have individual scores that vary by 50 points or more from bureau to bureau.

Considering how much these scores will impact your ability to get the mortgage and loan rates you want, it's worth spending the time and money to check yours out. And if you wonder how much a bad score can cost you, take a look at the following table.

HIGH SCORES, LOW RATES		
(For 30-year fixed $150,000 mortgage; rates as of July 2004)		
FICO Score	Rate	Monthly Payment
720–850	6.07%	$906
700–719	6.20%	$919
675–699	6.74%	$971
620–674	7.89%	$1,089
560–619	8.53%	$1,157
500–559	9.29%	$1,238

You can also now find out your credit score directly from all three credit bureaus, which have credit-scoring systems similar to FICO.

Equifax
www.equifax.com

Equifax offers several products and combinations of products ranging from $9 for a copy of your Equifax credit report to $39.95 for its three-in-one report with ScorePower® (your FICO credit score and your credit report from all three agencies plus a comparison of how your score stacks up to national averages and a simulator that shows how changes to your credit report could impact your credit score).

Experian
www.experian.com

Like Equifax, Experian offers several combinations of products and services, ranging from your Experian credit report for $9 to a three-bureau credit report that includes your credit score for $34.95.

TransUnion Corporation
www.transunion.com

The cost of your TransUnion credit profile will vary according to where you live but won't exceed $9. Like the others, TransUnion also offers a three-in-one credit profile; the cost is $29.95.

STEP THREE
GET PRE-APPROVED FOR A REAL ESTATE LOAN

There are actually two lessons to be drawn from the credit score table. The obvious one is that having a good credit score can save you a lot of money. The other is that even if you have a bad score, you can still get a mortgage. It's just that it will cost you more.

So however bad your situation may be, don't give up. This week visit all the banks in your neighborhood and tell them you want to be pre-approved for a mortgage. That way, you'll know in advance how much you'll be able to borrow—which is to say, how much you'll be able to spend on a property. Make sure you specify that you want to be preapproved, NOT simply prequalified. Being prequalified doesn't guarantee that you'll get a mortgage; preapproval does. Bring along the kind of proof of income I described to Brigitte and Travis: your most recent pay stub and bank statements, as well as your tax returns from the last three years.

Remember, if you are already a homeowner carrying a mortgage and are looking to buy a second home with the intention of renting it out, you will want to ask about refinancing so you can cash out some of the equity in your current home to use as a down payment. And be prepared to prove to the bank that you can expect the new house to generate a positive cash flow. (One way to do this is by showing the bank how much comparable houses in the same area are renting for.)

If you can't find a bank that is willing to work with you, then get yourself a mortgage broker. Ask your friends and family for recommendations or look in your newspaper's real estate section. You'll generally find pages and pages of ads from mortgage brokers who make their livings arranging real estate financing for people like you. (Before you take out a mortgage, always make sure to ask exactly what it's going to cost you—not just in terms of the interest you're going to pay but also in terms of up-front fees and points. In a perfect world, I suggest looking for a zero-point loan, which means the commission to the broker or banker who arranges the mortgage will be paid by the lender rather than by you directly.)

STEP FOUR
FIND A REAL ESTATE BROKER

If you're going to be investing in real estate, it's a good idea to have a broker who can do a lot of the heavy lifting for you. This means taking care of the endless paperwork that's involved in buying real estate as well as representing your interests in a transaction.

There are basically two types of brokers: one who represents the seller (the listing agent) and one who represents the buyer (your agent). Typically, the listing agent gets a 3% commission on a sale, and the buyer's agent gets a 3% commission on the purchase. As the buyer, you don't need to worry about this commission; it's the seller's responsibility to pay it.

Here's why it's important to have your own broker. If you walk in off the street without a broker and make an offer on a property, the listing agent will generally be happy to write it up for you. By doing so, the broker may get "both sides" of the commission (for a total of 6% of the purchase price). This is a bad deal for you and a great one for the broker. It's bad for you because the listing agent represents only the seller and can't be a dual agent—meaning no one is looking after your interests when the offer is written. Indeed, the sales contract will state that clearly. Nonetheless, the listing agent will get paid for your end of the deal.

So even if you go to open houses on your own, you should have a broker. You don't have to bring him with you, but you should establish a relationship with one so you can call him on a moment's notice to write up an offer for you.

By the way, open houses (which we'll cover in the next step) are a common place to find a broker. As you make the rounds, make a point of talking to the brokers who are running the open houses you visit. Tell them what you're looking for. Fill out their sign-up sheets. See who follows up. See who's hungry. Just keep in mind that most brokers who work open houses are new to the business and may not have the experience you want. Then again, they may really be hungry and willing to go the extra mile for you.

HOW TO FIND A TOP BROKER

I've always believed that success leaves clues. As a result, you should be able to find out who the top brokers are in any community within an hour. And often you can do it without leaving your home. When I started looking for real estate in downtown Manhattan, I did all my initial research online. In short order, I could tell who had the most listings and the most sales.

All I did was go to Google and search for "New York City real estate agencies." Then I compared web sites. It was clear who the big players were and who were the wannabes. In this way, I was able to identify the No. 1 real estate agent for downtown Manhattan.

If you don't like searching on the Internet, you can simply drive around the area you're interested in and note the agency names on all the For Sale signs you see. Again, success leaves clues. You'll see certain names over and over again on the listing signs. And read your junk mail. See who is spending money marketing in your area. As a rule, it's the veteran, successful brokers who spend money on advertising. For one thing, they're usually the only ones who can afford to do this. For another, they learned years ago that the best way to find clients is to spend money prospecting for them.

Finally, ask your friends for referrals. As I've said before, there's no recommendation more valuable than one based on personal experience.

But however you find your broker, don't sign any agreement that says you will work exclusively with him or her. If you do, you could find yourself in a situation where an agent who turned out to be a dud gets a commission on a deal they had nothing to do with closing. If you must agree to exclusive representation, at least make sure the contract contains provisions that allow you to cancel it—ideally, on one week's notice, but at least within 30 days.

Keep in mind that if you use a broker to sell a property, you will have to sign an exclusive agreement. In this case, make sure it provides you a 30- to 60-day out—so in the event the property is not selling, you don't get stuck with an ineffective listing agent for too long.

STEP FIVE
START GOING TO "OPEN HOUSES"

The fastest way to become a local real estate guru is to start frequenting "open houses." An open house is just what it sounds like: A homeowner who wants to sell his house opens the place up for inspection by prospective buyers (or their agents). Basically, it's an invitation to come through the house and "take a look." It's free and it's fun. Just don't get so hooked on it that you forget the point of the exercise—which is to actually buy a house.

When I lived in San Francisco, I rented an apartment in the Marina district. This was probably the single dumbest thing I ever did. I justified renting because I already owned a house in Danville that had a renter in it who was effectively paying my mortgage. All the real estate books said, "Find a home, buy it, then rent it, move somewhere else, then buy another home." That's just what I was doing—or so I told myself.

Every weekend I would go to open houses to get my finger on the pulse of the local real estate market. As time went on, I really did get to know the market. I knew exactly what was being offered in the Marina, what owners were asking, and what buyers were actually paying. I also got to know the local brokers, because I talked to them at the open houses I visited. I quickly learned who had the best listings, what kind of places were selling, and what kind weren't.

I felt very smart and knowledgeable. And, in truth, I was. Within three years, I knew more about Marina real estate than many of the brokers. I could go through a house and say to myself, "Oh, two years ago this sold for 'x,' and since then they redid the kitchen, so it's now probably worth 'y.'"

KNOWLEDGE WITHOUT ACTION COSTS MONEY

My problem was that the only homes in my price range in the Marina were one-bedroom condos like the one I was renting. At the time, places like these were selling for around $250,000, which I thought was insane. It seemed much cheaper to rent a one-bedroom condo than to own one. I'd look at two-bedrooms that were priced at $275,000 to $350,000 and think, "This is crazy. I could buy another home in the suburbs for that much money."

So I did nothing. Which was a terrible mistake. Within three years, the price of the condo I was renting jumped from $250,000 to $500,000! And I'd thought $250,000 was crazy. I started telling myself that the real estate market had to crash. It just had to.

Meanwhile, I kept looking at places in the Marina every weekend. I spent so much time looking that my girlfriend Michelle—who over the course of my compulsive house-hunting became my wife—started giving me a hard time. "Why do you keep looking?" she would ask me. "You're obviously never going to buy anything."

In all, I wasted four years renting in the Marina. When I finally bought my second home, it was a two-bedroom condo for $640,000. As I mentioned before, I later sold it for more than $900,000. That may sound good, but had I bought the place two years earlier, it would have cost me half as much and I would later have made nearly three times the profit.

So even though I did the right thing in the end, all those years of inaction cost me a lot of money!

Learn from my lesson. Go out this weekend and start looking at houses. Study the real estate ads, make a list, and plan to visit 20 open houses this weekend in the area you targeted in Step One. Then do it again the next weekend. Then do it again the weekend after that and the weekend after that.

THEN STOP LOOKING!

Within one month of weekend real estate expeditions, you should know your neighborhood. Looking at 100 open houses over the course of four or five weekends should give you a really good feeling for the market. You can look longer if you like, but it's really not worth it. Trust me on this.

STEP SIX
BUY A HOUSE AND START MAKING MONEY

There are two ways you can do this.

One is to move in, watch your home appreciate in value for at least two years, then sell it and collect the profit tax-free using the homeowner's tax break. Then repeat the process.

Many people don't seem to understand the homeowner's tax break. As I mentioned earlier in this chapter, if you sell a home that you've lived in for two out of the last five years, you can take up to $250,000 in tax-free profit if you are single—up to $500,000 tax-free if you are married.

THIS IS NOT A ONE-TIME DEAL

It used to be that you could take advantage of this terrific tax break only once during your lifetime. As a result, it was known as the "one-time homeowner's tax break."

Now you can literally do it every two years.

Here's what this means. Let's say you're single and you buy a home for $250,000. If you're fortunate enough to sell it two years later for $500,000, you've just made $250,000 tax-free. Let's say you then buy another home for $500,000, live in it for two years, and then sell it for $750,000. You've just locked in another $250,000 tax-free.

You can do this again and again and again.

Now, I know that in many areas of the country there is no way you are going to be able to take full advantage of your ability to collect tax-free real estate profits of $250,000 to $500,000 every two years. But even if you could do this no more often than once every 10 to 20 years, it's still worth considering. It's certainly a better alternative than sitting on a home you bought for $250,000 and then selling it someday for $1 million. That may sound like a great deal, but if you are single and you did this, you'd have to pay capital gains taxes on two-thirds of your profits (i.e., the taxable $500,000 above and beyond the tax-free $250,000).

BUT WHAT IF I DON'T WANT TO MOVE?

A colleague of mine was discussing this idea over lunch with her in-laws, and they said, "That stuff about getting rich in real estate doesn't apply to us. How can we be real estate investors? We love our neighborhood and we love our house. We don't want to sell it even if it *has* appreciated in value."

My colleague had a great suggestion. "So don't sell your house," she said. "Instead, use the equity you've built up in it. Borrow against your equity and use the money to buy a small house or condo that you can rent out. Your tenant will pay the mortgage on your new place, while you get rich!"

Her in-laws looked shocked, but they were definitely interested!

What my colleague had described to her in-laws is the second strategy. Use the equity in your current house to buy rental properties. As I noted earlier, as long as you have decent credit, a steady income, and can show that the rental property you want to buy will generate a positive cash flow, you shouldn't have any trouble finding a bank willing to lend you the money— even though you may still be paying off a mortgage on your current home.

CONSIDER MULTI-UNIT PROPERTIES

If you're really ambitious, you may want to consider buying a multi-unit property. By multi-unit properties, I mean two-, three- and four-family homes (or, as the professionals call them, duplexes, triplexes, and four-plexes). The strategy here is very simple. You buy a multi-unit home, keep one of the apartments for yourself and rent out the rest—the idea being that the cash flow from your rentals will more than cover all your expenses. If you do this correctly, you can make a lot of money very quickly—and you can often live rent-free.

BEING A LANDLORD CAN BE
EASIER THAN YOU THINK

Becoming a landlord is one of those things that, like getting a mortgage, may not be easy, but it doesn't have to be that hard, either. Consider the story of Lovelynn Gwinn. Back in 1998, everything was going great for Lovelynn. She had a terrific job working in the travel department at Warner Music and she had a terrific apartment in the Brooklyn Heights neighborhood of New York. The rent was high ($2,000 a month), but she had a nice roommate who split the cost with her. But then the roommate left, and suddenly Lovelynn had a problem. She couldn't find a new roommate to share the burden, and with an income of about $50,000 a year, she couldn't afford the full rent.

To make ends meet, Lovelynn took a second job at a record store. "I was working from 9:30 A.M. to 6:30 P.M. at Warner Music, then from 7 P.M. to 1 A.M. at Virgin Megastore," she recalls. "It was just too much." To make matters worse, she was broke all the time. "A friend asked me why I never had any money. I said, 'I don't have any money because it's all going to rent.'"

The friend happened to work for a bank, and knowing a little about personal finance, she told Lovelynn she should buy a house. At first, Lovelynn laughed off the idea. "I could never get a mortgage," she told the friend. "For one thing, I've got bad credit."

Now it was the friend's turn to laugh. "Everybody thinks they have bad credit," she said. And sure enough, when she ran Lovelynn's credit, it was just fine.

So then the question became how much of a house Lovelynn could afford. She only had $12,000 in savings, and she didn't think that would go very far as a down payment. Once again, she was wrong.

The first weekend Lovelynn went house hunting, she saw an article in the newspaper about a city program called Homeworks. One of many such programs sponsored by the City of New York, it sells run-down, repossessed buildings at cut-rate prices to developers who get all sorts of tax breaks and subsidies to fix them up and then resell them to individuals like Lovelynn at reduced prices.

NOT HER DREAM HOUSE, BUT A GREAT OPPORTUNITY

Working through Homeworks, Lovelynn was able to find a three-family brownstone in Harlem for $240,000. "This wasn't exactly my dream home," she says. "The neighborhood wasn't great, and the apartments were a little on the small side. But I figured this was a great opportunity."

Her idea was to rent out the other two apartments and use the proceeds to cover her mortgage payments. Of course, she had only $12,000 to offer as a down payment, which meant she needed a 95% mortgage. "It wasn't easy back then," Lovelynn says. "I had to go to a dozen different banks before I finally found one willing to work with me." But all it takes is one, and Lovelynn's perseverance eventually paid off. She got her mortgage—and her house—with a down payment of only 5%.

As it turned out, Lovelynn's decision to become a homeowner wound up changing her life in ways she never could have imagined. Two years after she moved into her renovated brownstone, Lovelynn was laid off from her job in the economic contraction that followed the 9/11 tragedy. By this point, however, she was making almost as much money as a landlord renting out the other two apartments in her brownstone as she had been at Warner Music, so she was able to ride out nearly two years of unemployment without breaking a sweat.

FROM TWO JOBS AND NO MONEY TO NO JOB AND PLENTY OF MONEY

In fact, she says, the only reason she finally went back to work was that she decided she was too young to be retired.

Appropriately enough, what Lovelynn wound up doing was getting her real estate license and becoming a real estate agent. "I get a kick out of help-ing people do what I did," she says. "And the thing is, it's so much easier to become a homeowner now than it was back in the late 1990s, when I did it. These days, if you have decent income and good credit, the banks will lend you up to $850,000 with no money down. So there really is no excuse not to do it."

Before she bought her brownstone, Lovelynn had absolutely no experi-ence in real estate. What she found was that being a landlord is no big deal. Basically, what it requires is common sense.

DON'T WORRY ABOUT PRICE— CONCENTRATE ON CASH FLOW

To begin with, she learned that you shouldn't be intimidated by the fact that a multi-unit house generally costs a lot more than a single-family home. What matters is the cash flow it can generate. "Don't focus on the total price of the house itself," Lovelynn says. "Focus on what it actually will cost to live month to month. If it pays for itself, what do you care what the total costs are?"

And while she points out that you've got to be comfortable with the responsibilities that go along with being a landlord—meaning you're the one who gets called when a pipe breaks at two in the morning—dealing with tenants doesn't have to be a nightmare. The trick is being selective about who you rent to (while keeping in mind, of course, that there are strict laws against discrimination on the basis of race, religion, age, and gender). You definitely want to ask applicants where they work and how much they make. And then verify their answers by calling their employers. You also want to get references from previous landlords and check them out, too.

"People are always afraid of who they're going to get as tenants," says Lovelynn, "but when I was going into it, I thought about the people I was friends with at work. They were all tenants, and they all paid their rent on time. That's what most people do."

Lovelynn's experience as the owner of—and tenant in—a multifamily home has been so positive that she's currently in the process of helping her sister buy a multi-unit property in Michigan. "I want to make it possible for her to do the same thing I did," she says. "Buying that three-family house changed my life."

KEY "START LATE" PRINCIPLES IN CHAPTER NINETEEN

- The combination of leverage, income, tax advantages, and appreciation makes real estate a uniquely valuable and productive asset.
- You can't make money just looking at real estate. You have to buy something.
- By buying a home, living in it for a while, and then either selling it or renting it out—and then repeating the process—you can make big money without having to spend very much.

FINISH RICH ACTION STEPS

Reviewing the principles we discussed in Chapter Nineteen, here is what you should be doing right now so you can Start Late and Finish Rich. Check off each step as you accomplish it.

❑ Decide where you want to buy real estate, check out your credit score, and get preapproved by a mortgage lender.

❑ Find a broker and start visiting open houses.

❑ If you are already a homeowner, use the equity in your home to buy a second home and rent the first one out. Let your tenant foot the costs of making you rich.

CHAPTER TWENTY

GET RICH
IN REAL ESTATE:
THE ADVANCED
COURSE

If all you did in real estate were follow the strategies I just described in Chapter Nineteen, you'd be in great shape to start late and finish rich. But if you have the interest and inclination, there is a lot more you can do—and a much richer future you can build for yourself—investing in real estate.

Beyond the basic six steps I just laid out, there are a variety of more sophisticated strategies you can employ buying, selling, and renting properties. They range from the simple and straightforward to the subtle and complicated. Not every one is right for everyone, but one (or more) of these may be right for you.

STRATEGY NO. 1:
LOOK AT NEW DEVELOPMENTS

One of the fastest ways to get rich in real estate is to be among the first to buy in a new development. This is especially true when the real estate market is hot, as it has been since the late 1990s. In fact, in recent years, developers have been selling out the first phase of new developments in just hours. In some parts of Florida where new developments are booming, it's not unusual to hear stories of people sleeping in their cars for days in order to be the first to put a down payment on a home that hasn't even been built yet.

Not too long ago, a friend of mine named Harry visited an area outside of Orlando to buy a few lots in a new golf-course development. He didn't intend to live there; rather, he figured he'd flip the houses as soon as they were built.

Unfortunately, Harry arrived at the development site later than he intended to. Though it was still a few hours before the office would open, there were already 500 people in line. The entire first phase of the development sold out in two hours, with most of the lots going for upward of $500,000.

Harry called me both excited and a bit miffed. "This developer sold more than $100 million worth of homes in just two hours," he said. "It's insane. There's no way these lots could be worth $500,000! Similar lots were going for $250,000 less than two years ago."

But that wasn't the biggest surprise. "Here's what's really crazy," Harry continued. "You're not going to believe this, David, but they're putting the second phase up for sale—and the same-sized lots are now going to be priced at $700,000! That's a $200,000 price increase in 48 hours!"

Obviously, there is some scary speculation going on, and you should never consider putting money into any development that isn't backed by reputable builders and financial institutions. Remember, it's not until you and the other buyers have put down your money that the developer actually has to build the development. The idea is that by the time he's done and the place is ready for occupancy, the market value of its condos or houses will have gone up significantly. All this depends on the developer being a reliable builder of quality homes, and the sad fact is that not all are. Still, if you're careful, you can achieve impressive returns investing in new developments—especially if you buy in the "first phase" and get in early. Stephanie, a member of my team at FinishRich, Inc., just did this a year ago—and her condo has increased in value from $350,000 to more than $500,000 in one year. Now the development is offering a new phase—and first-phase homeowners are being given first crack at buying at a discount.

MAKING A FORTUNE BY FLIPPING YOUR INTEREST

One of the great things about investing in developments is that you can tie up a development property with little or no money down. Few new developments ask for more than a 10% deposit. Many require less.

What's more, as long as your sales contract is "assignable," you can sell your interest in the property to someone else without even closing on the property. Recently, I got an e-mail from a reader who did just that.

David, just as you said, I got an "assignable right" in my contract. The condo cost $650,000. I put down 5% ($32,500). By the time the building was completed 18 months had passed and my company had transferred me to Atlanta. Fortunately, I had the ability to assign the right of the contract. I contacted my broker, who found a buyer for the condo in 48 hours. The condo was now worth over $900,000. I assigned the rights to my buyer and at escrow closing I walked away with a check for $250,000. And the buyer was thrilled because he bought the condo without it going on the open market, which would have gotten him into a bidding situation.

We all won.

IMPORTANT "BUYER BEWARE" CAVEAT

Just as the stock market booms and then busts, so too does real estate. Buying in a new development for "speculation" can truly backfire if the market cools down. You may be obligated to buy a home you don't want or lose your deposit if you don't close. So watch the market closely and keep in mind that real estate doesn't always go up.

STRATEGY NO. 2: LOOK FOR PROPERTIES THAT COME WITH TAX ABATEMENTS

One of the more interesting ways in which state and local governments try to promote real estate development in difficult areas is by offering builders tax abatements—that is, special tax breaks designed to entice otherwise wary investors.

For example, in the aftermath of 9/11, New York City decided to encourage development near what used to be the World Trade Center by giving massive tax breaks to new building projects downtown. Though these tax breaks initially go to the builders, they are ultimately passed on to whoever winds up buying the buildings.

As a result, purchasers of some new downtown condos face the happy prospect of having their property taxes reduced by as much as 90% over the next 10 years. Their actual savings should total in the hundreds of thousands of dollars.

And it's not just New York City that's doing this sort of thing. The use of tax abatements to encourage development is a national phenomenon. Check with local municipal housing departments or economic development agencies to see if there are any programs like this in your area. In addition, keep a sharp eye on the advertisements in your newspaper's real estate section and look for references to tax abatements or special tax code promotions. Some cities are creating redevelopment zones—and these offer not only tax abatements but also relocation credits!

STRATEGY NO. 3: USE "1031 EXCHANGES" TO DEFER TAXES ON RENTAL PROPERTIES

There is a catch to the homeowner's tax break: It applies only to personal residences. Once you start buying and selling rental homes, you'll have to find a different tax break to avoid having your profits eaten up by capital gains taxes.* Fortunately, one exists. It's called a **"1031 Exchange"** (1031 being the section of the tax code that defines it). Also known as a Tax-Free Exchange, Like-Kind Exchange, Delayed Exchange, or Starker Exchange (in honor of the real-estate investor T. J. Starker, whose challenge to the IRS led to the rule), it allows real estate investors to defer paying capital gains taxes when they sell rental properties.

Here's how it works. Under rule 1031, when you sell a rental property, you don't have to pay any taxes on the profits as long as you use all the proceeds to buy another rental property within 180 days. But the rules are very complicated. For one thing, when you sell the old property, you can't collect any of the money yourself. It must go immediately to a "qualified intermediary," or "QI" (also called an accommodator), who holds it in trust.

---

*A capital gain is basically the profit you make selling a property or business. Technically, it's the difference between the cost and the selling price, minus certain deductible expenses.

What's more, you've got to identify the new property you plan to buy within 45 days after you sell the old one.

So this is not something you should do without professional help. But it's definitely worth the trouble. After all, being able to defer or avoid the taxes on your real estate profits is one of the things that makes real estate such an incredible investment.

STRATEGY NO. 4: IF YOU OWN A BUSINESS, BUY A BUILDING FOR IT

We've already talked about the idea of starting your own business (if you're not already self-employed). As soon as you have one that makes money, you should consider buying a building to house it.

The best way I know to get rich in business is to own the real estate where your business is located. This is the classic "McDonald's formula." This formula was created by Ray Kroc, the driving force behind the world's largest fast-food chain. Kroc figured out early on that the business he was in wasn't just hamburgers. It was also real estate. He realized that if McDonald's owned the pads (that is, the land and buildings) on which its franchised restaurants stood, the company would eventually have millions and eventually billions of dollars' worth of real estate paid for by its franchisees. As a result of Kroc's insight, McDonald's has become a massive real estate player, the owner of a great deal of valuable property around the world.

BUSINESS OWNERS OFTEN GET RICH BY ACCIDENT

In the course of meeting and working with hundreds of business owners as a financial advisor, I learned a lot of amazing things. But nothing amazed me as much as the fact that most business owners who get really rich generally do so by accident. The accident isn't that someone happens to walk in the door one day and offer them a fortune for their business. This sort of thing rarely happens. Far more common, the accident is that when the owner first started the business, he or she happened to buy a building for it.

Here's a classic example:

For 20 years, Fred owned a furniture store. For most of that time, the store did well. But then the market changed, and Fred found that his type of store was too small to compete with the likes of IKEA and the other "big box" discounters. He began losing money, and after two years of trying to find a buyer for his store, Fred gave up and closed down.

Fortunately for Fred, he owned the building his store had occupied—and he discovered he could rent it out for $15,000 a month! Before long, Fred found a tenant willing to sign a ten-year lease. He now had more money coming in from rent than he had when his business was running profitably—and he didn't have to work. Instead, he played golf every day.

Then disaster struck. His tenant stopped paying the rent and eventually went bankrupt. At first, Fred was distraught; it seemed his luck had run out. But before very long he got an inquiry from a developer who was looking to redo the entire block. To make a long story short, the developer wound up paying $2 million for the vacant store, and Fred is now happily enjoying a comfortable and secure retirement.

Fred was able to start late and finish rich because he was lucky enough to have bought his real estate.

Lucky like a fox!

So be like Fred. Do whatever you can to buy the real estate your business uses—even if you have to start small. This is exactly what I've just done by buying a condo for my offices. Around the same time this book is published, FinishRich, Inc., will be moving into its new corporate headquarters. While we'll be increasing our office space fivefold, my mortgage payment will be less than what I was previously paying in rent. So now it's my personal net worth that will be growing—rather than a landlord's.

STRATEGY NO. 5: TIE UP A BIG DEAL WITH AN INEXPENSIVE OPTION

A good friend of mine named Andrew recently made $5.1 million in 120 days on a real estate flip. And he did it with an initial investment of only $150,000.

The secret to generating huge returns like this isn't complicated, but it can be risky. It definitely takes know-how and guts—plus bold action. Still, one deal can make you more money than a lifetime of work.

What Andrew did was use a $150,000 option to tie up a 1,300-unit apartment building that the owner was looking to sell for $72 million. What this means is that Andrew made the seller an offer to buy the building for the full $72-million purchase price, with a 90-day due-diligence period (and the deposit was refundable). The seller accepted his offer.

Now, Andrew didn't have $72 million, and he had no real intention of personally funding the purchase. But while he knew he couldn't afford to buy the building, he also knew that there had to be someone else out there who not only could but would. He just didn't know who it might be. So he tied up the property for 120 days and started looking.

Within a month, Andrew found someone who knew an investor who loved large apartment deals and was looking to place money from a 1031 exchange. Because of the strict rules that govern 1031 exchanges, the investor needed to park the money quickly. He looked at the property and decided he was inter-ested—so interested that Andrew was able to get him to agree to buy the building for $77.1 million. The deal was structured in a way that Andrew's company would receive more than $5 million in cash at the closing!

Andrew, who was 37 at the time, put together most of the deal via fax and phone while he was on vacation with me. We've been close friends since the third grade. He's the friend I bought my first home with for $220,000—the same friend who could barely afford to split the $25,000 down payment with me.

When Andrew let me know that this deal was close to getting done, it was with the classic "BlackBerry e-mail": *David—deal now 5.1 million— cash at closing.*

I immediately called to congratulate him. He said humbly, "I just got really lucky." My response: "Andrew, my friend, you've been working 80- to 100-hour workweeks since 1990. You've got nearly a decade and a half of experience. Your hard work, relationships, and knowledge are what created your luck—and you deserve every penny."

Andrew's example may be a bit extreme—but it's important to consider it as an indication of what is possible. As I mentioned, we bought our first piece of real estate together when we were in our early twenties. We scratched together $12,500 each to buy a home. We made almost nothing on that first home over five years, and I more or less stopped investing in real estate. But Andrew kept going—and today he's doing deals that are making him millions.

You start small and grow. You can do this, too—if you really want to.

The only thing that separates you from Andrew and a deal like the one I just described is knowledge and action. You just have to DREAM IT and THEN DO IT.

HOW TO TIE UP PROPERTY WITH OPTIONS

The mechanics of what Andrew did aren't complicated. The key is to get an "assignable right" to buy a property—and an exclusive period of time to tie it up while you find a buyer. The trick, of course, is to find an available property that you think you can flip for a higher price than the current owner is asking. Once you've done that, all you need to do is negotiate the key terms of your option—specifically, how much you're going to put down in cash and how long you have to close the purchase.

Deals like this can be small (for example, involving a single-family home) or large (involving a huge apartment building like Andrew's). The more sophisticated the deal, the better the team of real estate agents and attorneys you need around you. And you have to be willing to risk your down payment—which is not a small thing. Quite often, these deals don't work and the money (the deposit) can go "hard"—meaning the owner of the property keeps your deposit even though the deal doesn't close.

STRATEGY NO. 6: LET THE GOVERNMENT HELP MAKE YOU RICH

When it comes to things that sound too good to be true, I'm the ultimate skeptic. So when I started hearing that you can buy real estate often with little or no money down using special government loan programs, I really began to wonder.

Then, while researching my last book, *The Automatic Millionaire,* I learned about all the different real estate programs that are available to first-time homebuyers, veterans, low-income families, teachers, law-enforcement officers, and other special groups.

The more I researched these programs, the more intrigued I became. As I pointed out in Chapter Eleven, there are tons of government programs—federal, state, and local—designed to make it easier for people throughout the country to buy homes. In effect, the government has committed literally billions of dollars to help you get rich by investing in real estate. So why not take advantage of the situation?

WHERE TO FIND HELP FROM THE GOVERNMENT

The first thing you should do is go online and visit **www.hud.gov.** Do it now—or at least as soon as you finish reading this section of the book. This is the web site of the U.S. Department of Housing and Urban Development (HUD), the cabinet department whose mission is to increase homeownership, support community development, and increase access to affordable housing.

HUD is an amazing resource, and so is its web site. In addition to all the loan programs I described back in Chapter Eleven that are designed to make it easy for you to get low- or no-down-payment mortgages at reasonable interest rates, HUD funds counseling agencies throughout the country that can give you advice on buying a home, renting, defaults, foreclosures, and credit issues and reverse mortgages. You can find a full list of them on the web site or by calling toll-free (800) 569-4287.

The HUD web site also has a directory of—and links to—virtually every state and local agency or program aimed at aiding prospective home-buyers.

BUYING A HOME FROM HUD

Best of all, the HUD web site includes a listing—updated daily—of what are called HUD homes that are available for sale. These are homes acquired by HUD as a result of foreclosures on HUD-insured mortgages. As a matter of policy, HUD tries to sell these homes as quickly as possible at market rates, and most are within the price range of low- or moderate-income people. Anyone who has the cash or can qualify for a mortgage is eligible to buy one of these homes. As a rule, priority is given to purchasers who intend to use these homes as their primary residence, but if no such purchasers come forward, HUD will happily sell them to people looking for investment or rental properties.

HUD isn't the only government agency that sells homes. Agencies ranging from the Veterans Administration to the Secret Service regularly sell or auction off seized property that often includes real estate. While there are no guarantees, these sales can be a bonanza for bargain-hunters.

OTHER GOVERNMENT
SALES AND AUCTIONS

Federal Deposit Insurance Corporation. Among the assets the FDIC sometimes winds up acquiring from failed banks are a wide variety of homes. Under the FDIC Affordable Housing Program, the more modestly priced of these homes (both single- and multi-family) are reserved for sale to low- and moderate-income buyers. For details, you can call toll-free (800) 568-9161 or go online to www.fdic.gov/buying/owned/real/index. html. In addition, the FDIC auctions off more expensive properties to any interested party. For details, visit www.fdic.gov and click on "Asset Sales."

General Services Administration. The GSA auctions off real estate that was once used by the federal government, so most of what it has to offer are commercial properties such as office buildings, vacant land, and even former military bases. But it does sell the occasional house, so its auctions are worth checking out. An updated complete U.S. Real Property Sales List is available every two months. The Sales List also explains how the bidding process works. You can get it for free by writing to Properties, Consumer Information Center, Pueblo, CO 81002, or online at www.pueblo.gsa.gov/fedprogs.htm.

U.S. Department of the Treasury. Through a private contractor called EG&G Technical Services, the Treasury Department conducts more than 100 auctions a year of property seized in the course of criminal investigations by the U.S. Customs Service, the IRS, the U.S. Secret Service, and the Bureau of Alcohol, Tobacco, and Firearms. This property, which may have previously belonged to drug smugglers, money launderers, credit card swindlers, or pornographers, often includes homes—occasionally quite impressive ones. You can arrange to get free e-mail notification of upcoming auctions by registering at www.cwsmarketing.com/aa_ustd1.cfm. You can also get regular auction notifications by mail by subscribing at www.treas.gov/auctions/customs/rpsub.html or by calling the Treasury Department's Public Auction Line at (703) 273-7373. In addition, the IRS also auctions off real estate seized for nonpayment of taxes. For a current list of what's available, go to www.treas.gov/auctions/irs/real1.html.

The U.S. Department of Veterans Affairs. Like HUD, the VA acquires properties as a result of foreclosures on VA-guaranteed loans. Also like HUD, it tries to resell them as quickly as possible. Though VA houses are listed with local real estate agencies, a complete list is available at www.ocwen.com, the web site of Ocwen Federal Bank FSB of West Palm Beach, Florida, which handles the sales for the VA. You do not need to be a veteran to buy one of these houses.

STRATEGY NO. 7: LOOK AT LEASE-TO-PURCHASE DEALS

One of the easier ways to buy a home is to find a seller who will consider what is called a lease-to-purchase deal. Here's what you do. If you are considering renting a new home or renewing an existing rental agreement, tell the owner that in addition to signing a regular lease, you would also like an option to buy the property.

If he's amenable, you then draft a contract that stipulates not only the rent for a set period of time but also an agreed-upon purchase price. For example, say you are paying $1,500 a month renting a home whose current market value is $230,000. You can tell the owner, "I'm interested in renewing my lease for two years at $1,500 a month, but I'd also like a two-year option to purchase the house for $230,000, which as you know is the fair market value for the house." (If he doesn't accept, you can always offer more later if you want.) You add that if you do decide to exercise the option and buy the house, any rent you have paid to that point will be applied against the purchase price.

WHY WOULD AN OWNER AGREE TO A LEASE-TO-PURCHASE DEAL?

What's in it for the owner? Potentially a lot. Landlords make these kinds of deals all the time. Here's why:

- They're afraid the market may cool down and it may not be easy to sell a property.
- They're worried their property is going to be worth less in two years.
- They like the security of having a tenant locked into a two-year lease.
- They know a tenant who is thinking of buying the place is likely to take better care of it.
- You may have offered them an above-market price.

Despite all these reasons, you may find you'll have to sweeten the pot a bit to get your landlord to bite. One tactic is to offer to agree to a 10% hike in the rent. Chances are, the landlord will regard this as a no-lose deal. Not only is he getting higher rent, but you probably won't buy the place anyway. (Little does he know.)

By the way, don't assume you have to go out and create these opportunities. It's actually very easy to find one simply by looking in the "Houses For Rent" section of the classified ads. Keep an eye out for phrases like "rent to own," "lease to buy," "lease option to purchase," etc. There may even be a subsection head like "Lease to Purchase." All of these mean the landlord is looking for someone like you.

WHY A LEASE-TO-PURCHASE DEAL CAN MAKE YOU RICH

Say you've signed a two-year lease-to-purchase agreement under which you're paying $1,500 a month rent with an option to buy the house for $240,000. Two years go by, and the house is now worth $270,000—or $30,000 more than your agreed-upon purchase price. Now you can go to the bank and get financing to buy the home. The bank will happily loan you 80% of the purchase price, or $216,000. This means you now need to come up with only $24,000 in cash for a down payment, right? Wrong! You don't need to come up with anything, because under your agreement with the landlord, all the rent you paid would be applied against the purchase price.

So you don't actually have to raise $240,000 to buy the house, because you get to subtract out the $36,000 in rent payments you made over the past two years. All you need is $204,000. But since you've gotten the bank to finance 80% of the $270,000 purchase price, or $216,000, you are able to pay the seller the $204,000 you actually owe him, while you get a $12,000 check from the title company at the closing. You've just bought a home with no money down and gotten cash back at closing—how nice is that!

WHAT IF THE HOME DOESN'T APPRECIATE?

In the example I've used, the home increased in value by more than 17% in two years. That's hardly unheard of, but there's certainly no guarantee that it will happen all the time. Even so—even if the value of the house stays flat—lease-to-purchase deals still make sense. That's because as long as you can find a landlord willing to apply your rent toward a possible future purchase price, you come out ahead because your rent is no longer going down the drain. Instead of simply making the owner rich, it's building equity for you.

WHAT IF YOU'RE THE OWNER?

Someday (sooner than you think!) you may be a landlord yourself. There may be situations in which you might want to suggest a lease-to-purchase arrangement to a tenant. Let's say you own a rental property, but find yourself in a situation where the rental market is too soft for you to be able to charge enough to have a positive cash flow. A lease-to-purchase deal could solve your problem.

Here's how. You get your tenant to accept the increase you need to fix your cash flow by offering him a lease-to-buy arrangement under which all his rent payments can be applied to the purchase price. You stipulate a two-year lease and agree that the purchase price will increase by 5% a year.

You've instantly done two things: You've created positive cash flow, and you've guaranteed yourself a 10% increase in the value of your property over the next two years. At this point, the worst thing that could happen would be that your tenant exercises his option to buy in two years—in which case you've made money on both sides of the deal.

Under the best-case scenario, the tenant doesn't buy the property but he takes really good care of it because he was thinking about buying—and you've made extra money on the higher rent.

STRATEGY NO. 8: LOOK AT FORECLOSURES

The infomercials spend a lot of time on this topic. Truth be told, foreclosures are not the easiest way to buy property. First and foremost, properties that are actually foreclosed are usually a mess—both literally and figuratively.

By the time a bank forecloses, it's generally not the only creditor to whom the property owner owes money. Some of these creditors (such as contractors) may have put liens on the property. Also, the owner may have become discouraged and been either unwilling or unable to properly maintain his property. Even worse, he may have vandalized the place. It is not unheard of for buyers of foreclosed homes to find they have purchased a property where, in a fit of rage, the previous owner has poured cement down the drains and toilets, pulled out plumbing, smashed windows, stripped out wiring, and worse.

Still, people buy foreclosed properties every day and get rich doing it. So why not you?

THE ABC'S OF REAL ESTATE FORECLOSURES

The foreclosure process begins when, for whatever reason (usually a serious financial reversal, often related to medical problems), the borrower stops making payments on his mortgage. After a few missed payments, the bank (or other lender) advises the borrower that this is not acceptable—and that it plans to take action.

If there's no response, the lender notifies its attorneys to initiate action against the borrower. This typically happens within 30 to 90 days of not receiving payments—and after a barrage of letters and phone calls to the borrower to find out what's going on. The letters generally start out nicely, saying something like, "We value our relationship, appreciate your business, and apologize if this is a mistake on our part . . ." But over time they become increasingly aggressive as the loan falls further into arrears.

At this point, the final foreclosure countdown gets under way. It has four separate stages: Redemption, Default, Foreclosure, and Sale.

REDEMPTION. The lender's attorney contacts the borrower and gives him a deadline—known as the "cure date"—by which all missed loan payments must be paid back in full (usually with interest and penalty charges). If they are not, he warns, foreclosure proceedings will begin. While this is standard bank procedure, it is not legally required in most states. Indeed, many states allow formal foreclosure proceedings to start within 90 days of a late payment. And shockingly, in recent years, some homes have gone to a formal foreclosure for nonpayment of not just mortgage loans but condominium association dues—without the owner ever being informed.

DEFAULT. If the cure date comes and goes without the property owner doing anything about it, the lender will post a notice of default. At this point, a smart investor can swoop in and arrange what's called a "presale after notice of default." Often, the borrower will be eager to get out of the hole he's in without having a foreclosure on his record, and so you will likely be able to negotiate a very good deal for yourself. The best way to find properties in default is to have an "in" at the bank. Basically, you need to become acquainted with the people at your local bank who handle delinquent loans. They know who's behind on payments—and may even have a feeling for how receptive a particular borrower may be to an offer. (While some borrowers may be grateful for an offer, others may be highly offended—and tell you so in no uncertain terms.) One way to initiate this sort of relationship is to visit the bank and ask to speak with the manager. Tell him or her that you are a real estate investor who specializes in foreclosed homes and distressed property—and that you were wondering if the bank could keep you informed of properties in default. It probably wouldn't hurt to mention that you would be happy to do your banking business with them, and that in the event you wound up buying a default property with their help, you would of course give them the opportunity to handle your financing.

HOW THIS WORKS

When I lived in Danville, California, I knew an investor who focused on three suburbs and bought only preforeclosure homes. Over the course of a few years, he had cultivated relationships with the managers at three local banks—to the point where every week each of them faxed him a list of all the homes currently in default in his three markets of interest.

I remember him showing me the faxes, and his glee over a particular deal where he was confident he would be able to buy a house worth $500,000 for just $425,000—making a quick $75,000 in the process.

I couldn't understand why the banks gave him this information when they could just as easily foreclose the properties and flip the houses themselves. My investor friend laughed and said, "They don't want to take back these homes. Foreclosure is a nightmare for the bank. They have to pay attorneys, then they have to pay brokers—and worst of all, they have to report that they have nonperforming loans. I solve their problems!"

"But why give it to you?" I asked. "Why doesn't this guy at the bank just buy these things himself?"

He laughed again. "David, he's a nice guy, *but he works at a bank!* I take him to play golf and to nice lunches on a regular basis, and I solve his problems at work. He's thrilled."

While personal contacts can give you an unbeatable leg up on the competition, they are no longer as essential as they once were. There are a zillion newsletter services and web sites that also provide this information both locally and nationally.

WEB SITES THAT CAN HELP YOU FIND DEFAULTS AND FORECLOSURES

www.bargain.com
www.federalrealestate.net
www.foreclosure.com
www.foreclosurefreesearch.com
www.foreclosurenet.net
www.foreclosures.com
www.webreo.com

Bear in mind that most of these sites don't give away their data for free (although some offer free trials). They are all subscription services that charge between $19.95 and $39.95 a month for the information they provide. While this may seem costly, all it may take is one good deal to justify the investment.

FORECLOSURE. If the borrower doesn't cure the delinquent payments after the default notice has been posted, the lender will exercise his rights under the trust deed he holds and foreclose on the mortgage, taking possession of the house. If the former owner is still living there, the lender will get a court order to have him evicted. It is not a pretty picture, which is why most homeowners will go to any length (such as agreeing to a presale after notice of default) to avoid it.

SALE. Since most lenders have no interest in keeping the property they repossess, most foreclosed homes are ultimately sold at a public auction. This takes place after a period of time (usually 30 to 120 days) prescribed by state law. During this period, the sale will be announced through legal advertisements and public notices. Often, though not always, the property will be auctioned at the county courthouse. Sometimes the auction will take place at the property itself. In some cases, these auctions are conducted over the Internet.

ATTEND A FORECLOSURE AUCTION— AND WATCH WHAT HAPPENS

The best way to learn how to buy properties at a foreclosure auction is to go to one and observe. To find one in your area, visit your local courthouse; a schedule of upcoming foreclosure sales should be posted prominently. You can also look in the "Legal Announcements" or "Public Notices" listings in the classified ads section of your local newspaper. They generally contain listings for numerous foreclosure auctions. In addition, look in the Friday edition of the *Wall Street Journal*, which lists upcoming national foreclosure auctions.

By visiting a few auctions, you'll get a feeling for what is required, what the pace is like, and what kind of opportunities exist.

As you'll see, bidders at most foreclosure auctions must be prepared to put down 10% of the purchase price in cash or certified check. At IRS auctions, successful bidders are often required to come up with as much as 20% of the purchase price in cash.

A WORD TO THE WISE

Buying homes at foreclosure auctions is by no means a "no-brainer." It's a complicated business. Indeed, one reason I want you to go to a few foreclosure auctions as an observer before you actually start bidding on anything is that you will quickly see that many of the people who attend these auctions are true professionals. Often the bank that held the mortgage on the property will go to the courthouse and bid on its own property. So you need to know what you are getting into.

BEFORE YOU BEGIN BIDDING AT A FORECLOSURE AUCTION

Just because you've finally gotten the hang of the procedure at a foreclosure auction doesn't mean you should immediately start bidding on properties. Before you offer to buy anything, inspect the property personally. And do a title search. This will cost you money, but you want to be sure that you are bidding on a home that is free and clear of additional liens.

WELL DONE—YOU'VE GOT A NEW ROAD MAP TO WEALTH

This chapter on real estate was designed to introduce you to many of the ways smart investors use real estate to grow their wealth. Over the course of your lifetime, you may use one of these ideas, some of them, or all of them to help you start late and finish rich.

The secret to building wealth in real estate is to simply get started! There will always be a reason not to invest in real estate. By the time you read this book the real estate market could be cooling down. We could be experiencing inflation, or terrorism, or a new war. The world is uncertain. But real estate is a unique investment that has proven throughout history to be very solid. It's certainly helped to create countless millionaires. Now it's your turn.

KEY "START LATE" PRINCIPLES IN CHAPTER TWENTY

- Depending on your situation and inclination, there are a variety of slightly more sophisticated strategies you can employ to make serious money investing in real estate.

FINISH RICH ACTION STEPS

Reviewing the principles we discussed in Chapter Twenty, here is what you should be doing right now so you can Start Late and Finish Rich. Check off each step as you accomplish it.

❑ Check out new developments, properties with tax abatements, properties you can option and flip, government sales and auctions, lease-to-purchase deals, and foreclosures.

❑ If you own your own business, buy a building for it.

Congratulations! Having finished Part Four, you now know how to turbocharge your income—which, combined with spending less and saving more, will make it much easier than you dreamed to start late and finish rich. But while you're nearly there, your journey isn't quite over. In the next section, we'll complete what you need to know by talking about how to turbocharge your life by giving more and being more.

PART FIVE

GIVE MORE,
LIVE MORE

CHAPTER TWENTY-ONE

IT'S NEVER TOO LATE TO GIVE MORE

Everyone can be great because everyone can serve.
—Dr. Martin Luther King, Jr.

Over the last twenty chapters, you've read—and, hopefully, learned—more about how to start late and finish rich than most people will read and learn in their entire lifetime. It would be easy at this point to feel you've found out all you need to know and decide it's time to call it quits. Please don't make this mistake.

In this final section of the book, we're going to talk about how **to give more and live more.** This may seem a far cry from figuring out your Latte Factor or learning the ins and outs of paying yourself first or growing your income, but it is every bit as important as those concepts—or anything else we've covered so far. The truth is that while money can help make your life easier, it can't always bring you happiness. Real happiness comes from inside of us. It comes from living a life of meaning. And deep down inside, we all know this.

This is why I often say that while finishing rich is an important and worthy goal (I'm all for you having tons of money!), I also know that *having a purpose bigger than money is critical to long-term happiness, joy, and personal fulfillment.* Having nice stuff is great, but living a life of meaning is even better. So with that in mind, I'd like you to consider the possibility that your life is meant to be lived with a purpose higher than simply accumulating wealth—and that purpose is to give more. If you are already giving, then I'd like to suggest that maybe you consider giving even more.

Just as it's never too late to start saving, **it's never too late to start giving—or living more.** The more you give, the more you really live. And the more you live, the more joy enters your life.

What kind of giving am I talking about? Well, let me suggest that the world really needs your help and that you are in a position to make a difference. Yes, you. *You can make a difference*—and the way to start is with the life-changing idea of tithing.

THE WORLD NEEDS YOUR HELP

The one incredible universal truth that has stood the test of time is that *the more you give, the more you receive.*

This notion—that the more we give back to others, the more comes back to us—is not simply a religious doctrine; it is virtually a law of nature. If you are looking to attract more wealth and happiness into your life, the fastest way I know how is to give more.

By giving, I don't simply mean donating money to some worthy cause. That's certainly one way of doing it. But you can also give by donating your time and energy and expertise.

However you do it, the truth is that the world needs your help—*and it needs it now.*

WHY THE WORLD NEEDS YOUR HELP

We live in a great country—the greatest, some will tell you, in the world. Yet did you know that even in the United States, one of the most prosperous nations of all time, some 33 million people don't know where or when they're going to get their next meal? Did you know that more than 8 million Americans regularly go hungry? Or that 3.5 million Americans have no place to live? Or that by 2012, the homeless population is expected to double in size?

On a global basis, the situation is far bleaker. Roughly one out of every five human beings on the planet—that is, more than 840 million people—are malnourished. Upward of 153 million of them are children under the age of five. According to the Food and Agriculture Organization of the United Nations, some 6 million children die each year as a result of hunger and malnutrition. Every day, some 40,000 children under age five die from hunger and preventable diseases. That's 24 children a minute.

FORTUNATELY, PEOPLE ARE HELPING

Faced with such dire facts, many people simply choose to ignore them. But many more people step up to the challenge. According to the Bureau of Labor Statistics of the U.S. Department of Labor, nearly 64 million Americans—or roughly 29% of the population—did some sort of volunteer work in 2003. At the same time, American individuals, estates, foundations, and corporations gave an estimated $241 billion to charitable causes, according to Giving USA 2004, a study released by Giving USA Foundation.

But while these statistics are impressive, the truth is they could be better. When I think about the Latte Factor and how we spend money on little things we don't really need, I wonder what would happen if for just one day no one in the country bought lattes but instead gave the money to charity.

Imagine what would happen if we got every fancy coffee place in America—starting with Starbucks—to create a "Latte Factor-Help The World Day." Just imagine how much money could be raised to help the homeless!

Could something like this make a difference? We'll probably never know. But I do know that if *you* were to start contributing something today, you could.

And that's the way we change the world—one person at a time.

TITHING—THE GREATEST GIFT
YOU WILL EVER KNOW

With this in mind, let's look at the concept of proactive giving called "tithing." Technically, tithing is voluntarily giving one-tenth of one's income to charity—usually through a church or other house of worship. But I like to think of it more generally as simply devoting any regular percentage of your income or time to any worthy cause or causes.

In the year since I wrote *The Automatic Millionaire* (which includes a chapter on tithing), I've been surprised to learn that not everyone has heard of tithing. And many people who have assume it's strictly a religious thing. In fact, tithing is mentioned in both the Old and New Testaments. But you don't have to be religious to believe in its importance. For at its core, tithing is simply the deeply meaningful act of deciding today that you will send a portion of what comes into your life back out to help others.

IS THE SECRET TO BECOMING RICH THE "GOLDEN MAGNET" OF GIVING?

Over the years, I've spent a lot of time studying the rich and the superrich (whom I define as people whose net worth exceeds $10 million, not including real estate). The more I've learned, the more I've become convinced that most people who achieve great wealth have at least one thing in common—giving.

When I first heard the billionaire investor and philanthropist Sir John Templeton make this point, I wondered if it could really be true. (Templeton himself was a famous tither—who started giving to charity on a regular basis long before he became rich.) Could the secret to being rich really be as simple as "give more and more will come back to you"? Does giving away wealth really attract wealth?

Some 10 years later, I can say that I am certain of it. Time and again, I've come across examples of superrich individuals who made a point of donating a portion of their earnings to charity—even *before* they became rich. Indeed, virtually every self-made billionaire I've ever studied echoes Templeton in declaring that tithing or giving was a principle of their life well before they had any money.

As a result, I've come to believe that the giving of your time or money to help others is more than the "golden rule." It is the golden magnet. I have seen this happen in my life and in the lives of hundreds of people around me. It's a simple, observable fact: Those who give lead more abundant lives.

HOW ONE COMPANY DECIDED TO TITHE— AND BECAME A BILLION-DOLLAR SUCCESS

You recently completed a chapter about how to start your own business. Hopefully, it inspired you to consider doing just that. Well, here's a great story about one new venture that incorporated tithing in its original business plan—and within four short years achieved a market capitalization of more than $1 billion. Could it be that the idea of donating a portion of its income helped to jump-start this company's success?

The company is called **Salesforce.com**. It was founded by a very successful visionary named Marc Benioff. While I don't know Marc personally, one of my best friends from college is married to his sister. On the golf course a few years back, my friend told me how his brother-in-law was in the process of creating a new company that could make traditional contact-management software obsolete by putting the contact-management system online (so no software or network would be required). As my friend shared with me what this new company was trying to do, it seemed clear Benioff was onto something that could transform the way business is done in the twenty-first century. But equally impressive, as Benioff toiled away building his company, he did something I'd never seen done before—he committed 1% of Salesforce.com's equity to a foundation that would give back to help others. He also committed 1% of the company's profits (in product donations) and 1% of his employees' time to help others. He then went around giving interviews and speeches, pointing out that if more corporations both in the United States and abroad were willing to set aside a percentage of their stock, profits, and time to helping others, the world would quickly become a better place. Benioff called this "Compassionate Capitalism," and he wrote a book on the subject, using the phrase as his title.

WHAT IF EVERY COMPANY IN THE WORLD GAVE BACK?

What a great idea! What if every company gave back to the world a small percentage of its stock and profits and time? It wouldn't have to be a lot. In fact, it could be a tiny percentage, like Benioff's 1%. But cumulatively and over time, the impact would be huge—especially if everyone started doing it. Imagine if Wal-Mart or Microsoft had tithed just 1% of their equity from day one.

In June 2004, just four years after Benioff started Salesforce.com in a small office, he was able to take the company public. Overnight, his net worth swelled to an estimated $250 million, as the market valued Salesforce.com at roughly $1 billion. On that basis, the endowment of the charitable foundation Benioff established was suddenly worth some $10 million.

But even before that happened, the foundation was supporting charitable programs in 13 countries that positively impact 50,000 families. Equally important, 85% of Salesforce.com's employees had already taken advantage of Benioff's "time giveback program," volunteering their time to make a difference in their communities. And Salesforce.com was offering its products to nonprofit organizations for free.

My guess is that this is only the beginning for Salesforce.com. Was it a coincidence that this company did so well so quickly? Or did tithing make a difference? There's no way of knowing for sure, but my gut tells me that Benioff's decision to tithe his company's equity certainly didn't hurt. Indeed, it had to have helped. Companies go public every day. One of the things that made this one stand out is that it was built to give back.

See how giving can change your life and help others at the same time? With this in mind, let's take a close look at how to manage your giving.

DECIDE ON A PERCENTAGE AND MAKE IT AUTOMATIC

For starters, you can decide today that you're going to send a percentage of your income back out to help others. What percentage? That's up to you.

Many people suggest the traditional tithing route in which you take 10% of your gross income even before you pay yourself first and donate it to helping. *Then* you make your contributions to savings. In effect, you're deciding to pay yourself *second*.

I'm not so sure about this practice. My experience is that it turns many people off from giving anything. I say you decide. One alternative is to continue to pay yourself first—but at the same time commit to giving a percentage (even if it's only 1%) to help others.

The best way I know of to do this is to make the process automatic by arranging to have a percentage of your income automatically deducted from your paycheck or checking account and transferred to a reputable charity.

What's a reputable charity? It's an organization that doesn't use up your contribution on administrative expenses but actually spends the vast bulk of the money it collects on the people or causes it's supposed to be helping. Most experts agree that a charity should pass through at least 70% to 75% of what it raises—meaning its administrative expenses should never exceed 25%.

I personally never give money to any charity until I've had a chance to look at its financial records. If you're going to give money to an organization, you deserve to know how the organization is going to spend it. So ask to see the financials and make a point of finding out what percentage of the money raised actually goes to the people the charity claims to be helping. If a charity won't show you its records, find one that will.

INTERNET RESOURCES TO HELP YOU DECIDE WHERE TO GIVE

There is no end to the great resources on the Internet that will help you figure out what groups deserve your support. Here are a few favorites:

www.justgive.org

This is a great place to get started. JustGive is designed to help you identify the charities that are most meaningful to *you*. At this site, you can find information on more than 850,000 nonprofit groups and get access to complete reports and financial records. You can even funnel donations through the site, and if you register, it can also help you keep track of all your contributions.

www.give.org

This is the web site of the Better Business Bureau Wise Giving Alliance. It collects and distributes information on hundreds of nonprofit organizations that solicit nationally or have national or international program services. The BBB Wise Giving Alliance won't recommend one charity over another, but it will provide the information you'll need to make your own informed decision. So before you make any donations, be smart and check out what this site has to say about the organizations you may be considering.

www.guidestar.org

Established in 1994, Guidestar describes itself as an interactive "marketplace of information" for nonprofit organizations, donors, foundations, and businesses. Guidestar provides an incredible amount of information about the operations and finances of nonprofit organizations. Click on the "Donor" link to access Guidestar's four-step plan to help you make smart choices not only concerning *which* organizations to support, but also *how much* you can afford to give.

www.irs.gov

Before you donate money to any organization, you should make sure it is recognized by the IRS as a bona fide tax-exempt charity under section 501(c)(3) of the Tax Code. To do this, visit the IRS web site, click on "Publications," and scroll to Publication #526, "Charitable Contributions," in the drop-down menu. This booklet, which you can access immediately online, covers everything you need to know about charitable giving and how you should document donations for tax purposes. You can also call the IRS toll-free at (800) 829-3676 to have a copy mailed or faxed to you, or to ask any additional questions.

GIVING BACK A PERCENTAGE OF YOUR TIME

People ask me, "What about giving my time to charities? Does donating my time count?"

Of course it does. In fact, donating your time can often be more useful than donating your money. There are tons of charities that need helping hands far more desperately than they need additional dollars.

And from your point of view, donating your time can be incredibly meaningful. I've given both money and time to charities—and though both count and both help, the experience of giving my time has had far more impact on my life than the experience of writing checks.

YOU CAN ALSO CHOOSE TO GET REALLY INVOLVED

You can give a little of your time or you can give a lot.

I've never seen a charitable organization that wasn't looking for enthusiastic volunteers. All too often, people assume that to be really involved with an organization you need to be rich and powerful. This is simply not true.

Take the story of Marissa. She came up to me after I delivered a speech on giving and confessed that her dream was to be on the board of a major charity in her city. Unfortunately, she added, she was sure the organization wouldn't want her because she wasn't rich. As she put it, "I can't buy my way onto the board."

This prompted me to ask Marissa a really simple question: "Have you tried to volunteer your services to the organization?"

Marissa said she hadn't.

"Then don't assume anything," I replied. As I told her, my experience is that while charitable organizations are always looking for money and connections, they are equally interested in enthusiasm. And you can often make up with enthusiasm and dedication what you can't offer with money or connections.

Marissa said she'd give it try. A year later, I received an e-mail from her. She was now chairwoman of the charity's big annual fund-raising event. "You wouldn't believe how much time this has taken up of my life," she wrote me, "but I've never been happier. I've met so many incredible people. I have even gotten a new job as a result of someone I met through the organization. But while it's been unbelievable for networking, the most important thing is that I feel like my life has more significance. I just feel better as a person."

SOMETIMES GETTING INVOLVED CAN COMPLETELY CHANGE YOUR LIFE

When he was a boy, Darren Port's best friend had diabetes, so in 1993 Darren decided to sign up for a "walkathon" sponsored by the New York chapter of the Juvenile Diabetes Foundation. This led Darren to get involved in the organization. Before long, Darren's youth and enthusiasm were attracting attention, and he was being tapped to do more. Soon, people twice his age were looking to him for leadership. By 1996, he was named chairman of the Walkathon.

As a result, Darren started to become well known in New York philanthropic and business circles. As he told me recently, "The people I've met in the last 10 years as a result of donating my time to charity have not only become close friends, they've also led to amazing business relationships. I've got a Rolodex filled with the names of some of the most important people in the city. Because they appreciate what I've done, I know I can count on their help if I ever need something."

Then Darren said something to me that is really important to know:

"Charities are driven by the people who get involved!"

As a result of his work with the Juvenile Diabetes Foundation, Darren has found his passion and his purpose. He recently founded a new company, called **PoweredbyProfessionals.com,** that is transforming how charities raise money. In just a year, he's helped worthy groups raise more than $3 million.

ARE YOU READY TO GET INVOLVED?

Here are some great web sites of organizations that can help you get started volunteering your time to help others.

www.networkforgood.org

Network for Good is an "e-philanthropy" site that lists worthy organizations to which you may want to donate your money or time. It also provides information about how to get involved with issues you care about. The site's goal is to connect people to charities—or, as the group puts it, it's dedicated "to using the virtual world to deliver real resources to nonprofits and communities."

www.volunteermatch.org

VolunteerMatch is a nonprofit online service that will match your individual interests, location, and schedule with community-service opportunities in your area. It has already generated hundreds of thousands of volunteer referrals nationwide.

www.volunteersolutions.org

Volunteer Solutions is another matching service that helps connect individuals to volunteer opportunities in their communities. You can search for opportunities based on your interests, skills, and location, or simply by entering a keyword. You can also register to receive e-mails that list volunteer opportunities that match your specific profile.

www.idealist.org

This is the web site for Action Without Borders, a service dedicated to connecting people, organizations, and resources to "help build a world where all people can live free and dignified lives." The site will enable you to search more than 40,000 nonprofit and community organizations in 165 countries, along with thousands of volunteer opportunities in your area and abroad.

www.charities.org

America's Charities is a nonprofit federation of both national and local charities. Its member charities receive donations through workplace-giving campaigns. Visit this site to find out how your company can sponsor a workplace-giving campaign for employees.

www.nationalservice.org

The Corporation for National and Community Service provides opportunities for Americans of all ages and backgrounds to serve their communities and country through three programs: Senior Corps (age 55 and older), AmeriCorps (age 17 and older), and Learn and Serve America (for students). You can access any of these three organizations through this one site.

www.nvoad.org

The National Voluntary Organizations Active in Disaster (NVOAD) coordinates planning efforts by many voluntary organizations that are involved in responding to disasters. Click on the "Members" link at their web site to get a list of the many fine groups that participate. The list consists of links to each member's web site, where you can learn more about them and how you can help.

www.mentoring.org

The National Mentoring Partnership is an advocate for mentoring and a resource for mentors and mentoring initiatives nationwide. Its web site allows you to explore available mentoring opportunities as well as to sign up for online training to become a better mentor.

www.campfire.org

Camp Fire USA is a not-for-profit youth development organization that currently serves some 735,000 children annually. Its mission is to build caring, confident youth and future leaders. Visit its site to find out how you can volunteer your time or make a donation.

www.savethechildren.org

Founded in 1932, Save the Children is a nonprofit child-assistance organization that strives to make lasting positive change in the lives of children in need. It operates in 17 states and more than 40 countries throughout the developing world to help improve the health, education, and economic opportunities of children and their families. In addition to allowing you to make online donations, the web site also offers many other ways for you to get involved in Save the Children's mission.

www.ymca.net

With more than 2,500 branches, the YMCA is the nation's largest not-for-profit community service organization, working to meet the health and social service needs of nearly 19 million men, women, and children in 10,000 communities throughout the United States. Y's are for people of all faiths, races, abilities, ages, and incomes. The YMCA web site offers ways to get involved either as a volunteer or as a donor.

www.americaspromise.org

America's Promise—the Alliance for Youth is a collaborative network that strives to fulfill what it calls the "Five Promises" for every young person in America: Caring Adults, Safe Places, Healthy Start, Marketable Skills, and Opportunities to Serve. This site offers many ways to donate your time and resources and to make a difference in the life of a child.

www.score.org

SCORE, which describes itself as "Counselors to America's Small Business," is a nonprofit association that provides entrepreneurs with free, confidential business counseling. Advice and workshops are offered at 389 chapter offices nationwide by volunteers who are experienced entrepreneurs and/or corporate managers and executives. If you want to share your business expertise and give back to your community, you might consider volunteering your services to SCORE or donating funds to the SCORE Foundation. This web site explains how you can do either.

www.standupforkids.org

Stand Up For Kids is a national volunteer organization committed to the rescue of homeless and at-risk youth. Run almost entirely by volunteers, it provides food, clothing, shelter, help in finding housing, education assistance, vocational development, counseling, health services, transportation to self-help meetings, and legal assistance. Volunteers also conduct life-skills training, such as budgeting, banking, apartment cleanliness and safety, shopping and cooking, nutrition, and hygiene. The web site offers many ways to get involved.

www.doctorswithoutborders.org
Doctors Without Borders is a private, nonprofit organization that delivers health care to remote, isolated areas where resources and training are limited. It also provides emergency aid to victims of armed conflict, epidemics, and natural and man-made disasters. You can volunteer to help or make a donation at its web site.

www.aarp.org/volunteer/
The American Association of Retired Persons (AARP) is a nonprofit advocacy organization for people age 50 and over "dedicated to enhancing quality of life for all as we age." An entire section of the AARP web site is devoted to community service, and it provides plenty of information about how you can donate your time and talents in your own community.

WHY THE "HAVE MORES" HAVE MORE

There's a hero in all of us that keeps us honest and makes us great.

I hope this chapter has inspired you to find your hero and give some of your money or time (or both!) to help others.

Over the years, I've seen firsthand that the "have mores" give more. I've also seen that the fastest way to feel rich is to give more—and that those who give more become rich faster. I don't think it's a coincidence. Research shows definitively that people who give of their time and money to help others, live longer, happier, and wealthier lives.

What more could you ask for?

CHAPTER TWENTY-TWO

START LATE, LIVE RICH!

So far on this journey, we've covered how to spend less, save more, earn more, and give more so you can start late and finish rich. All of this is important, but in truth my heartfelt goal for you involves much more than just money. What I really hope is that learning how to be smart with your money will help you **LIVE RICH**.

What do I mean by live rich? I mean living a life that's in line with your values—a life where you spend more time than you're spending now being the person you really want to be.

DON'T POSTPONE LIVING RICH—*START TODAY*

Here's a great truth about your life. You only get one. So why not LIVE A GREAT LIFE?

Your life isn't a dress rehearsal. Your life isn't a practice run. You can have a practice marriage, a practice career, and a practice business. But you don't get a practice life.

THERE IS NO
"DO OVER" BUTTON

If you screw up a computer game, you can always hit the reset button. But life doesn't have a reset button. So the question I have for you right now is this: *Are you having fun?*

Are you living a life you love—a life that brings you joy, fulfills you, and is in line with your core values? Are you the person you want to be? Are you doing what you long to do?

Are you living rich?

Be honest. There's no one watching you read this book right now. It's just you and me and your soul here. What did your soul answer?

Let's try the question again so you don't fly right by this. . . .

ARE YOU LIVING RICH?

This is not a small question. In fact, it's about as big as they come. The question of whether you're living rich—whether your life is fun—is not something we're normally raised to ask ourselves. It's the kind of question that if you stop and really answer it, can shake up your whole life.

We've been led by decades of marketing to believe that we will lead the good life when we are rich or retired. Not before.

We will be happy when we have more stuff. Not before.

We've been led to believe that in order to live rich, we must *be* rich. But you know what? It's simply not true. It's nothing more than an advertising message designed by smart, sophisticated Madison Avenue marketers who are ruining many people's lives.

Don't let it ruin yours.

The truth is that life doesn't start when you retire. Life doesn't and shouldn't start when you've got a lot of money in the bank. The truth is that your life has already started.

So what does it mean for YOU to live rich? In a few pages I'll ask you some questions that are designed to help you answer this for yourself. I'll also provide you with an exercise to help you move toward what matters most to you. But first let's look at why retirement is NOT always about living rich.

THE MYTH OF RETIREMENT

I believe retirement—at least the way it's been marketed to us—is a myth.

Here's how the myth goes:

You can and should put off what is really important in your life now—because someday, sometime in the future, if you save enough money, you'll get to do what you really want to do, give, and be.

Here's the truth about retirement:

If you put off what you want to do with your life for decades, with the idea that you'll enjoy your life after you retire, *you will ultimately miss your life!*

The happiest retirees are people who have lived full and meaningful lives. The only thing that changes for them when they reach retirement age is that they are able to start tapping their retirement funds without being penalized, and maybe they bid *adios* to their regular jobs. Otherwise, they simply continue doing what they have always done—leading full and meaningful lives.

In contrast, people who have put off having a life generally find retirement a shock. This is particularly true of men, many of whom find it such a shock that they literally drop dead within months of retiring.

RETIRE, RETIREMENT, RETIRING— WHO CAME UP WITH THIS?

The ironic thing about the concept of retirement is that even the definition of retirement is screwed up.

Here's how *Webster's New World Dictionary* defines the three words most people have been trained to want.

---

re-tire (ri-tïr), *v.i.* [RETIRED (-tïrd´), RETIRING],[Fr. *retirer; re-,* back + *tirer,* to draw], **1.** to go away or withdraw to a private, sheltered, or secluded place; hence, **2.** to go to bed. **3.** to give ground, as in battle; retreat; withdraw, **4.** to withdraw oneself from business, active service, or public life, especially because of advanced age . . .

re-tire-ment (ri-tïr´mənt), *n.* **1.** a retiring or being retired; withdrawal, removal, etc. **2.** privacy; seclusion. **3.** a place of privacy or seclusion.

---

re-tir-ing (ri-tür´iñg), **_adj._** [ppr . of _retire_], **1.** that retires. **2.** drawing back from contact with others, from publicity, etc.; reserved; modest; shy.

LIVING TO RETIRE IS NOT LIVING

If you read these definitions of retirement, you'll see there's something amiss. Retiring and retirement are described in terms that are almost entirely negative: it's all about seclusion, isolation, inactivity. That said, the good news is that people today are living longer then ever before. According to a recent study, anyone who reaches the age of 65 has a 25% chance of living to at least 92. (Married people who reach 65 have a 25% chance of living to be 97!) Moreover, the fastest-growing segment of our population is currently people over 90.

As a result of increasing longevity, the entire notion of retirement is undergoing a forced change. Today's 60- and 70- and 80-years-olds are not shuffling off to the shuffleboard court. A growing number of them are running, biking, jogging, rafting, race-car driving, having sex, volunteering, working—you name it, they're doing it and having fun in the process.

So what it means to retire is really changing and will continue to change, because older people (who are not feeling so old) are no longer willing to be put out to pasture. And that's a good thing. Many people in their sixties, seventies, and eighties are learning that life can really start at anytime—and that it is NEVER TOO LATE to live rich.

THE JOY CAN START NOW—
IT DOESN'T HAVE TO WAIT

The fact is, you don't have to have a fully funded 401(k) account to have joy. What really matters is that you have consistent joy in your life _now_, that you have some fun _now_—that you forget the idea that you're supposed to wait until you retire to have those things.

You can start going for it today. All it takes is knowing yourself and knowing what you want. And the best way I know to learn those things is by asking yourself some questions. Starting with . . .

WHEN WAS THE LAST TIME
YOU EXPERIENCED JOY?

There are some questions that stop you dead in your tracks. This is definitely one of them.

I know it stopped me.

It happened in 2001, while I was watching *The Oprah Winfrey Show* on TV. Oprah was telling a story about how she had been out running with her trainer one day back in 1992, and her trainer asked her if she could remember the last time she had experienced joy. Oprah thought about it and realized it had been more than seven years earlier!

When she shared this on her show, I couldn't believe it. Here was Oprah, a rich and famous woman, someone who was changing the world—and joy was missing in her life?

Oprah went on to explain how the trainer's question made her remember how much joy she had felt while she was filming *The Color Purple* in 1985, and how the memory of that joy and its meaning ultimately inspired her to change her own life. As she put it, it led her to take her TV show out of what she called the "yak, yak, yak" genre and transform it into a platform to help people truly lead better, more meaningful lives. The world is a better place today because of how this one woman was inspired by that question about joy.

THE NEXT DAY THE JOY QUESTION
HIT ME HARD

After I finished watching Oprah that day, I tried to go back to whatever I was doing. But that question—"When was the last time you experienced joy?"—continued to rattle around in my head.

The next day it hit me . . . hard.

I remember driving up to my office at Morgan Stanley, where I ran my financial planning business back in 2001. It was 5:45 in the morning. I had been on the road for three straight weeks, on a tour to promote my second book, *Smart Couples Finish Rich*. As a result, I now had three weeks of work to catch up on and a list of 27 clients who had scheduled appointments to see me my first week back.

As I sat in my car in the dark parking garage, I heard a voice in my head ask, "When was the last time *you* experienced joy, David?"

The answer came to me, clear as crystal: It had been two weeks earlier, while I was giving a speech in Virginia in front of more than a thousand couples.

Then the same internal voice asked, "When was the last time you had joy in the office you're about to enter?"

I couldn't remember the last time.

I sat in my car for fifteen minutes and watched the digital clock on my dashboard hit 6:00 A.M. I was 33 years old. I had two best-selling books, a hugely successful financial planning business, a wonderful wife, and money in the bank—and I was exhausted. What was I doing to myself? Why was I still working as a financial planner? It wasn't fun anymore. I wasn't getting the same fulfillment out of helping people one-on-one as I got helping thousands at a time. That's where the joy was. Not in my office, but out on the road, teaching, lecturing, writing, broadcasting, helping large numbers of people.

I'd like to be able to tell you I quit that very day, but sometimes it's not that easy. I had built a large business with hundreds of clients I cared about deeply as well as a team of loyal, hardworking employees. It would take me a full year to be really honest with myself about what gave me joy.

The more honest I became, the more I was motivated to decide to make a change. Ultimately, I decided to leave a business that was earning me a wonderful living. I also decided to leave San Francisco, where my wife and I had both been born and raised, and move to New York City, where we knew no one. Why? So I could focus the rest of my life on teaching people about how they could live and finish rich.

This decision wasn't based on money but on a sense of purpose and a sense of meaning. At the time, there was no way to know whether my income in this new life I was choosing would be one-tenth of what I had been earning as a partner of The Bach Group. But I did it anyway because I wasn't happy, and the idea that I should wait another 30 or 40 years to be happy just didn't make any sense to me. It didn't make sense to wait to live rich.

So far, my decision to follow my heart seems to have worked out pretty well.

HOW TO TAKE BETTER CARE OF YOURSELF

Most people really believe that if they just had more money, the things that make them unhappy would disappear and their lives would be better. The truth is that your life can be better without your somehow getting more money. It can be better today, but you need to make some decisions and take some actions.

You don't need me to tell you what will make you happy. *Only you know the truth.*

ASK BETTER QUESTIONS, YOU WILL GET BETTER ANSWERS

Most people ask themselves the wrong questions. If you ask yourself a question like "Why does my life always stink?," your brain will search the files in your head and come up with an answer. It's just like Google, the great Internet search engine, except it's better. But like Google, your brain answers only the questions you ask it.

So I want you to ask yourself some better questions. I know from experience that doing this can lead you to some amazing discoveries—and motivate you to do what it takes to create a new life for yourself.

The questions I have in mind are similar to the questions I asked myself back in 2001 when I discovered the "when was the last time you experienced joy?" question.

Are you ready? Let's go.

THE "LIVE RICH" QUESTIONS

What makes you happy?
Be honest. Think about all areas of your life.
What makes you happy at work?
What makes you happy at home?
What makes you happy with friends and family?
What makes you happy when you are by yourself?
What do you love to do?
What would you do with your life today if you were not afraid of failure?

What is not working in your life?

What are you currently doing that prevents you from experiencing joy?

What is working in your life?

Who is not working in your life? Often there are people in our lives who don't add value. In fact, they subtract from our life's joy. Be honest.

Who right now in your life is subtracting value from your life and adding misery to it?

Can you fix any of these relationships or should you let them go out of your life?

What relationships *are* working in your life? Just as there are people who don't work in our lives, there are people in our lives who do. They bring value and joy to you. The clearer you are about why these people bring joy into your life, the easier it will be to appreciate and enjoy your relationships with them—and attract more people like them into your life.

If we were getting together one year from today, what would have to happen for you to be able to tell me that you now have more joy in your life?

What is the single most important thing you've learned about yourself as a result of answering these questions?

WRITE IT DOWN

Later, after you've taken the time to think about these questions, consider writing out your answers in a journal. Getting your answers down on paper will really help you connect to your truths. You'll find—as many of my students and clients have—that in putting them down on paper, your answers become clear more quickly and the actions you need to take more obvious and easier to initiate.

THE PURPOSE OF YOUR LIFE IS JOY

This may sound far-fetched, but it's not. I believe you are here to have a life of meaning and joy—to do great things, to be a great person. To live rich.

How do you find this fulfillment? You don't find it. You live it.

Joy is not out there somewhere under a rock. It is not found in any one specific thing, like getting a new job, starting a new marriage, losing 30 pounds, or having a child. It is inside of you waiting to come out. Joy comes from doing what you are meant to be doing with your life.

This is your mission in life: to find what you are meant to be doing while you are here. It is the hardest thing there is to do, and it is the most important thing to do. If what you are doing today doesn't create joy in your life, then you may not have found what you are meant to be doing. If you have not found what you are meant to be doing, it can be tough to live rich.

HOW TO CREATE THE "LIVE RICH FACTOR" IN YOUR LIFE

I believe each of us has the power to discover our purpose and become joyful in the process of journeying toward that purpose. It is not easy, however. Nothing important and meaningful ever is.

What you need to do is create what I call the "LIVE RICH Factor" in your life. I call it this because those who find the purpose that leads them to joy are truly the luckiest people in the world because they are living richly.

There are four basic principles involved in creating your LIVE RICH Factor.

PRINCIPLE ONE
BECOME CONNECTED WITH YOUR TRUTH.

The hardest thing to do is to be honest with yourself. We lie more to ourselves than to anyone else. You must tell yourself the truth about whether or not you are happy. If you are not happy, you must admit it to yourself. To really be connected to your truth, you must tell yourself the truth and you must tell the world the truth. You must have what I call "truth congruence"—which means that who you are on the inside matches who you show to the world on the outside. *The Live Rich Questions* I posed earlier can lead you to be instantly honest with yourself—provided you answer them honestly. (You did do this, right? If not, make sure you do after you finish reading this book.)

PRINCIPLE TWO
STOP JUDGING YOURSELF.

You are your own harshest critic. I said this earlier, but it needs to be said again. Many people talk to themselves in a way they would never accept from a stranger, a friend, or a loved one. If this describes you, try stopping the negative conversations you have with yourself immediately. For one week, simply commit to saying "Stop it!" when you think a negative thought about yourself. If you are in the habit of saying negative things to yourself, you will find this is one of the most difficult exercises you will ever do. Carry a pad with you at all times and make a mark each time you catch yourself "thinking negative." You'll find that as the days go on your negative thinking can quickly be reduced. The motivational expert Zig Ziglar uses a phrase I love about people having "stinking thinking." Your job is to cut out that stinking thinking.

PRINCIPLE THREE
STOP JUDGING OTHERS.

It's hard to be joyful when you're always judging others. In fact, it's close to impossible. Judging others creates a huge amount of stress in our lives. It affects our marriages and our relationships with our kids as well as the way we relate to friends, coworkers, and society in general.

We are not here to judge one another.

The next time you find yourself upset at someone or some situation, catch yourself and ask, "Are you judging?" Judging others is often an unconscious habit. But it's a habit that can be changed the moment you decide to stop doing it.

PRINCIPLE FOUR
PURSUE FUN WITH A VENGEANCE.

It's okay to pursue fun. It's what children do.

My greatest joy these days is the simple pleasure of going to the park with my little son, Jack. The park is free; the time I spend with Jack in the park is priceless.

Why do we stop pursuing fun as we get older? Fun shouldn't be squeezed into a few weeks of vacation each year. It shouldn't be squeezed into the last chapter of your life when you will supposedly have enough money to "retire." Fun deserves to be a part of your life now. Most of the things in life that are fun can be done for little or no money.

But fun doesn't just happen. You must make having it a priority in your life or it will go missing. And life is too short to not have it.

CONGRATULATIONS— YOU HAVE SHOWN UP

You've really come a long way since you began reading this book. Together, we've gone on a journey that has included learning how to spend less, how to save more, how to earn more, and how to live and give more.

Many people buy books like this one with great intentions, but most never actually follow through. If they do pick up the book, they may flip through several pages and then put it back down again. Others will skim the book and think about some of the ideas.

Then there are the people like you who actually read the book all the way through, think about what they've read, and *act on it!*

It is the acting on the new ideas and insights you've acquired that will change your life. Many people make the mistake of judging new ideas before they even try them. That's too bad, because to get new results in life, you have to show up with new ideas and new effort.

I hope I've inspired you to try some new ideas and to make some new efforts. I hope I've inspired you to believe you have a chance to have a new beginning.

YOU CAN DO IT . . . PROVIDED YOU DON'T MAJOR IN MINOR THINGS

If it's so easy to start late and live and finish rich, why do so many people think it's impossible? The answer is that most people are too busy to put time and energy into what matters most.

We clutter up our lives with things that we think are important instead of living what is really important.

We major in minor things.

This book is meant to be a road map to a life of more wealth, more freedom, and more joy. While it shouldn't be too hard, you can't follow this map without making an effort. Which is as it should be, because life is not effortless.

Life is rich—but life is not easy.

Few people tell the truth about this.

For many of you, this book will be the key to a new beginning. You will experiment with these new ideas and try them on for size. Your results will be proportionate to the energy and effort you put in.

As you try out these ideas, I'd love to hear from you—about your successes, inspirations, and insights. You can e-mail me at success@ finishrich.com. I wake up each morning and read the e-mails my readers send me. Your e-mails are my favorite part of the day—they inspire me to do what I do. They also enable me to learn more each day as you, my readers, share with me what is working—and not working—in your lives. I want you to know from my heart that I have incredible respect for you. Though ours is a journey worth pursuing and sharing, relatively few people are willing to put in the effort that it requires. You are a special person who has chosen to live more, do more, and be more.

Until we meet again: Enjoy your life and your journey. *Remember, as long as you start today, it is not too late for you to live and finish rich.*

Your journey is just beginning—have fun—and **LIVE RICH!**

CHAPTER TWENTY-THREE

YOU STARTED LATE ...
BUT YOUR KIDS
DON'T HAVE TO

If only I had started earlier.

If only someone had taught this to me when I was young.

It would have been so much easier.

Well, now you know how to catch up. And since you do, the million-dollar question for you is this: Who can you go to and teach right now about what you've learned so they don't wind up starting late on their journey to living and finishing rich?

Do you have children? Nieces or nephews? Younger neighbors or co-workers?

The fact is, you now know more than enough to really help a younger relative or friend start *young* and finish rich.

You can teach someone else to save more, spend less, earn more, and—most important—live and give more.

Just think how much better the world would be if we started teaching our kids about money in school—when they are still young enough for it to make a real difference in their lives. Unfortunately, our school systems are not generally required to provide financial education, nor are they set up or funded to do so (at least not yet). So we as smart adults have to take matters into our own hands and do it ourselves. Here's how.

ELEVEN LESSONS TO RAISE SMART KIDS TO *LIVE* AND FINISH RICH

LESSON NO. I
TEACH THEM TO "OWN THE PLACE"

When I was seven, my grandma taught me a lesson that would ultimately shape the course of my life. One day at McDonald's, my favorite restaurant in the whole world, she said to me, "David, there are three types of people who come to McDonald's: the people who work here, the people who eat here, and the people who own the place. If you want to be rich, you want to own the place."

Later that night, she opened the *Wall Street Journal* and showed me how to look up the price of McDonald's stock and explained what it meant to buy shares in a publicly traded company. "If you started saving your allowance," she said, "you could buy stock in McDonald's, and when your friends ate there, you could make money from them."

That was all it took. I was hooked.

Over the next few months, I saved my allowance as well as my birthday money, and with a little help from her and my father (the stockbroker), I bought my first share of McDonald's stock. When I turned nine, I realized what was true of McDonald's was probably also true of Disneyland—and soon I bought some stock in Mickey Mouse's house.

The rest, as they say, is history. I've been investing ever since.

The moral for you is this: The time to teach your kids about money and investing is now. The message is simple: Every product or service you buy is provided by some company—and as my grandma said, when it comes to companies, you can be an employee, a consumer, or an owner.

Teach your kids to become owners.

This is not difficult. Look around you. Are your kids playing video games? Well then, teach them that they can buy stock in the company that makes the video games (e.g., Electronic Arts). Are they listening to music on their iPods (Apple Computers), or composing their book reports on Word (Microsoft), or yakking on their cell phones (Samsung or Nokia or Verizon)? The point is that every day they are making companies rich. Teach them how to own these companies and they will make themselves rich as well.

You may create a future millionaire.

LESSON NO. 2
TEACH THEM TO PAY THEMSELVES
FIRST . . . AUTOMATICALLY

You can't get rich if you don't Pay Yourself First. You now know this. But your kids don't. Teach them that the moment they earn a dollar, they should Pay Themselves First.

To keep it simple, explain that the secret to becoming rich is to pay yourself first 10% of what you earn. If they earn $10, they should save the first dollar they are paid and live off the remaining nine. Explain that if you do this, you will never have to worry about money—ever! Share with them the truth that you've learned from Chapter 9, that the only way people consistently save money when they become adults is to pay themselves first automatically.

Pay Yourself First . . . Automatically is so simple a concept that it should be ingrained in us in school. We shouldn't be allowed out of the eighth grade without knowing it. Unfortunately, you won't find it on any curriculum, so it's up to you to teach it today to a child you love.

LESSON NO. 3
TEACH THEM THE "MIRACLE" OF COMPOUND INTEREST

One of the most astonishing facts of life is what has come to be known as the miracle of compound interest. Show your child what this means. Kids may not get it when you say, "Pay Yourself First." They may not get it when you tell them that it's easy to become a millionaire if you start saving when you are young.

You have to show them the math.

So show them the math. Literally. Show them the table on page 39 in Chapter Three and let them see what an enormous pile of money they can accumulate if they start saving just a few dollars a month when they are young.

Tell the kids you're mentoring that the smartest financial decision they will ever make is to buy a home. Hammer this message into their heads. Do they get a kick out of watching Donald Trump on *The Apprentice*? Tell them what made Trump rich was real estate and that it all starts with buying their first home. Share with them how to go do this. If you skipped over the section on real estate and buying a home, go back and read Chapters 11 and 12.

Also teach your kids the power of a biweekly mortgage payment plan—how it can change their lives by enabling them to pay off their mortgages years early, thus saving them tens of thousands (maybe hundreds of thousands) of dollars.

LESSON NO. 5
TEACH THEM ABOUT CREDIT CARDS
AND THE PERILS OF DEBT

One way that we are truly failing our kids is by raising them to be credit card addicts. Our children see us using our credit cards irresponsibly. What they don't see is the stress and pressure that the resulting debt creates in our lives.

Teach them how credit cards also have a "miracle of compound interest"—only in reverse.

According to a survey by college loan provider Nellie Mae, the average college student owes $2,700 on his credit cards—with 10% of them owing more than $7,000. Share with your kids that trying to pay off a $7,000 credit card debt at a typical 20% rate by making the minimum monthly payment will take them more than 34 years and cost them more than $20,000.

Explain that credit cards are okay if they are used responsibly, but that the minimum payment they see on their bills is a trap designed to keep them in debt forever. Most important, explain that if they are late paying their credit card bills—or worse, simply stop paying them at all—they will ruin their credit records, which can make life really, really difficult. Explain how a bad credit record can affect their ability to get a job (because employers routinely check the credit reports of job applicants, and judge them accordingly) as well as their ability to buy a home or car (because having a bad credit record makes it much harder to get mortgages or car loans).

In short, make them understand that just because a bank or a store is willing to give them credit cards doesn't mean they can really afford to use them.

LESSON NO. 6
TEACH THEM ABOUT THE LATTE FACTOR

While you know all about the Latte Factor, chances are that the kids you are mentoring don't. So explain the metaphor to them today. Make it a game. Ask them to track their Latte Factor for one day (you can download the Latte Factor Challenge form from **www.finishrich.com**) and then report back to you on what they spent their money on. Have them run the Latte Factor Calculator to figure out what a huge nest egg they could amass if they saved the money they now spend on things they don't really need.

They'll be shocked—and motivated—when they discover that doing this could really make them millionaires. I know because I get e-mails daily from young people who tell me that a parent or mentor encouraged them to go through this exercise, and what an eye-opener it was for them. It really is a wake-up call.

LESSON NO. 7
TEACH THEM THAT IF THEY CAN'T PAY CASH FOR SOMETHING, THEY SHOULDN'T BUY IT

We live today in a "have it now" society. Your kids are watching MTV, and what they see there are pop stars with their "bling-bling." With their $100,000 watches and gold necklaces, these people are not the role models you want your kids to emulate. Teach them that many of these "bling-bling" guys and gals will be broke in ten years. It's the truth and your kids need to know it.

Teach them that it's not about the money. Your kids may think they want to be rich—and that's a great motivator—but what they really want (and what you should want for them) is freedom. Teach your kids that the real reason they should be saving their money—instead of spending it on luxuries they can't really afford—is that saving leads to financial security, and financial security provides freedom. Explain how having money in the bank will give them the ability to do what they want to do when they want to do it.

LESSON NO. 8
TEACH THEM TO TITHE
A PERCENTAGE OF WHAT THEY EARN

Teach the child you mentor the importance of giving back. Tithing shouldn't have to be taught in churches or temples; it should be taught at home. Our kids need to learn at a young age why it's so important to give back a percentage of what they earn. Teach them to do this and together we'll make the world a happier and better place.

LESSON NO. 9
TEACH THEM WHAT YOU DID WRONG WITH YOUR MONEY

Chances are if you bought this book, you started later on your financial life than you wish you had. Tell the child you mentor the truth. What did you do wrong? What would you do differently if you had the chance? You've got decades of real-life experience, so share what you've learned. Give the gift of your hard-won knowledge to someone you love. You may change their life forever.

LESSON NO. 10
TEACH THEM THAT IF THEY DON'T CONTROL THEIR OWN
DESTINY, SOMEONE ELSE WILL

Too many parents raise their kids to go to school, earn good grades, and get a good job. This is not a formula for living rich.

The rich teach their kids to be owners. The middle class teach their kids to be employees.

So teach your child to be an entrepreneur. The fact is that these days it's far riskier to be an employee than to be an entrepreneur.

In this uncertain and competitive world, entrepreneurship is the key to prosperity and security—and ultimately it will be the key to your child's future. The world needs more dreamers, more doers, more builders—and that means more entrepreneurs.

LESSON NO. 11
TEACH THEM TO DREAM BIG DREAMS

The world needs more dreamers. Let the adults be realistic. We need our kids to believe and know that they really can be "anything" and "anyone" they want to be. Our greatest purpose in life is to use the gifts our creator gave us to be who we were put here to be. For many of our kids, this means dreaming of a life bigger than the one they are currently living.

Please—as an adult, be a dream creator and not a dream stealer. Your words of encouragement to a young person may shape not only the child's destiny, but the world's. You don't know who you are talking to when you speak to a young person. You might be speaking to the next Dr. Martin Luther King or President John F. Kennedy or Oprah Winfrey or Michael Jordon or Lance Armstrong. You don't know what the child you love can do. Only the child can know, and she or he might not know it yet. SO ENCOURAGE THE DREAM!

WHO WILL YOU TEACH TODAY?

Mentor a child to become a dreamer who lives and finish rich—*please.* Commit right now to do this. Fill out the commitment form on the following page. Sign and date it, and then share with me what happens when you take action. You can submit your story to me on our web site at **www.finishrich.com** or e-mail me at success@finishrich.com.

Better yet, have the person you mentor send us their story so we can use their successes to encourage other young people to dream bigger and live richer.

Thanks—I'm proud of you!

THE MENTOR COMMITMENT

I, _____, hereby commit to teach _____ (insert child's name) to be smart with his or her money. I will share this book and the lessons I've learned no later than _____(insert date).

Signed, _____

Date _____

A START *YOUNG,* FINISH RICH SUCCESS STORY

I will be a senior in high school in Baltimore, Maryland. My summer reading for my Economics class included your book, *The Automatic Millionaire.* Out of the eight ridiculously boring books plus yours (which I don't count as boring) that I have to read before the start of term, I chose to read your book first because, even at seventeen, I have a love affair with money that would make my boyfriend jealous.

Your book is, without a doubt, the worthwhile read of my life. The most basic and necessary aspects of a consumer society are never taught in school. Most young people I know are intimidated by money because they are under the impression that it's too complicated. Thus they get stuck in the cycle of, as you said, "living paycheck to paycheck."

This book really gave me a clear direction for my financial future. Hopefully, by starting early, I'll be another automatic millionaire you helped. I want to be able to take care of my parents the way they cared for me, so that will be my incentive to be successful with your plan. So thank you for sharing your expertise with America. We desperately need honest and simple financial advice. I look forward to retiring a millionaire! Thanks again.

Kat Harrington
Baltimore, MD

THE FINISH RICH
ANNUAL SURVEY

The Finish Rich Annual Survey was conducted for FinishRich, Inc. by Temple University in June, 2004. This survey included more than 1,000 people between the ages of 21 and 69. Respondents were nearly evenly split between men and women, of whom:

- 68% are married or cohabitating.
- 70% have dependent children.
- 55% have a college degree or have completed post-graduate work.
- 72% are employed or self-employed.

SUMMARY

- "Living paycheck to paycheck" keeps more than 70% of respondents from saving.
- Over 90% of respondents wish they had started saving while in their twenties.
- Half of all respondents feel they are "starting late."

- Only 56% are saving for retirement.
- 96% feel that Social Security will cover less than half their retirement expenses; 80% believe Social Security will cover less than a quarter.
- Two thirds believe they will have to work to at least age 70.
- Three quarters believe they will be less well off than their parents were at retirement.

THE STORY BEHIND THE NUMBERS

A quick analysis of the key findings:

How well are Americans saving?
Americans aren't saving enough.

- As expected, older people tend to have more saved than younger people, but overall saving levels tend to be low—more than half of all people polled report less than $10,000 in total savings (excluding the value of their homes). Three in ten report less than $1,000 in total savings.
- Roughly half of all people polled are concerned about their current level of savings, but don't feel they can contribute any more, mostly due to income level, costs of raising a family, and education costs.
- Roughly eight out of ten people save 10% or less of their income each year.
- Nine out of ten people report they would have started saving in their twenties if they could "do it all over again."
- One out of five report that they cannot save due to credit card debt.

How do Americans feel about their retirement?
Most Americans are pessimistic about their ability to retire.

- Low savings rates, high debt, longer lives, and rising medical costs will dramatically affect Americans' ability to retire. Roughly half of all people polled feel they will not be able to retire until they are at least 70. Fifteen percent say they do not ever expect to be able to retire.
- Only three out of ten people polled are confident Social Security will be there for them upon retirement.

- Only three out of ten people polled contribute the maximum amount allowed by their employer to their 401(k).
- Roughly nine out of ten people polled feel they will NOT meet their retirement goals.

Are Americans using debt wisely?
Most Americans have significant levels of credit card debt.

- Over two-thirds of Americans polled are in debt and use credit cards to fund "day-to-day" expenses.
- Approximately eight out of ten people have at least two credit cards.
- Two-thirds of people report they have at least $5,000 in credit card debt.
- One out of five cannot save at all due to credit card debt.

Do Americans feel they have a good plan for the future?
Most Americans feel they are financially ill prepared for the future.

- Eight out of ten people polled do not have a written financial plan.
- Roughly half of all people polled are concerned about their current level of savings, but don't feel they can contribute any more in the future, mostly due to income level, costs of raising a family, and education costs.
- Seven out of ten Americans report that they would need at least three years of expenses to quit their job, but most have less than three months of expenses in savings.

Do Americans expect Social Security to be there for them?
Not a chance, Jack.

- Only three out of ten people polled are confident Social Security will be there for them upon retirement.
- Eight out of ten people feel that Social Security will only cover 25% or less of their retirement expenses.

ACKNOWLEDGMENTS

To everyone who has helped me to help others live and finish rich, I say a sincere—THANK YOU.

Start Late, Finish Rich is the seventh book I've written in the *FinishRich Series®* in seven years. Today there are over two million books in print, translated into ten languages, as the message of "living and finishing rich" reaches around the world and changes lives. This has not been accomplished on my own—there have been so many who have helped me along the way. This is merely a short list—and if I've left you out on paper, please know I haven't left you out in my heart.

First, to my loyal readers, I send a profound thanks. Thank you for e-mailing me on a daily basis and telling me your success stories. Thank you for coming to my seminars, sometimes driving hours to meet me. Thank you for taking the time to stop me on the street to let me know about how my books are helping you. Most important, thank you for letting me know what it is you need and then giving me the opportunity and privilege to deliver it. You've taken me on a ride I never expected, and I am so grateful.

To Oprah Winfrey and her incredible team at Harpo—God bless you! To have the privilege to launch the message of *The Automatic Millionaire* on your show—and then a few months later to do a second show on *Smart Couples Finish Rich*—was a dream come true. You helped me to reach the world with my message, and I will never forget it. Not a day goes by that I don't receive an e-mail, a letter, or a phone call from someone who wants to let me know how the shows we did changed their life. To Ellen, Katy, Candi, Paul, Dana, and Becky—you are a team of "stars" that I will always be grateful to—you are the hardest-working, smartest people in television, and it is a true joy to work with you.

To my team at the Doubleday Broadway Group—where do I start? It's been an amazing partnership, and in 2004 you did publishing as well as any author could ask for. To my publisher, Stephen Rubin, I say a sincere, deep thank you for listening to me and my ideas—and working on almost all of them (not a small thing). To my editor, Kris Puopolo, we've now done four books together. What an honor it's been. You are world-class; my books are what they are because of your intelligent input and your championship attitude. To David Drake, my PR guru, we are now working on book number six! Thank you for helping me reach the world for the last six years; I would never be here without you! There are so many others to thank—Michael Palgon, Bill Thomas, Beth Haymaker, Chris Fortunato, Jean Traina, Catherine Pollack, and Janelle Moburg. Thank you all for working so tirelessly to make the FinishRich Series such a success.

To Allan Mayer, we've now worked on five books together. This one was really tough, with a really tight time frame, but we pulled it off—and then some. I'm so proud of our work together and our partnership, and I thank you for it. In truth, "thank you" feels small compared to how much we've done together and how many people we've helped—but thank you!

To Jan Miller, my agent and advisor, you've coached me to say "no" in the last few years to 95% of the opportunities that have come my way. That is integrity at its best—and you've been right every time. I know your clients always say "thank you,"—but, honestly, THANK YOU. You've really helped me make this happen. To Shannon Miser-Marvin, you and Jan have coached me since 1997—and I'm so grateful for your guidance. To Stephen Breimer, thank you for having my back on every deal we do. I feel very protected, and I am grateful for your guidance. To Harry Cornelius, we continue to do what we do, and you continue to "be right" about what is possible—thank you!

Next, there's my growing team at FinishRich, Inc.—a dream team that supports me and makes all of this possible. First, to Liz Dougherty—the honest truth is that without you much of this would not have been possible. Thank you for working harder than anyone could ever ask. To Stephanie Oakes, who came on board during the firestorm, you stuck it out and thrived—and I'm so grateful for your contributions. To my dear friend Steven Krein, who came on when I was at the brink of imploding from growth and opportunity, you truly saved the day. We will be able to help millions of people going forward because you "get it." To Unity Stoakes, Jim Pharo, and Jennifer Carcano, who came to help not really knowing what we were doing but feeling it was right, thank you for believing in our mission and working so tirelessly to help others. To team FinishRich, Inc., now and in the future—seriously, thank you! To the thousands of financial advisors who continue to teach the FinishRich Seminars®—my deepest gratitude goes out to you for your dedication to helping others and spreading the message of my books.

To my friends and family, you know who you are and you know how much I love you. I'm the luckiest guy in the world to have you in my life, and I'm forever grateful for your love and encouragement. Special thanks go out to my parents, Bobbi & Marty Bach. Every child should be so lucky to have parents who love and cheer them on like you have with me. I am able to do what I do today because of your profound love and support.

Last, to my wife, Michelle. Any sane wife would have told her husband he was crazy to want to leave a secure career to move to New York to write books and try to change the world. But you said, "I just want you to be happy, and I think we should do this." Now that our gamble is paying off—and coming to seem like such an obvious thing to do—I realize how risky it was, and I'm so profoundly grateful to you for supporting my desire to do this. You are the best, and I love you. To Jack, my little one-year-old—wow! You bring joy to your mother and me. Thanks for coming into our lives. We love you.

Finally, to those of you I haven't yet met, thank you for being interested in my message of hope. I'm grateful for the chance to be your coach, and I look forward to meeting you someday.

Live Rich,
David Bach
New York

Finishing Rich is as Easy as 1-2-3-! at FinishRich.com

Step 1 Go to our web site at **www.finishrich.com.** There you can join our FinishRich Community by registering for my powerful FREE FinishRich Newsletter. Each month I'll send you my thoughts on the economy as well as useful ideas to help you succeed both personally and financially—AND you'll receive any updates we make to any of the FinishRich books.

Step 2 Attend a FinishRich Live Event in your area. Each month, courses based on my books are taught throughout North America, and 95% of them are FREE. Find the updated listing at www.finishrich.com.

Step 3 Download the FREE *Start Late, Finish Rich* audio program called "The Five Secret Questions to Start Late and Finish Rich." These Five Questions are designed to get you to take immediate action toward realizing your dreams and going for the life that you deserve.

How to Reach Us

Go to **www.finishrich.com** or e-mail us at *success@finishrich.com*. I love hearing about your successes, and I learn from your suggestions and questions. I promise—if you send it, we will read it!

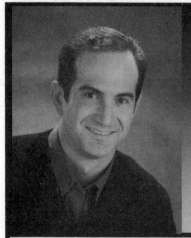

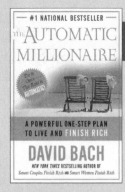

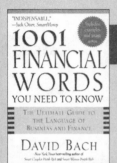

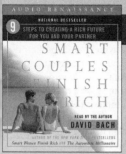

What Others Are Saying About David Bach's Books

I just wanted to take a minute to tell you how much I enjoyed your book, *The Automatic Millionaire*. I have never been interested in finance, investing, saving, or planning for retirement. In fact, I thought those who took an interest in money matters were self-indulgent, stingy, and shallow.

However, my 50th birthday (!) is only a few years away so "retirement" started to really enter my awareness. I saw you on the *Today* show and thought *The Automatic Millionaire* sounded so easy that maybe even I could do it. A few weeks later I saw the book and purchased it. It was an informative and easy read...and surprisingly uplifting!

In a few short weeks, I've opened an ING Direct account with automatic payroll deductions, increased my employer-matched retirement fund payroll percentage (TIAA-CREF), and made substantial headway in paying off my credit card debt (now at $1,200 and falling rapidly). I'm excited to begin this adventure—thank you!

Tom Mantoni
Eaton, PA

After reading *The Automatic Millionaire*, I called my bank and increased my monthly mortgage payment so that it will end up being more than 2 extra payments per year, automatic, of course. I also called ING Direct and set my savings account on automatic deduction from my bank 2 times per month. My husband called his HR department and increased his 401(k) contributions to 12% per month.

I am 68. Tom is 61. But it's never too late, right?

Thanks so much,

Thomas H. Claus and Gail Ingis-Claus
Fairfield, CT

Your book, *Smart Women Finish Rich*, has changed my life. I read it three months ago and since then I have paid down $3,000 in credit card debt, renegotiated the rate on that credit card, established an "Emergency Basket" that already has over $1,000 in it, and opened a Roth IRA to be funded each year. Before reading your book, I had no savings whatsoever and the balance of my credit card was around $4,000. I just want to thank you for teaching me how to fund my future and my dreams!

Christi Dean
Newbury Park, CA

Thank you so much! I always thought I had control and knew what to do with our money, but I really didn't. My wife was only contributing 6% into her 401(k) while I was contributing only 8%. We had all of our savings earning less than 1%. After reading your book, we moved 6 months' worth of joint expenditures into a money market account, earning over 2% (and only going up from here). I upped my 401(k) contribution to 10% and my wife and I opened up 2 separate Roth IRA's for retirement, maxing them out by automatically deducting money every month. We are only 27 years old, we own our own home, and are on our way to financial freedom.

Thank you!

Jim and Kim O'Hara
Melville, NY

Smart Women Finish Rich inspired me in a way you could never imagine. I completed the worksheets, examined my goals, and organized my financial folders. I started a savings account while further reducing my spending. Progress was apparent, but I wanted more! Then I read *The Automatic Millionaire*. Again ...wow! I can do this! Bottom line...entire credit card debt has been paid off, resulting in excellent credit reports. My biweekly mortgage payments are significantly decreasing my principal. I started contributing to a retirement account at work, raising my contributions every time I get a raise (I'm up to 17%). I have an automatic deduction to a savings account as well AND I'm having fun! I have become a certified diver, learned to play golf, and am living life to the fullest. People now ask ME, a single woman, how I do so well financially. I tell everyone about your books and the Latte Factor. I'm such a believer in the principles of your books, I even give *Smart Couples Finish Rich* as an engagement present. Now that's a gift that keeps on giving!

Kathleen Milner
Plymouth, MA

I read *Smart Women Finish Rich* two years ago about the same time my divorce was final. I had some credit card debt, no savings, was not contributing to my 401(k), and was renting a very small house for my daughters and myself. Your book put me on a path to financial independence. Along this path, I have found my self-esteem renewed and my self-confidence returned. It was difficult for me to see past the daily financial struggle of living paycheck to paycheck. With your advice, I have been able to accomplish the following:

✓ Organized financial filing system
✓ Paid all recurring bills automatically
✓ Increased my 401(k) contribution to 12% (company contributes 3%)
✓ Purchased a home and refinanced mortgage to a 15-year loan
✓ Rolled over two 401(k) plans from previous employers into a traditional IRA
✓ Purchased additional life insurance
✓ Began taking my daughters on an annual vacation (St. Louis, Chicago, Disney / Orlando)
✓ Paid all credit card bills in full each month maintaining a zero balance
✓ Purchased a new car, only financing $10,000 over 3 years.

I still have a few things on my "Finish Rich To Do List" but I believe I am definitely on the right path. I must admit that I love the journey and I feel very grateful that you have shared your financial knowledge with me. In turn, I have shared your book with several friends and family members hoping to help others as you have helped me.

Amy Manske
Prairie Village, KS

Your book, *Smart Couples Finish Rich*, was a gift from my Dad and it is changing our lives. My husband and I read the first 100 pages the first few days we had the book. We quickly drew out our value circles (a life-changing exercise in itself) and reorganized our filing system. We have big goals and dreams and in order to get there we have to take care of BIG debts standing in our way but since starting your book, we can see the light! Now more than ever, we are on our way to success. We are thrilled with your ideas and we can't wait to start teaching our son about investing early. Thank you, thank you, thank you!! This is one of the best gifts my Dad could have gotten us.

Michelle Collazo
Tucson, AZ

Your book inspired me to take many steps toward becoming an Automatic Millionaire. In one week I have started paying 10% more on my 15-year mortgage, increased my 403(b) to 10% and consolidated my debt at 0% interest and it is all AUTOMATIC. I feel less stress and anxiety over my financial future.

RJ Sykes
Houston, TX

Following the steps outlined in *Smart Women Finish Rich* inspired me to pay off my debt in its entirety, revamp my ailing credit history and save toward retirement when beforehand, I'd been living paycheck to paycheck for most of my life. Right now I'm experiencing yet another layoff, which before reading your books would have set me back for years. I now have the luxury of choosing from good options and can support myself for a couple of years, if necessary. I'm looking forward to becoming an automatic investor in the near future. Thank you so much for the information and inspirational books.

Kristin Wall
Stockton, CA

On behalf of me and my future wife, I wanted to thank you for making my life automatic. My father has been trying to teach me about money for years but I always thought it was too complicated or that I didn't have the extra income to make a difference. Little did I know that it was so easy. I was a quarter of the way through *The Automatic Millionaire* when I was so moved by your *"How many hours per day do you work for YOURSELF"* formula that I literally got up, went to my computer, and cranked up my 401(k) contribution from 4% to 15%! At the same time I also set up an additional deduction to my savings account. My fiancée and I live the exact same lifestyle as we lived before. However, our lives are richer knowing that there will be a pot of gold waiting for us at retirement. We're also looking to buy our first home next year and it makes it so much easier knowing that the money is there waiting for us. *The Automatic Millionaire* should be mandatory reading for every high school and college student across the country. The information is too good to pass up and it sure as heck beats chemistry. From the bottom of my heart…thank you. You've changed my life.

Chris Kesler
Austin, TX

The Automatic Millionaire
Home Study Course

In this home study audio program packed with how-to tips, David takes a personal approach to the insights he shared in *The Automatic Millionaire*. You'll be coached by David as though he's in your home, car, or office as he reveals even more strategies, secrets, and tactics to help you turn an ordinary income into a lifetime of financial freedom…easily and automatically. The complete Automatic Millionaire Home Study Course is filled with critical tools and additional information you won't find anywhere else, including:

✓ <u>8 extraordinary audio sessions</u>
✓ <u>An Exclusive Bonus Session: How to Put Your Financial House in Order</u>
✓ <u>Accompanying Workbook on CD-ROM</u>

Best of all, with The Automatic Millionaire Home Study Course, you'll have David Bach as your personal, one-on-one financial coach. Through these audio sessions, he'll be available to you whenever you need him, so you'll never forget your focus or lose momentum. You can check in anytime you want a strategy review, a shot of power, or a fresh dose of inspiration. And you can listen anywhere—while you're commuting, traveling—or even exercising!

Also included in the Automatic Millionaire Home Study Course is a copy of the #1 Bestseller, *The Automatic Millionaire,* and our exclusive Latte Factor Travel Mug.

ABOUT THE AUTHOR

David Bach has helped millions of people around the world take action to live and finish rich. He is the author of the #1 *New York Times* business bestseller *The Automatic Millionaire* as well as the national bestsellers *Smart Women Finish Rich, Smart Couples Finish Rich,* and *The Finish Rich Workbook.* Bach carries the unique distinction of having all four books in his FinishRich Series appear *simultaneously* on the *Wall Street Journal, BusinessWeek,* and *USA Today* bestseller lists. He is also the author of *1001 Financial Words You Need to Know,* the first financial dictionary published by Oxford University Press. In all, his books have been published in ten languages with more than two million copies in print worldwide.

Regularly featured on television and radio as well as in newspapers and magazines, Bach has appeared twice on *The Oprah Winfrey Show to* share his strategies for living and finishing rich. He is also a regular contributor to CNN's *American Morning* and has appeared regularly on ABC's *The View,* NBC's *Today* and *Weekend Today* shows, CBS's *Early Show,* Fox News Channel's *The O'Reilly Factor,* CNBC's *Power Lunch,* CNNfn, and MSNBC. He has been profiled in numerous major publications, including the *New York Times, BusinessWeek, USA Today, People, Reader's Digest, Time, Financial Times,* the *Washington Post,* the *Wall Street Journal, Los Angeles Times, San Francisco Chronicle, Working Woman, Glamour,* and *Family Circle.*

David Bach is the creator of the FinishRich® seminar series, which highlights his quick and easy-to-follow financial strategies, from which millions have benefited. In just the last few years, more than half a million people have attended his Smart Women Finish Rich® and Smart Couples Finish Rich® seminars, which have been taught throughout North America by thousands of financial advisors in more than 2,000 cities. Each month, through these seminars, men and women learn firsthand how to take financial action to live a life in line with their values.

A renowned financial speaker, Bach regularly presents seminars for and delivers keynote addresses to the world's leading financial service firms, Fortune 500 companies, universities, and national conferences. He is the founder and CEO of FinishRich, Inc., a company dedicated to revolutionizing the way people learn about money. Prior to founding FinishRich, Inc., he was a senior vice president of Morgan Stanley and a partner of The Bach Group, which during his tenure (1993 to 2001) managed more than half a billion dollars for individual investors.

David Bach lives with his wife, Michelle, and son, Jack, in New York, where he is currently working on his eighth book, *Smart Homeowners Finish Rich*. Please visit his web site at **www.finishrich.com**.